ENV BOOKS SERIES

WASTE DISPOSAL AND MANAGEMENT

Editors

Dr. Pawan Kumar 'Bharti'
Environmental Scientist
Society for Environment, Health, Awareness of nutrition & Toxicology (SEHAT)
Chauhan Bhawan, Vikas Colony, Jamna Palace, Haridwar-249401 (UK), India
E-mail: *gurupawanbharti@rediffmail.com*

Dr. B. Tabassum
Assistant Professor
Department of Zoology
Govt. Raza PG College, Rampur (UP) - 244 901 (India)

Dr. Priya Bajaj
Assistant Professor
Department of Zoology
Govt. Raza PG College, Rampur (UP) - 244 901 (India)

Associate Editors

Dr. Virendra Kumar
Plant Protection Officer, Kanpur, (India)

Mr. Jaswant Ray
Dept. of Zoology, Mewar University, Chittodgarh, (Rajasthan), (India)

Ms Faiza Naeem
Govt. Raza PG College, Rampur, (India)

DISCOVERY PUBLISHING HOUSE PVT. LTD.
NEW DELHI-110 002

Published by:
Tilak Wasan

DISCOVERY PUBLISHING HOUSE PVT. LTD.
4383/4B, Ansari Road, Darya Ganj
New Delhi-110 002 (India)
Phone : +91-11-23279245, 43596064-65
Fax : +91-11-23253475
E-mail : discoverypublishinghouse@gmail.com
sales@discoverypublishinggroup.com
web : www.discoverypublishinggroup.com

***First Edition:* 2015**

ISBN: 978-93-5056-729-6

Waste Disposal and Management

Printed at:
Infinity Imaging Systems
Delhi

ENV Books Series, India

Calls lengthy and error free chapters for further volumes of books on various environmental issues.

(Send your manuscripts to envbooks@gmail.com)

Founding Editor (Editor-in-Chief)

Dr. Pawan Kumar 'Bharti'

Society for Environment, Health, Awareness of Nutrition & Toxicology (SEHAT-India)

1775, Sohanganj, Near Clock Tower, Delhi-7, India

E-mail: *gurupawanbharti@rediffmail.com*

Other Titles by Editor-in-Chief:

1. **Agriculture Ecology and Environment (2014)**
   Bharti, P.K. and Olubukola O. Babalola (eds.)
   (ISBN: 978-93-5056-480-6).
2. **Water Resources and Agriculture (2014)**
   Bharti, P.K. and Ezeaku Peter Ikemefuna (eds.)
   (ISBN: 978-93-5056-481-3).
3. **Aquatic Ecology and Biotechnology (2014)**
   Bharti, P.K. and Zaki, M.S.A. (eds.)
   (ISBN: 978-93-5056-451-6).
4. **Fisheries and Toxicology (2014)**
   Zaki, M.S.A.; Bharti, P.K. and Chauhan, A. (eds.)
   (ISBN: 978-93-5056-452-3).
5. **Agriculture and Environmental Biotechnology (2014)**
   Bharti, P.K. and Chauhan, A. (eds.)
   (ISBN: 978-93-5056-479-0).
6. **Aquaculture and Fisheries Environment (2014)**
   Gupta, S.K. and Pawan K. Bharti (eds.)
   (ISBN: 978-93-5056-408-0).

7. **Environmental Conservation and Biotechnology (2014)**
Chauhan, A. and P.K. Bharti (eds.)
(ISBN: 978-93-5056-512-4).

8. **Agro-forestry and Climate Change (2014)**
Bharti, Pawan K. and Singh, Narayan (eds.)
(ISBN: 978-93-5056-514-8).

9. **Microbial Applications and Environment (2014)**
Bharti, Pawan K. (ed.)
(ISBN: 978-93-5056-515-5).

10. **Microbial Ecology and Habitat (2014)**
Bharti, Pawan K. (ed.)
(ISBN: 978-93-5056-514-8).

11. **Freshwater Ecosystem and Xenobiotics (2013)**
Bharti, P.K.; Zaki, M. and Chauhan, A. (eds.)
(ISBN: 978-93-5056-299-4).

12. **Biodiversity of Aquatic Ecosystem: Significance, Threat and Conservation (2013)**
Bharti, P.K. and Kaoud, H.A.H. (eds.)
(ISBN: 978-93-5056-297-0).

13. **Advances in Agriculture and Ecology (2013)**
Bharti, P.K.; Chauhan, A. and Ezeaku Peter Ikemefuna (eds.)
(ISBN: 978-93-5056-362-5).

14. **Aquatic Biodiversity and Pollution (2013)**
Bharti, P.K.; Chauhan, A. and Kaoud, H.A.H. (eds.)
(ISBN: 978-93-5056-359-5).

15. **Environmental Health and Problems (2013)**
Bharti, P.K. and Gajananda, Kh. (eds.)
(ISBN: 978-93-5056-263-5).

16. **Climate Change and Biodiversity (2013)**
Bharti, P.K. and Chauhan, Avnish (eds.)
(ISBN: 978-93-5056-360-1).

17. **Advances in Biotechnology and Ecological Sciences (2013)**
Bharti, P.K., Chauhan, A. and Ray, J. (eds.)
(ISBN: 978-93-5056-358-8).

18. **Soil Quality and Contamination (2013)**
Bharti, P.K. and Chauhan, Avnish (eds.)
(ISBN: 978-93-5056-361-8).

19. **Eco-toxicology and Eco-technology (2013)**
Bharti, P.K. and Zaki, M. (eds.)
(ISBN: 978-93-5056-313-7).

20. **Environmental Biotechnology and Application (2013)**
Bharti, P.K. and Chauhan, Avnish (eds.)
(ISBN: 978-93-5056-262-8).

21. **Aquatic Environment and Toxicology (2013)**
Bharti, Pawan K. (ed.)
(ISBN: 978-93-5056-236-9).

22. **Environmental Pollution and Biodiversity (2012)**
Bharti, P.K.; Chauhan, Avnish and Kumar, P. (eds.)
(ISBN: 978-93-5056-149-2).

23. **Prakriti me Aushadhi (*in Hindi*) (2012)**
Singh, J.R.; Bharti, P.K. and Bharti, B.
(ISBN: 978-93-5056-200-0).

24. **Climate Change and Agriculture (2012)**
Bharti, P.K. and Chauhan, Avnish (eds.)
(ISBN: 978-93-5056-148-5).

Preface

India is the second largest nation in the world, with a population of 1.21 billion, accounting for nearly 18% of world's human population, but it does not have enough resources or adequate systems in place to treat its solid wastes. Its urban population grew at a rate of 31.8% during the last decade to 377 million, which is greater than the entire population of US. India is facing a sharp contrast between its increasing urban population and available services and resources. Waste management is one such service where India has an enormous gap to fill. Proper waste disposal systems to address the burgeoning amount of wastes are absent. The current waste management services are inefficient, incur heavy expenditure and are so low as to be a potential threat to the public health and environmental quality. Improper waste management deteriorates public health, causes environmental pollution, accelerates natural resources degradation, causes climate change and greatly impacts the public life quality.

The per capita waste generation rate in India has increased from 0.44 kg/day in 2001 to 0.5 kg/day in 2011, fuelled by changing lifestyles and increased purchasing power of urban Indians. Urban population growth and increase in per capita waste generation have resulted in a 50% increase in the waste generated by Indian cities within only a decade since 2001. There are 53 cities in India with a million plus population, which together generate 86,000 TPD (31.5 million tons per year) of MSW at a per capita waste generation rate of 500 grams/day. The total MSW generated in urban India is estimated to be 68.8 million tons per year (TPY) or 188,500 tons per day (TPD) of MSW. Such a steep increase in waste generation within a decade has severed the stress on all available natural, infrastructural and budgetary resources.

Large cities collect about 70 - 90% of MSW generated, whereas smaller cities and towns collect less than 50% of waste generated. More than 91% of the MSW collected formally is landfilled on open lands and dumps. It is estimated that about 2% of the uncollected wastes are burnt openly on the streets. About 10% of the collected MSW is openly burnt or is caught in landfill fires. Such open burning of MSW and landfill fires together releases 22,000 tons of pollutants into the lower atmosphere of Mumbai city every year. The pollutants include carbon monoxide (CO), carcinogenic hydro carbons (HC) (includes dioxins and furans), particulate matter (PM), nitrogen oxides (NOx) and sulfur dioxide (SO2).

The nature is beautiful. Tempo of modern life however means imbalance in nature. Our habits regarding waste disposal are self-oriented and uncivilized. Once we are out of our house, we forget everything about hygiene and sanitation. Health, cleanliness, waste and waste management are interrelated. India is considered as one of the dirtiest country in the world, since there is no integrated waste management system. There is a need about integrated waste disposal and its management at different levels, in houses, at schools and colleges and at public places with concern about health and hygiene. Scientific approaches with short term and long term strategies should be developed about handling of waste, drainage, sewage, drinking water and eatables to maintain clean surroundings. Since the environment related problems are highly complicated requiring expert knowledge for a satisfactory solution. Sanitation is the cornerstone of good health. It brings dignity, self esteem and safety.

Random Waste Management has a direct relationship with clean air, clean water, clean food and quality of lifecycle. Waste Management practices differ from country to country, for urban and rural areas, for metropolitan cities to towns, for domestic and Industrial waste, for hazardous and non-hazardous waste and bio-degradable and non-biodegradable wastes. Irrespective of the source and type of waste, there is a need for proper and integrated waste management at all stages collection, transportation, segregation, treatment, recycling and disposal.

It gives us great pleasure to present before our readers the proceedings of National Conference on Random Waste Disposal: Socio-ecological Impacts and Concerns; निर्मल भारत: स्वस्थ भारत (NBSB-2014). This compendium is a proceeding of national conference on Random waste disposal: Socioecological impacts and concerns held on 12 January, 2014 at Mohammad Ali Jauhar University, Rampur (UP) and organized by Raza (PG) College Rampur (UP), India.

This book provides comprehensive coverage of the fundamental principles and current practices and trends in the field of waste generation and disposal practices, environmental pollution, ecological changes and solid waste management. This book updates the subject matter, illustrations and problems to incorporate new concepts and issues related to waste disposal, waste minimization, resource recovery from waste, recycling of waste, ecological stress and solid waste management (SWM).

Particularly thanks are due to all contributors and publisher also for their contribution and assistance. We hope this book will provide a multi-disciplinary forum to explore emerging areas in the field of waste disposal and management.

– Editors

(envbooks@gmail.com)

Acknowledgement

Though this is a short episode in the long journey of quest, thousands of hands were there to help, to mitigate any disaster and making it memorable experience. This seems to be an occasion, where, we cannot fully depend on words. Still...

"A Journey of a thousand miles begins with a single step"

Behind every success there is certainly an unseen power of Almighty *'God'*. Firstly we are very much thankful to Almighty *'God'*, whose gracious blessings enabled us to complete this work.

We are highly thankful to *Department of Science and Technology* (*DST*), New Delhi for providing financial support to conduct National conference on Random Waste Disposal: Socio-ecological Impacts and Concern.

Words at our command are not adequate, either in the form of spirit or thought, to convey the depth of our profound gratitude to *Honbl'e Mohmmad Azam Khan Sahab*, Founder and Chancellor, Mohmmad Ali Jauhar University, Rampur, whose motivational support, affection, inspiration, excellent guidance and constructive criticism, during the entire course have helped us to complete this herculean task. Indeed this book is our dedication to his passion towards education and social reformation.

We are also indebted and express our heartfelt regards to our patrons *Prof. Mohd. Yunus* (Vice chancellor, Mohammad Ali Jauhar University, Rampur) and Director of our conference *Dr. Ashwani Kumar Goyal* (Joint Secretary, Higher Education, Lucknow). We are grateful to *Dr. N.B. Khan* (Former Director, Higher Education, UP Govt.), *Dr. Paramatma Singh* (Principal, Govt. Raza PG College, Rampur), *Dr. M.A. Siddiqui*, (Dean, Department of Zoology, Mohmmad Ali Jauhar University), *Dr. Mohd. Javed* and *Dr. A.K. Saxena* (Govt. Raza PG College, Rampur) for their encouragement and untiring efforts and to all the participants, our dedicated team of faculty members for their help and co-operation. We are also whole heartedly thankful to *Mr. Pavan Kumar*, Department and Science and Technology, New Delhi for his inspiration and indebted support.

In the last but not least we are indeed grateful to our respected and beloved parents, who inspired us at every step and gave us steadfast and unflinching moral support, encouragement and showered packets of selfless love at each and every moment, we would have not achieved this goal without their blessings and support.

– Editors

Contents

WASTE DISPOSAL AND MANAGEMENT *Pages:* 1-13
Edited by: **Dr. Pawan Kumar 'Bharti'; Dr. B. Tabassum;** and **Dr. Priya Bajaj**
ISBN: 978-93-5056-729-6
Edition: **2015**
Published by: **Discovery Publishing House Pvt. Ltd., New Delhi (India)**

1

Solid Waste Management at Indian Research Stations Over East Antarctica

Pawan Kumar 'Bharti' [1,2,3*]

ABSTRACT

India has a permanent scientific research station in the Antarctica and the Maitri station is located on Schirmacher Oasis in the Central Dronning Maud Land, while Bharti station is located in Larsemann Hills, Ingrid Christenson Coast over East Antarctica. However, the activities due to operation and maintenance of the research stations in Antarctica have impacts on the Antarctic environment. Besides, the scientific stations also generate waste materials and few of them are discharged into the Antarctic environment, which may create negative impacts on the Antarctica. The assessment of waste materials emanating from various sources was carried out. The present paper attempts to highlight the solid waste management and handling practices observed during XXX ISEA in austral summer at Bharti as well as at Maitri station over East Antarctica.

Key words: Antarctica, environmental pollution, Solid waste Management, Indian research stations, Indian Antarctic programme.

1 Member, 30th Indian Scientific Expedition to Antarctica
Bharti Island, Larsemann Hills, Christenson Coast, East Antarctica

2 Antarctica Laboratory, R & D Division, Shriram Institute for Industrial Research, 19, University Road, Delhi - 110 007

3 Society for Environment, Health, Awareness of nutrition & Toxicology (SEHAT-India), 1775, Sohanganj, Near Clock Tower, Delhi-110 007, India.

INTRODUCTION

Antarctica is the coldest continent on the earth. The Indian Ocean, Pacific Ocean and Atlantic Ocean surround the continent. Antarctic continent covers 10% of the earth surface and has a surface area of nearly 14 million square kilometer. It also has 70% of the Worlds fresh water resources in the form of ice sheets. Thick ice sheets cover the whole continent (almost 98%). As a result of the environmental conditions, the remaining (~ 2%) portion without ice cover is basically the barren soil and rocks .The Antarctica Conservation Act (ACA) was made in the year 1978 and is intended to conserve and protect the natural environment of Antarctica. It also addresses the proper material management especially of waste generated by several countries to explore the potential of Antarctica in the wake of rising human activity. Many countries have set up scientific research stations in Antarctica. There are about 65 scientific research stations in summer and 30 research stations in winter, which are currently operating for scientific investigations.

STUDY AREA

A. Maitri Station

The Schirmacher Oasis is situated at about 100 km inside Princess Astrid coast of Queen Maud Land between the ice shelf and the continental ice dome in Antarctica. The valleys are ice-free because the mountains block the flow of ice from the polar plateau and low precipitation and strong winds lead to little accumulation of snow in the area. Schirmacher oasis region has three types of lakes, viz. Pro-glacial Lake, Land-locked lake and Epi-shelf lake. During summer, the polar ice melts and water often flows into the lakes. The lakes occupy closed basins and vary in surface area, depth and ice-cover thickness.

The India Scientific station 'Maitri' is located at Latitude 70°45′ 53″ South; Longitude 11° 44′ 03″ East in the Schirmacher Oasis in Central Dronning Maud Land of east Antarctica. It is approximately 80 km from the ice edge. It is situated in an area of barren rock and is surrounded by a number of lakes. The closest station to the Maitri is the Russian Station Novolazarevskaya. Maitri is relatively large station complex, spanning an area of approx. 1000 × 500 meter.

Indian permanent Scientific Base Maitri in east Antarctica was established in 1989 on a rocky ground of Schirmacher Oasis. It has facilities to conduct scientific research throughout the year in several fields viz. atmospheric sciences, earth sciences, geomagnetism, human physiology and medicines, meteorology, ecology, glaciology, geology, biological and environmental sciences.

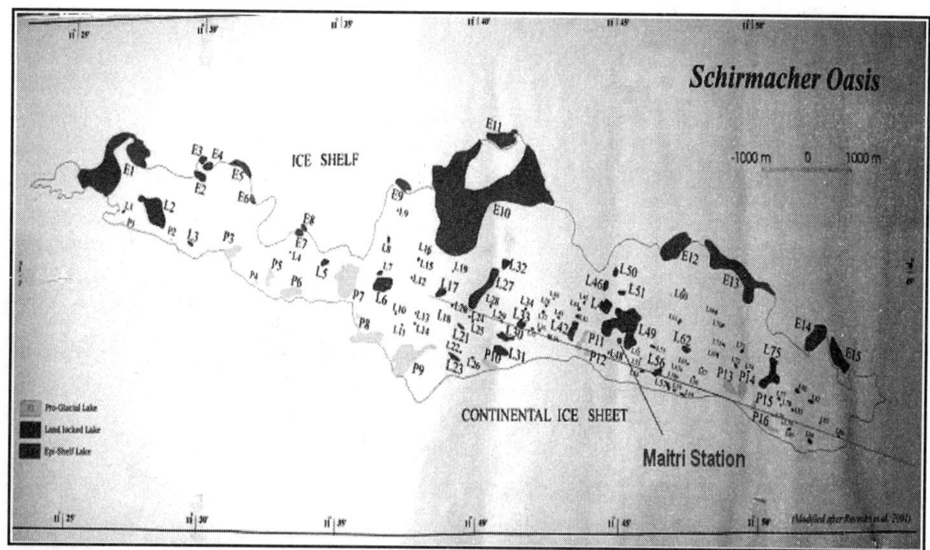

Fig. 1.1: **Map Showing the Location of Maitri Station in Schirmacher Oasis**

B. Bharti Station

Larsemann Hills is at the Ingrid Christensen Coast of east Antarctica (69° 21′ 00″ S to 690 27′ 00″ S and 750 57′ 00″ E to 76° 27′ 00″ E). It is an ice-free Antarctic coastal oasis, located between the Amery Ice Shelf and the Vestfold Hills. Isolated islands, peninsulas and nunataks occur along the coastal continental ice. The areas are mainly exposed hilly and rocky terrains. There are two main peninsulas in the Larsemann Hills, of east Antarctica (i) Broknes Peninsula; and (ii) Stornes Peninsula. In between these two peninsulas, there are numbers of promontory, islands of varying shapes, sizes, heights and water bodies.

Bharti Island (690 24′ to 690 26′ S; 760 10′ to 760 15′ E), is situated over the Larsemann Hills of east Antarctica. The ice patches over the lake and the rocky regions are typical characteristics of the oases regions. The poplar ice is also seen in the background of the Bharti Island, which is one of the main feeders of fresh water to various lakes in this oasis region. This promontory is sandwiched in the northern direction by McLeod Island; eastern direction comprises the Quilty bay, north-eastern direction by Fisher Island, western direction is the Stornes peninsula and the southern direction by the Antarctic continent and polar ice caps.

The Indian Research Station at Larsemann hills, east Antarctic is located on an ice-free rocky area, situated between Quilty Bay on the east and Thala Fjord on the west. The Larsemann hills provide a unique opportunity for studying the environmental impacts of research facilities run by three nations (Australia, China, and Russia) as well for the new Indian Scientific Base at Bharti Island.

Fig. 1.2: **Map Showing the Location of Bharti Station in Larsemann Hills**

The main aims of the project work were to carry out detailed environmental monitoring and assessment including solid waste management and disposal studies at existing Indian Scientific Stations Maitri as well as Bharti over east Antarctica.

MATERIALS AND METHODS

Preliminary studies on solid waste generation, separation, handling, storage, disposal and management was carried out at Maitri and Bharti Polar Research Stations as per the standard methodologies as described by Bharti (2012a). The percent composition of generated solid waste was also evaluated manually, while its segregation and storage activities were noticed on the basis of general public survey.

Ash samples were also collected from toilet & food incinerators for physico-chemical characteristics & metal content and analysed using standard methods described by Furman et al. (1922). A preliminary study was conducted to make an inventory of waste materials generated at Maitri station.

WASTE DISPOSAL POLICY AT INDIAN POLAR STATIONS

Indian Scientific Bases have developed a waste management policy, which outlines ways to minimize waste and how specific waste materials should be disposed off in safe ways. Waste disposal policy Includes:

- Reduction of waste amount introduced to Antarctica to the minimum extent.

- All waste should be separated into categories and clearly marked.
- All categorized waste should not mixed and keep in a separate container
- Waste should stored in the marked containers after segregation

ENVIRONMENTAL MONITORING

The environmental monitoring and impacts assessment studies at Indian stations was carried out with keeping in view of various activities pertaining to the logistics operations and subsequent operation of the Indian stations. The types of activities are presented in Table 1.1. A matrix was prepared to identify the impacts of various activities on environmental components, which shows the interactions of various outputs of station with the environmental elements. These includes use of polar vehicles, power generations, incineration of food and toilet waste, water effluent, waste water discharge, helicopter, field equipments, etc. The estimation of air emission can be calculated as per the guidelines based on fuel consumption (Emergency of Manual of Antarctica). Proper preventive and mitigation measures have also been proposed for Antarctica circumstances.

Table 1.1: Output of the Activity from Operations at Maitri Station

Sl.No.	Actions	Output					
		Air Pollutant	Wastes	Noise	Oil Spills	Heat	Mechanical
1.	Snow Vehicles	✓	✓	✓	✓	✓	✓
2.	Generator	✓	✓	✓	✓	✓	✓
3.	Incinerator	✓	✓	✓	✓	✓	✓
4.	Helicopter	✓	✓	✓	✓	✓	✓
5.	Field Equipment					✓	✓
6.	Waste Disposal	✓	✓				
7.	Human activity			✓			✓
	Maitri Station	✓	✓	✓	✓	✓	✓

WASTE MANAGEMENT

Proper waste management and disposal are given high priority at the Indian station. The waste management at Indian Research Stations is in accordance with Antarctica waste management policy. Since the size of the Indian Scientific Expedition to Antarctica varies from year to year, the amount of waste generated each year varies accordingly. Maitri station has comprehensive schemes for separating, storing and back loading of solid waste, while the appropriate plan regarding solid waste generation, management and disposal at Bharti station is about to plan.

The overall waste materials at Indian stations are separated into few categories. These are as follows:

- Biodegradable waste like Food & Vegetable waste, paper & cartoon packs, tissue paper, etc.

- Non-degradable waste like glass, aluminum, metal cans, etc.
- Hazardous wastes: Paints, waste oils and fuels, medical wastes, electronic waste, chemicals waste, etc.
- Sewage waste water
- Incinerated ash of toilet and food waste
- Waste oil

Solid Waste Management at Maitri Station

The foods and toilet waste generated at Maitri Station are burnt in an oil-fired incineration at high temperature. Food waste is incinerated in a designated area at the Maitri Station. Human toilet waste is incinerated once in a day. ATF is used as fuel for the incineration of food and toilet waste. The release of flue gas from incineration of waste may contribute environmental impact through emission released. The ashes from the incinerator are collected in drums, stored and transported out of the Antarctica once in a year. Samples of food and toilet waste ash were also collected and detail analysis of ash samples was carried out at Shriram Institute for Industrial Research, Delhi

All type of waste materials except sewage waste is annually removed from the Antarctica. Further, incinerator ashes of food and toilet waste at Maitri station are separated, collected in containers and brought back to India for appropriate disposal or utilization. All types of the waste materials generated at Maitri station are presented in Table 1.2, which gives an overview of annual waste production at Maitri station.

Table 1.2: Solid Waste Generation at Maitri Station (In Tons)

Sl.No.	Waste Generated	Estimated		
		Monthly	Summer	Annual
1.	Kitchen cum Food	0.4	2.0	4.5
2.	Waste water effluent	50	250	700
3.	Packaging waste	0.15	1.0	1.7
4.	Glass waste	0.10	0.4	1
5.	Oil Waste	0.13	0.5	1.4
6.	Ash	2.0	10	2.6
7.	Chemical waste	0.08	0.5 Ton	1 Ton
8.	Electrical/Electronic	0.1	0.5	1.2
9.	Medical waste	0.01	0.04	0.11
10.	Metal/Scarp	1.25	7	15
11.	Misc.	0.83	4	10
	Total	**55.06**	**275.94**	**738.51**

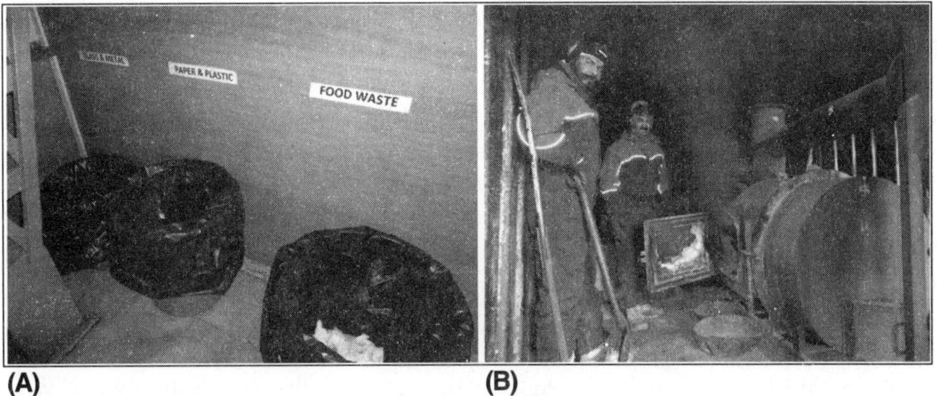

(A) (B)

Fig. 1.3 (A-B): **Segregation and Incineration of Solid Waste at Maitri Station**

SOLID WASTE MANAGEMENT AT BHARTI STATION

During the construction of Bharti station, all the solid waste were separated and compacted and stored in a large container. All the solid waste material generated at Bharti station was brought back from Antarctica.

To support the continuing scientific research and, stay of scientist and logistic staff, generators run throughout the study period to supply power to the station site. ATF is used as fuel to run generators, Cranes, Piston bullies, snow scooters and boilers. The supporting activities like storage of food material, cooking of food, maintenance of generators, cranes, snow scooter, piston bullies, supply of drinking water, temperature regulation inside temporary shelters, waste disposal, etc. are regular phenomenon. These activities may pose a little extent impact surrounding environment, but environment regulations are to be strictly adhered to in Antarctica. All the solid waste is stored in a separate container and brought back to the real land. There are few separate bins for degradable and non-degradable types of solid waste. After separating, waste was dumped into a container, which was inside the ship. Percent composition and quantum of solid waste generated in kitchen and dining hall at Bharti station is given in tabular form.

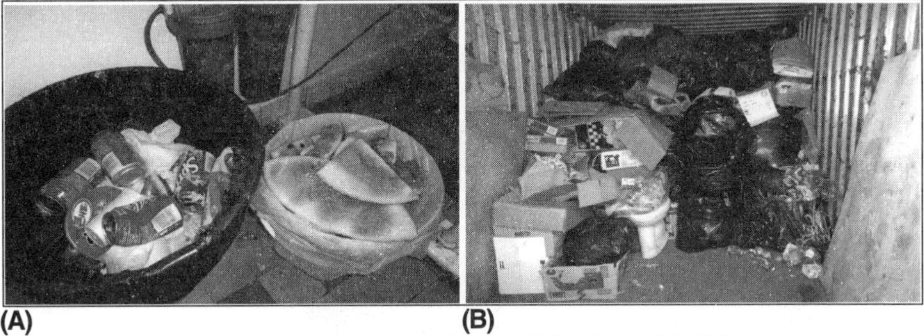

(A) (B)

Fig. 1.4 (A-B): **Segregation and Storing of Solid Waste during Construction of Bharti Station**

A significant quantity of solid waste was generated during the XXX ISEA Voyage at two locations, i.e. Indian Kitchen and Dining hall of ship. The presented data shows the quantity and composition of degradable as well as non-degradable waste originating from kitchen and dining area of ship. The composition of solid waste was computed statistically and the constituents are given in the tabular form. A weekly report on the quantity of solid waste generated was prepared for all the consecutive months. All the degradable and non-degradable waste was packed and stored in appropriate containers of sufficient capacity.

Significant volume of solid waste was generated in the Kitchen and dining hall area during the XXX ISEA. The data of solid waste generation is given in tabulator form in the last section of this chapter. Solid waste was collected from both points, segregated, sorted and stored in a large container to bring it back.

67% of degradable and 33% non-degradable waste was estimated in Kitchen area, while 72% degradable and 28% non-degradable solid waste was generated in dining area. It was observed that 5-9 kg/day degradable and 4-5 kg/day non-degradable solid waste was generated in kitchen, while 4-5 kg/day degradable and 3-4 kg/day non-degradable solid waste was generated in dining area during the month of November 2010. 5-7 kg/day degradable and 3-5 kg/day non-degradable solid waste was generated in kitchen, while 5-7 kg/day degradable and 4-5 kg/day non-degradable solid waste was generated in dining area during the month of December 2010.

But during the month of January 2011, 3-5 kg/day degradable and 4-6 kg/day non-degradable solid waste was generated in kitchen, while 3-4 kg/day degradable and 4-6 kg/day non-degradable solid waste was generated in dining area. The fluctuation in the generated quantum of degradable and non-degradable waste was due to the scarcity of fresh fruits and vegetables in the last months of expedition. All the waste material was brought back by ship after completion of expedition.

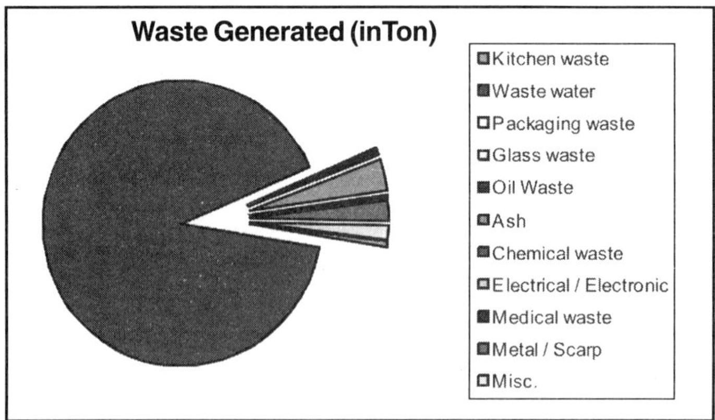

Fig. 1.5: **Annual Waste Generated at Maitri Station, Schirmacher Oasis**

Table 1.3: Percentage Composition of Solid Waste in Kitchen of Ship at Larsemann Hills (Bharti Station)

Sl.No.	Materials	% Composition
1.	Metal Scrap and glass	8
2.	Cartoon and packaging Paper	10
3.	Plastic and Polythene	15
4.	Food Residue	35
5.	Bones	10
6.	Fruits and Vegetables residue	15
7.	Others	7
	Total	**100**

Table 1.4: Percentage Composition of Solid Waste in Dining Hall of Ship at Larsemann Hills (Bharti Station)

Sl.No.	Materials	% Composition
1.	Metal Scrap and glass	12
2.	Cartoon and packaging Paper	10
3.	Plastic and Polythene	8
4.	Food Residue	25
5.	Bones	8
6.	Fruits and Vegetables residue	35
7.	Others	2
	Total	**100**

Table 1.5: Solid Waste per Capita at Ship during 30th ISEA (in Kg)

	Degradable	Non-degradable
Kitchen waste	390	364
Dining Hall waste	482	380
Total	**872**	**744**
Per capita (kg)	38	32

Table 1.6: Generation of Solid Waste in Kitchen of Ship at Larsemann Hills (Bharti Station)

Sl. No.	Month/Week	Amount (kg/day) Degradable	Amount (kg/day) Non-degradable
1.	November 10, week 1	5-7	4-5
2.	November 10, week 2	5-7	4-5
3.	November 10, week 3	8-9	4-5
4.	November 10, week 4	8-9	4-5
5.	December 10, week 1	6-7	4-5
6.	December 10, week 2	6-7	4-5
7.	December 10, week 3	5-6	3-4
8.	December 10, week 4	5-6	3-4
9.	January 11, week 1	4-5	5-6
10.	January 11, week 2	4-5	5-6
11.	January 11, week 3	3-4	4-5
12.	January 11, week 4	3-4	4-5
	Total (kg)	**482**	**380**

Table 1.7: Generation of Solid Waste in Dining Hall of Ship at Larsemann Hills (Bharti Station)

Sl. No.	Month/Week	Amount (kg/day) Degradable	Amount (kg/day) Non-degradable
1.	November 10, week 1	4-5	3-4
2.	November 10, week 2	4-5	3-4
3.	November 10, week 3	4-5	3-4
4.	November 10, week 4	4-5	3-4
5.	December 10, week 1	5-6	4-5
6.	December 10, week 2	5-6	4-5
7.	December 10, week 3	6-7	4-5
8.	December 10, week 4	6-7	4-5
9.	January 11, week 1	3-4	5-6
10.	January 11, week 2	3-4	5-6
11.	January 11, week 3	3-4	4-5
12.	January 11, week 4	3-4	4-5
	Total (kg)	**390**	**364**

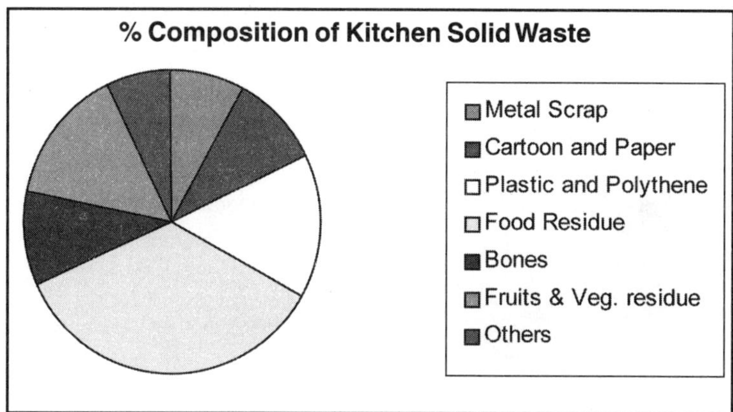

Fig. 1.6: **Percentage Composition of Solid Waste in Kitchen of Ship at Larsemann Hills (Bharti Station)**

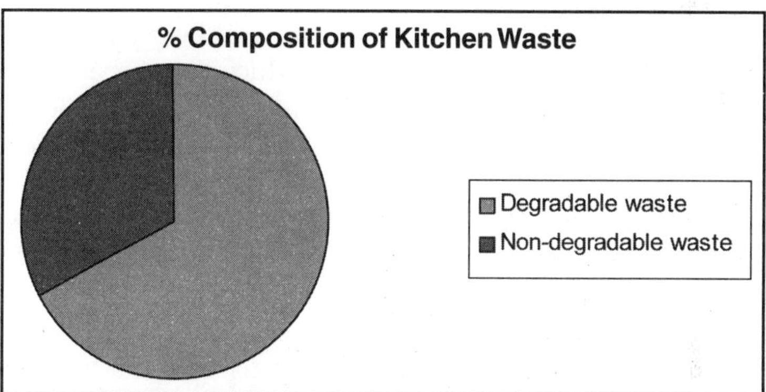

Fig. 1.7: **Percentage Composition of Solid Waste in Kitchen of Ship at Larsemann Hills (Bharti Station)**

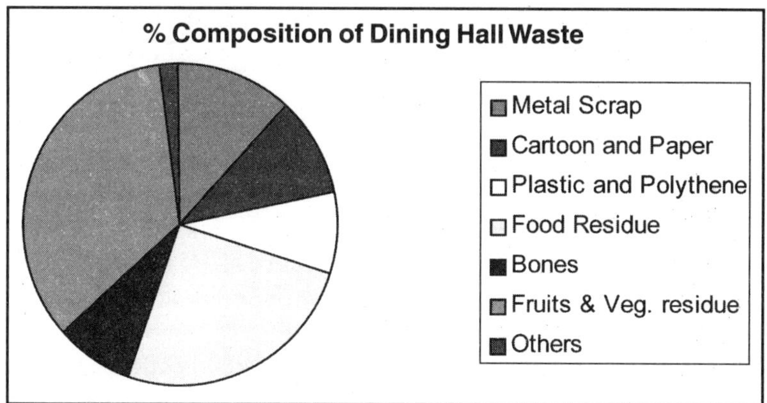

Fig. 1.8: **Percentage Composition of Solid Waste in Dining Hall of Ship at Larsemann Hills (Bharti Station)**

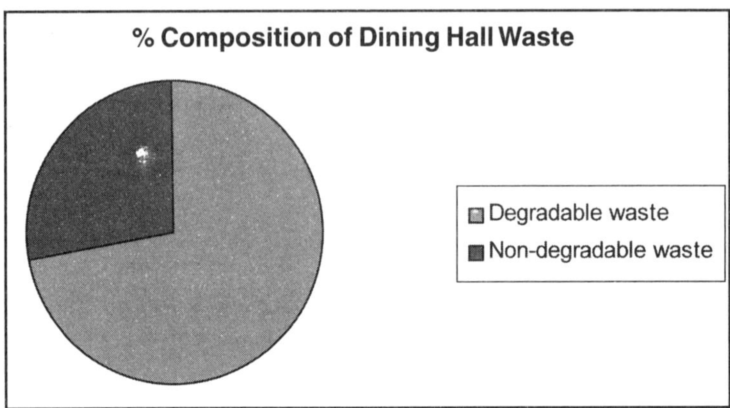

Fig. 1.9: **Percentage Composition of Solid Waste in Dining Hall of Ship at Larsemann Hills (Bharti Station)**

RECOMMENDATIONS

- All expedition members to reduce paper uses. Less packaging is to be brought to Maitri station and this will reduce the garbage generation.
- A waste compressor machine or baler should to be installed at Maitri station. The compressor would reduce waste volume significantly.
- Ensuring adequate onsite supervision of the activities at research stations annually by environmental specialist.
- Cumulative impacts of various activities on the environment components particularly at station sites should be monitored.
- Polythene packing materials, paper, wood packaging, metal chips, aluminum foil and other packaging materials shall not be disposed off into the open pit or ice-shelf or into the sea. The use of plastic bags on Indian Scientific bases over East Antarctica should be minimized.
- The compactor for fuel drum and solid waste should also be installed, wherever it is feasible to reduce the volume of waste to facilitate its storage and removal for reuse, recycling, disposal and back-loading to India.

CONCLUSION

The solid waste management and environmental assessment studies carried out at Indian Scientific Bases, Maitri and Bharti stations located in east Antarctica throws light on the status of air, water quality and waste generated in and around Indian research stations. Despite all care, there is always accidental contamination as well as transport of solid and liquid waste in study area due to strong winds, surface velocity of water & seepage or percolation process, which can directly or indirectly affect the quality of water, ice and soil. Further, round the year maintenance combined with increased scientific and logistics activity every year results in waste generation at the Maitri station. A zero discharge system should be developed & implemented at Maitri station to avoid and minimize the pollution load in east Antarctica.

REFERENCES

Bharti, Pawan K. (2012a): Solid Waste and River Ecology, *Lambert Academic Publishing GmbH & Co. KG, Saarbrucken, Germany*, pp: 65 (ISBN: 978-3-659-12852-3).

Bharti, Pawan K. (2012b): Environmental Monitoring and Assessment during the Construction of Indian Scientific Base (Bharti Station) in Antarctica, In: Biodiversity Conservation and Environmental Management (Eds.- Khanna et al.), *Biotech Books*, Delhi, pp: 81-97 (ISBN: 9788176222624).

Bharti, Pawan K. (2012c): Anthropogenic Activities and Global Climate Change, In: Climate Change and Agriculture (Eds.- Bharti, P.K. and Chauhan, A.), *Discovery Publishing House Pvt. Ltd.*, Delhi, pp: 1-22 (ISBN: 9789350561485).

Bharti, P.K. and Gajananda, Kh. (2013): Environmental Monitoring and Assessment in Antarctica, In: Environmental Health and Problems (Eds.- Bharti, P.K. and Gajananda, Kh.), *Discovery Publishing House Pvt. Ltd.*, Delhi, pp: 178-186 (ISBN: 93-5056-263-4).

Bharti, Pawan K., Bhupesh Sharma, N. Pal, R.K. Singh and U.K. Niyogi (2014): Environmental Monitoring at Maitri Station, East Antarctica. In: Proceedings of National Seminar on Environmental Issues and Challenges, Ramjas College, University of Delhi, India.

DCEE (2004): Draft Comprehensive Environmental Evaluation for the Concept of Upgrading the Norwegian Summer Station Troll in Dronning Maud Land, Antarctica to Permanent Station, Norwegian Polar Institute, Polar Environmental Center, Tromsa, Norway.

Erich R., Gundlach; John J., Gallagher; John Hatcher & Tom Vinsor (2000): Planning and Hazards Oil Spill Response in Antarctic's. International Oil Spill Conference, 241-244.

Furman, N. Howell; Welcher, F.J. and Scott, W.W. (1922): Standard Methods of Chemical Analysis, Princeton N.J. Van Nostrand, Eight Warren Street, New York, Third Edition, pp: 1397.

Sharma, B.; Bharti, P.K.; Pal, N.; Singh, R.K.; Niyogi, U.K. and Khandal, R.K. (2011): Waste Management Practices at Indian Research Station 'Maitri', East Antarctica, In: 'Proceedings of Brainstorming Session on Polar Sciences' Published by Indian Meteorological Department, MoES, Govt. of India, pp: 67-76.

SIIR (2010): Long Term Environmental Monitoring and Impact Assessment Study at New Scientific Base at Larsemann Hills, 27th, 28th, 29th ISEA Combined Report to NCAOR, Submitted by Shriram Institute of Industrial Research, Delhi.

SIIR (2012): Long Term Environmental Monitoring Study at New Scientific Base Bharti at Larsemann Hills, 27th, 28th, 29th, 30th ISEA Combined Report to NCAOR, Submitted by Shriram Institute of Industrial Research, Delhi.

Web help:

http://en.wikipedia.org/wiki/climate-of-Antarctica.

http://quest.arc.nasa.gov/antarctica

http://www.usap.gov/sciences. support

http://antarctica.ac.uk/

http://www.esri.com/news/arcnews

http://www.eia.doc.gov/emeu/cabs/antarctica.html

WASTE DISPOSAL AND MANAGEMENT *Pages:* 14-30
Edited by: Dr. Pawan Kumar 'Bharti'; Dr. B. Tabassum; and Dr. Priya Bajaj
ISBN: 978-93-5056-729-6
Edition: 2015
Published by: Discovery Publishing House Pvt. Ltd., New Delhi (India)

2

Efficacy of *Catharanthus roseus* Extract Against Cadmium Contamination Induced by WEE Disposal in Groundwater

B. Tabassum and **Priya Bajaj**

ABSTRACT

Processing (disposal and recycling) of Electrical and Electronic Wastes (WEE), including computers, televisions, mobiles, laptops, AC, refrigerators, batteries, inverters and electric wires etc. have emerged as a critical global environmental health issue because of their massive production value and insufficient management policies. In developing countries including India, processing of WEE occurs through informal and non-standardized procedures. This leads to environmental exposure of cadmium and other heavy metals. Potential exposure of population to cadmium through WEE has induced a number of problems, especially in pregnant women and children. Indiscriminate exposure to cadmium and its persistence in environment warrants for the intensive studies and require effective protection measures.

The current study has been planned with the aim to establish *Catharanthus roseus*, a well known medicinal plant as an herbal protective measure against sub-acute (21 days) cadmium contamination. All the experiments were performed to elucidate the effect of plant extract on hepato-renal system of albino rats (*Rattus norvegicus*) on account of its biochemical closeness to human.

Cadmium intoxication significantly increases Liver Weight, Serum Urea, Uric acid, BUN, Creatinin, K^+, A/G ratio, Cholesterol, triglyceride, Total Lipids, transaminases,

Toxicology Laboratory, Department of Zoology, Govt. Raza PG College, Rampur (UP) - 244 901, (India).

phosphatases and dehydrogenases while decreases Body weight, kidney weight, Serum Na^+, Cl^-, Albumin, Globulin and Total Proteins. These alterations were retained to the normalcy by pretreatment with *Catharanthus* extract without any ill effect of its own.

Key words: WEE, Cadmium, *Catharanthus roseus*, Groundwater contamination.

INTRODUCTION

Present scenario is encountering with a major global challenge due to pollution. No component of environment, whether atmosphere or hydrosphere or lithosphere has been left unpolluted. Somehow, these pollutants are remarkably constituted by heavy metals including cadmium, lead, mercury etc. A number of anthropogenic (extensive uses of electronic and electrical appliances) as well as natural activities percolate these metals to groundwater table. There are about 35 heavy metals virtually present everywhere, slowly absorbing and eventually causing dreadful diseases.

Cadmium is the second most hazardous heavy metal occurring in both elemental as well as compound forms. It is a major pollutant of ambient air and water, introduced through a number of occupational activities. Among which, unsafe processing of electronic and electrical wastes are important one, comprising about 40% of total exposure. It is a highly toxic metal with a very high Bio-concentration factor (BCF>100) that is why; its industrial application is regulated by standards of USEPA (United States Environmental Protection Agency). WHO (World Health Organization) Permitted groundwater cadmium concentration is 0.005 mg/L and Acceptable Daily Intake (ADI) is 10-20 μg/day only. The reality is far away from these standards; in developing countries like India, this permitted limit for cadmium is fell down to 0.03 mg/L almost sixty times to the international standard and still not achieved at most of the places.

More than 10 million pound cadmium is tossed all around the world per year. Major sources of cadmium exposure are mining, batteries, electronic and electrical goods, electroplating, vapor lamps, engraving, fertilizers, smoking, soldering, and old galvanized PVC water supply pipes. Recently electronic and electrical wastes have arisen as the biggest source of cadmium exposure. An estimated 50 million tons of EE-wastes are produced every year all around the world. Devices like mobiles, laptop, computers, televisions, refrigerators; AC, resistors, marine and aviation equipments, nickel cadmium batteries etc are sharing a huge part in today's lifestyle. Among these sources, Ni-Cd batteries are the most serious one, containing about 6-18% cadmium. About 86% cadmium is used in rechargeable batteries, necessary component of all electronics and electrical instruments. Informal Processing (recycling and disposal) of these goods results in significant health hazards to workers and communities.

The production of electrical and electronic equipment (EEE) is one of the fastest growing global manufacturing activities. Rapid economic growth, coupled with urbanization and a growing demand for consumer goods, has increased both the consumption and the production of EEE.(Ramesh Babu *et al.,* 2007). EEEs are made of a multitude of components, some containing toxic substances that have an adverse impact on human health and the environment if not handled properly. Often, these hazards arise due to the improper recycling and disposal processes used. It can have serious repercussions for those in proximity to places where e-waste is recycled or burnt. (e-Waste Guide, 2008)

Developed countries are exporting these scrap goods to developing countries at a very high rate and India and china are the major dumping grounds for the purpose. In India, Delhi and Bangalore are such major sites. Lower environmental standards, cheap labor, high population density and relatively high value of recovered raw material at these places; cause the global expansion of pollution generating activities. Uncontrolled burning, disassembly and disposal of these goods cause a variety of environmental problems such as groundwater cadmium contamination.

Fig. 2.1: **Dumping Sites and Piles of WEE**

Cadmium exposed to environment, is absorbed in human body mainly through inhalation route (15%) but oral absorption (6-8%) is also significant. Inside the body, it primarily encounters with liver and then exported to kidneys via blood, so are the most affected tissues. All their major metabolic functions of body are altered by acute and sub acute exposure to cadmium that can be inferred by biochemical and hematological estimations and further proved by histo-pathological examination of affected tissues.

Current global challenge on cadmium exposure and reports of agencies like USEPA and 8th International conference on cadmium are warning continuously to reduce the exposure of cadmium and even a number of efforts have been made till now in this direction. Among those, restricted industrial application and socio-legal campaigning against unsafe WEE processing are the most important one. USEPA has declared standards for their eco-safer processing, according to which, various units of WEE equipments, after shredding and dismantling should be recycled separately and hazardous smoke thus released should be captured, contained and treated to mitigate environmental threat.

Although reduction in exposure chances is a better way to avoid intoxication, but endogenous protection mechanisms provided through herbal ingredients are also effective to overcome toxic insults without any side effect of their own. USEPA and other organization are trying to reduce the cadmium exposure and awaking the public for safer disposal of EE-wastes, but severity of hazard is demanding to introduce some dietary supplement to protect from the ill-effects of cadmium toxicity. Past few decades has seen considerable changes in opinion regarding ethno-pharmacological therapeutic applications.

Mainly with such a background, this work aims to establish some herbal protection against cadmium contamination, that could be available easily and supplemented with metabolic impairments. A common herb, Sadabahar or Rose Periwinkle (*Catharanthus roseus*) has been selected for the purpose. The studies would be performed in model organism, albino rats on account of its simple general behavior, easy rearing and biochemical closeness to human.

Sadabahar is a very common, evergreen sub-shrub or herbaceous ornamental plant bearing oval to oblong shining green leaves and white to dark pink flowers. It is the native of Madagascar areas, but now cultivated throughout the world. The extract from different parts of this plant has been used to treat a wide assortment of diseases including diabetes, malaria, leukemia and other diseases. It is known for a number of pharmacological actions as antimicrobial, wound-healing, ant carcinogenic, vaso-dialating activities. This plant has more than 400 known alkaloids and extract is safer to use up to 4 g/kg bodyweight.

Fig. 2.2: Catharanthus Roseus **Plant**

MATERIALS AND METHODS

Experimental Animals: Adult male Wister albino rats (*Rattus norvegicus*) of almost same age and weight (100 ± 10 gm), were procured from inbred colony. They were acclimatized at room temperature with 12 hr dark/light cycle and at 24 ± 4°C. The rats were fed on standard diet and water *ad-libitum*. All experiments were performed as per animal institutional ethical committee (360/01/CPSEA/2001).

Experimental Chemical: The experimental compound cadmium chloride was obtained from Merck, India and its LD_{50} was calculated to be 88 mg/Kg body weight by log dose /probit regression line method (Finney, 1971).

Experimental Plant: Experimental plant is *Catharanthus roseus* or sadabahar, a member of family- Apocyanaceae. *Catharanthus* plants were collected from local fields and identified. For preparation of aqueous crude extract, known quantities of wet leaves and twigs were homogenized with distilled water in a mixer grinder and centrifuged at 1000×*g* for 15 min, supernatants were freeze dried and used as crude extract (yield 20-24% of wet wt). Further, the extract was analyzed by HPLC (High Performance Liquid Chromatography) to find the major constituents. A safety trial was performed to set the safe dose of extract and it was found to be 200 mg/100 gm body weight.

Experimental Design: The experiment was performed at sub-acute level for 21 days. All the rats were divided into four groups and caged separately, as following:

Group I: **Control** (Given Saline only)

Group II: **Cadmium treated** (Given 0.42 mg/kg body weight $CdCl_2$)

Group III: ***Catharanthus* + Cadmium treated** (Given 200 mg/kg body weight *Catharanthus* 2 hrs prior to 0.42 mg/kg body weight $CdCl_2$)

Group IV: ***Catharanthus* treated** (Given 200 mg/kg body weight *Catharanthus*)

Experimental Methods: All the rats were weighted before and after the experiment to estimate the change in body weight. At the end of designated days the animals were sacrificed, their Liver and kidneys were taken out, weighted and further assessed. The blood samples were collected from direct cardiac puncture under aseptic conditions and centrifuged at 1000 g to determine the biochemical parameters:

- Nitrogenous wastes
  - Urea (Newman & Price, 1999)
  - Uric acid (Newman & Price, 1999)
  - Blood urea nitrogen (BUN) (Newman & Price, 1999)
  - Creatinine (Teitz *et al.*, 1994)
- Electrolytes
  - Sodium (Na^+) (Bassir, 1971)

- Potassium (K^+) (Bassir, 1971)
- Chloride (Cl^-) (Skeggs & Hachstrasser, 1964)

- Protien profiles (Dumas *et al.*, 1975)
  - Albumin
  - Globulin
  - A/G (Albumin/Globulin) ratio
  - Total proteins
- Lipid profiles
  - Cholesterol (Roeschlau *et al.*, 1974)
  - Triglycerides (Cole *et al.*, 1997)
  - Total lipids (Folch *et al.*, 1957)
- Metabolic enzymes
  - Aspartate aminotransferase (AST) (Rietman & Frnkel, 1954)
  - Alanine aminotransferase (ALT) (Rietman & Frnkel, 1954)
  - Alkaline phosphatase (ALP) (Bessy *et al.*, 1946)
  - Acid phosphatase (ACP) (Hillman, 1971)
  - Lactate dehydrogenase (LDH) (Babson & Babson, 1973)

Statistical Analysis: The data obtained from various biochemical tests were analyzed using one-way analysis of variance (ANOVA) followed by student Newman–Keul's (SNK) test. Results were expressed as Mean ± SEm. Differences with $P<0.05$ were considered as significant (Glantz, 1992).

RESULTS

Table 2.1 shows a significant increase in Liver Weight, Serum Urea, Uric acid, BUN (Blood Urea Nitrogen), Creatinin, K^+, A/G ratio, Cholesterol, triglyceride, Total Lipids, AST (Aspartate aminotransferase), ALT (Alanine aminotransferase), ALP (Alkaline phosphatase), ACP (Acid Phosphatase) and LDH (Lactate Dehydrogenase) while a significant decrease in Body weight, kidney weight, Serum Na^+, Cl^-, Albumin, Globulin and Total Proteins. These alterations in biochemical parameters are significantly retained to the normalcy by pretreatment with *Catharanthus* extract and this herbal extract did not show any ill effect of its own in the Group IV as compared to control.

DISCUSSION

Cadmium is a highly toxic metal, Found in Lithosphere. WEE (Electronic and Electrical Wastes) are the major issue in consideration regarding cadmium exposure. It is the main component of almost all electronic and electrical devices like light-sensitive resistors, corrosion-resistant alloys for marine and aviation environments, and nickel-cadmium batteries. The most common form of cadmium is found in Nickel-cadmium rechargeable batteries. These batteries tend to contain between 6-18% cadmium. The sale of Nickel-Cadmium batteries has been banned in the European Union except for medical use.

When not properly recycled it can leach into the soil, harming microorganisms and disrupting the soil ecosystem. Exposure is caused by proximity to hazardous waste sites and factories and workers in the metal refining industry. The inhalation of cadmium can cause severe damage to the lungs and is also known to cause kidney damage.

Table 2.1: Biochemical Alteration in the Serum of *Rattus norvegicus* against Sub-acute Cadmium intoxication and *Catharanthus roseus* Extract Pretreatment

(Values are expressed as Mean ± SEm)

Sl. No.	Biochemical Parameters	Group I: Control	Group II: Cadmium Treated	Group III: *Catharanthus* + Cadmium Treated	Group IV: *Catharanthus* Treated
1.	Body Weight(g)	104±0.58	84±1.15*	101±1.53	102.67±1.33
2.	Kidney Weight(g)	0.861±0.01	0.687±0.02*	0.847±0.03	0.834±0.02
3.	Liver Weight(mg)	3.34±0.12	4.34±0.12*	3.33±0.16	3.37±0.13
4.	Urea(mg/dl)	16.37 ± 0.12	19.27 ± 0.61*	16.33 ± 0.15	16.87 ± 0.47
5.	Uric Acid(mg/dl)	1.65 ± 0.02	1.76 ± 0.02*	1.66 ± 0.01	1.68 ± 0.01
6.	Creatinine(mg/dl)	0.42 ± 0.02	0.58 ± 0.03*	0.41 ± 0.02	0.47 ± 0.02
7.	BUN(mg/dl)	7.64 ± 0.05	9.36 ± 0.10*	7.63 ± 0.07	7.77 ± 0.28
8.	Na^+(mEq/L)	141 ± 0.58	132 ± 0.58*	142 ± 1.15	140 ± 1.15
9.	K^+(mEq/L)	4.17 ± 0.01	5.84 ± 0.07*	4.21 ± 0.01	4.30 ± 0.03
10.	Cl^+(mEq/L)	103 ± 1.00	93 ± 0.57*	101 ± 1.15	99 ± 1.00
11.	Albumin(g/dl)	3.52 ± 0.05	2.63 ± 0.04*	3.60 ± 0.06	3.35 ± 0.07
12.	Globulin(g/dl)	3.22 ± 0.07	1.29 ± 0.02*	3.23 ± 0.01	3.17 ± 0.01
13.	A/G Ratio	1.09 ± 0.01	2.04 ± 0.01*	1.11 ± 0.02	1.06 ± 0.02
14.	Total Proteins(g/dl)	6.75 ± 0.12	3.91 ± 0.06*	6.83 ± 0.06	6.52 ± 0.07
15.	Cholesterol(mg/dl)	5.67±0.36	9.07±0.36*	6.2±0.39	5.17±0.38
16.	Triglycerides(mg/dl)	47.88 ± 2.16	73.09 ± 6.79*	58.23 ± 4.18	46.27 ± 2.08
17.	Total Lipids((mg/dl))	63.8±0.79	85.87±1.23*	67.07±1.04	61.8±1.67
18.	AST(IU/L)	109±1.15	183±1.00*	113±1.33	107±1.00
19.	ALT(IU/L)	77±1.00	105±1.00*	79±0.58	75±1.53
20.	ALP(IU/L)	181.67±0.88	221.67±1.45*	186±1.0	183±.058
21.	ACP(IU/L)	244.33±0.88	288±0.58*	246.67±0.88	242.33±0.88
22.	LDH(IU/L)	87.53±0.52	156.1±1.10*	89.67±0.88	87.33±0.88

(i) Melting of Batteries

(ii) Burning of UPS

(iii) Burning of Electric wires

EXPEDIENT METHODS OF RECYCLING OF WEE

Prevalently in the expedient method of recycling and disposal of electrical and electronic-wastes (WEE), the equipment is simply tossed onto an open fire in order to melt plastic and to burn away invaluable metals. This releases carcinogens and neurotoxins into the air, while bone fire refuses intoxicate the water ways and groundwater table. Unsafe exposure may cause leaching of cadmium and other metals from landfills and incinerator ashes. Around 70% of cadmium in landfills comes from discarded electronics and electrical equipments.

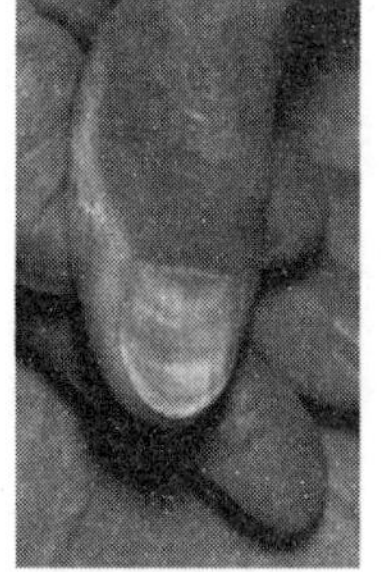
(i) Deposition of Uric Acid crystals in nails

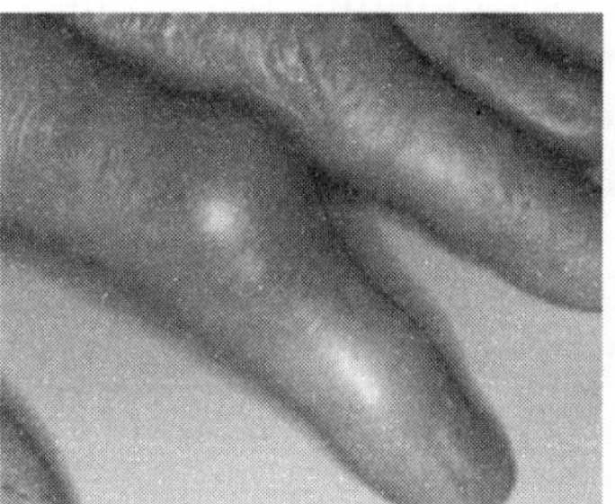
(ii) Gout affected hand-joints

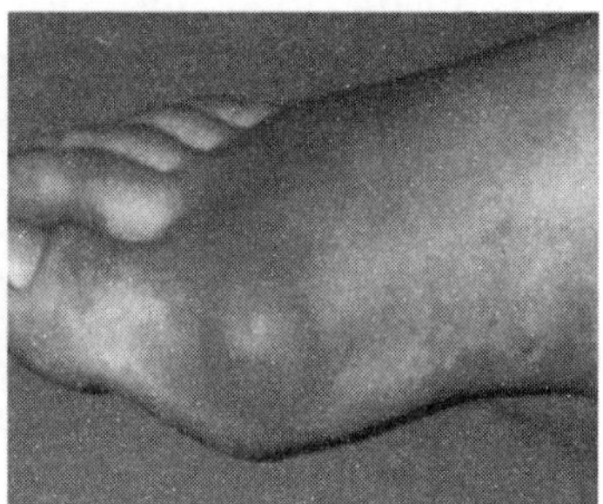
(iii) Gout affected leg-joints

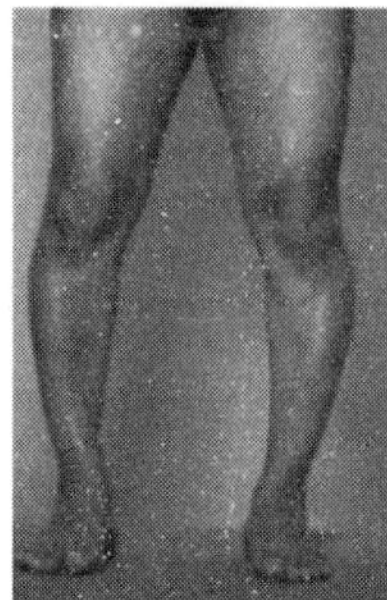
(iv) Osteomalacia

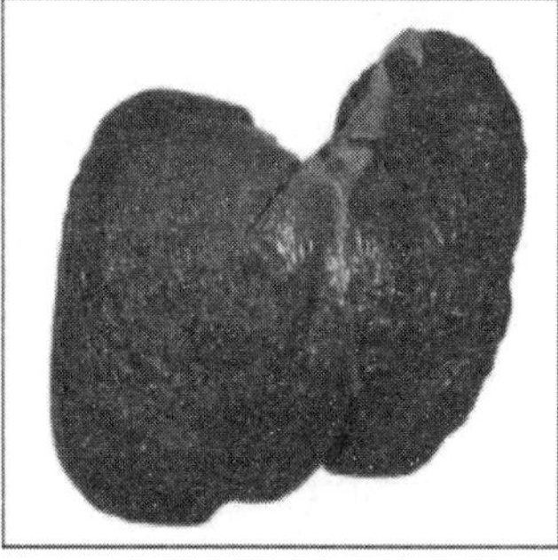
(v) Liver-Cirrhosis

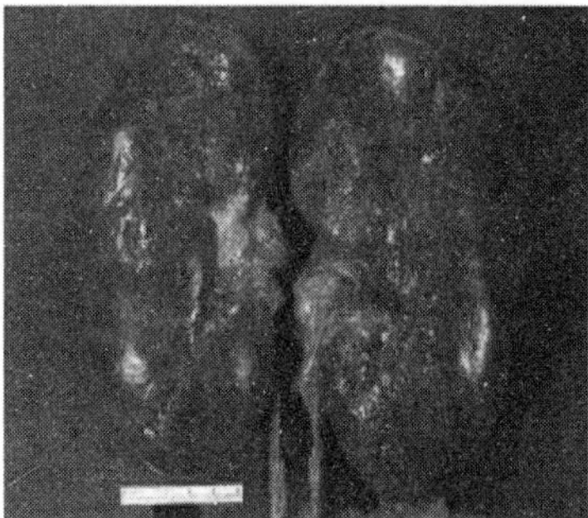
(vi) Kidney shrinkage

Cadmium is widely distributed in the body bound mainly to red blood cells. It accumulates (approximately 50 - 70 % of body burden) in the kidney and liver, where it induces the production of metallothionein that binds approximately 80 - 90 % of cadmium in the body. Accumulation of Cadmium makes such a dangerous and minimizing effect on body functions (Shaikh etal., 1999). Cadmium toxicity is symptomized by osteomalacia, osteoporosis, joint pain, gout, kideny-shrinkage, liver-damage, renal faluire, muscular-fatigue, anosmia, anaemia, carcinogenesis and sometimes coma. Ingestion of higher amounts may even cause death.

SYMPTOMS OF CADMIUM TOXICITY

The detailed mechanisms for the toxic effects of cadmium are still largely unknown. However, it is thought to involve interferences with antioxidant enzymes, alteration in thiol proteins, inhibition of energy metabolism alteration in DNA structure and affectation of some enzyme activities. Long-term exposure to Cadmium increases lipid peroxidation and causes inhibition of SOD activity indicating oxidative damage in liver and kidney. The various toxic effects induced by Cadmium in biological systems have been linked to increased lipid peroxidation. (Patra et al., 1999)

Rate and health effects of cadmium depend on its route of exposure. Cadmium is a cumulative toxin with a slow rate of elimination, accumulating mainly in the liver and kidneys. Cadmium poisoning is not reversible. It stays in the system for a very long time and excreted very slowly via metallothionein, the major excretory protein of kidney. Its biological half-life is 10 years, staying for a larger part of life (Longe, 2005). Besides cadmium's long half-life, the body lacks ability to metabolize it properly. Replacement of zinc and calcium inside the body is also an important mechanism of cadmium toxicity (Sutoo *etal.,* 2002).

Cadmium is known to increase oxidative stress by being a catalyst in the formation of reactive oxygen species, changing body metabolism of different biochemicals. Toxicity is caused by lipid peroxidation, free radical production and depleting glutathione and protein-bound sulfhydryl groups. Cadmium inhibits glutathione peroxidases resulting in reduced defense against the lipid peroxidation. (Novelli *et al.*, 2000, Congui *et al.* 2000) Cadmium also stimulates the production of inflammatory cytokines and downregulates the protective function of nitric oxide formation (Navas-Acien *et al.* 2004).

Thus cadmium toxicity is attributed to its slow rate of elimination, longer biological half life and no proper mechanism of body metabolism. Cadmium causes its injurious effects by acting as a catalyst in the generation of reactive oxygen species (ROS) (Zwennis *et al.*, 1992). Having been absorbed from the alimentary tract, metal forms durable combination with the protein thionein forming metallothionein, which play an important role in further metabolism of this m *et al.* Cadmium-Metallothionein complexe reaches kidneys for its elimination, so considered to be the most susceptible organs for metals (Choudhary *et al.*, 2001 and Hollis *et al.*, 2001).

In the present study, rats exposed to cadmium had significantly lower body weight and Kidney weights. Cadmium toxicity is manifested as loss of apetite, food-avoidance, leading to starvation that results in reduced body weight (Itokawa *et al.*, 1974). Increased protein catabolism (Siddhu *et al.*, 2004) and increased lipid peroxidation of polyunsaturated fatty acids of tissues and body fluids (Mata *et al.*, 1996) may also be attributed to reduced body weight and kidney weight.

Assessment of liver weight is also an important standard for toxicity measurement and it is found to be increased after subacute cadmium stress. Hepatomegaly and increased lipid and cholesterol content and decreased lipoprotein synthesis in liver may increase liver weight (Institoris *et al.*, 1999; Hamid, 2006).

The kidneys are critical target organ for cadmium toxicity (Cherian *et al.*, 1985 and Friberg *et al.*, 1986). Most studies on cadmium toxicity, therefore, centers on the detection of early signs of kidney dysfunction which results from oxidation. For general evaluation of kidney function, serum nitrogenous wastes and Protein profiles are generally considered (Denham *et al.*, 1975). According to the Anetor (2002) and Dioka *et al.* (2004), the serum nitrogenous waste concentration is determined largely by the efficiency of renal clearance. Accumulation of cadmium in the kidney results in loss of tubular function, leading to tubular proteinuria. Cadmium interferes with glomerular filtration rate (GFR) and tubular re-absorption and secretion (Soisungwan *et al.*, 2004).

Cadmium intoxication causes production of oxygen free radicals that increases oxidative stress and lipid peroxidation. The lipid droplets deposit in the pores of endothelial layer of glomerulus. This eventually produces endothelial injury, due to which glomerular filtration rate (GFR) decreases. Anetor (2002) also revealed that production of oxygen free radicals by cadmium induces tubular necrosis. Tubular necrosis increases tubular permeability, resulting in diffusion and back leak of the filtrate across the tubular basement membrane back into the interstitutium and circulation, which in turn leads to an apparent decrease in GFR. Under these circumstances excretion rate is decreased and retention of nitrogenous waste in serum is increased (Klassen, 1996 and Verbeka *et al.*, 1996).

The results of the study clearly indicate that Cadmium intoxication caused significant hyponatremia, hypochloremia and hyperkalemia which may be due to loss of renal tubular functions and glomerular injury (ATSDR, 2008). Generation of highly reactive oxygen species aftermath of cadmium exposure may result in systematic mobilization and depletion of the cell intrinsic antioxidant defence. Formation of reactive oxygen intermediates beyond the scavenging capacity of these antioxidant defence mechanisms results in accumulation of harmful free radicals and likelihood of oxidative damage to critical biomolecules, such as membrane proteins and lipids. This peroxidation in tubular epithelium leads to decrease in membrane fluidity and membrane integrity which delocalizes the enzyme Na-K ATPase from basolateral to apical membrane, while in glomerular filtration membrane decreases glomerular filtration rate (GFR). Thus both decreased GFR and backleak of filtrate leads to imbalanced serum electrolytes. (Schnellman and Kelly, 2008)

Besides cadmium damages juxtaglomerular apparatus, due to which renin secretion gets decreased, and probable disturbance in renin – angiotensinogen pathway generally causing aldosteron reduction resulting in electrolyte imbalance (Rhods and Tadnner, 1995; Wang and Giebisch, 1996 and Ellison, 2008).

Cadmium promotes lipid peroxidation, producing free radicals which damage the glomerular filtration membrane andultimately reduces GFR (Hussain, 2002). Damage in tubular epithelium causes diffusion and backleak of the filtrate across the tubular basement membrane back into interstitium and circulation. Thus both decreased GFR and backleak of filtrate leads to imbalanced serum electrolytes.

Glomerular membranes are highly selective, completely excluding the proteins like albumin, globulin and other plasma proteins. Cadmium damages the slit diaphragm of this membrane causing leakage of plasma proteins, in turn reduces the serum level of proteins. Loss of fixed negative charge from the GFM due to Cadmium intoxication may be another region for Proteinurea and therefore reduced serum protein profile. GFM bears fixed negative change. These negative charges impede the passage of negatively charged macromolecules by electrostatic repulsion and favors positively charged molecules by electrostatic attraction (Marya, 2003).

Liver, the key organ for lipid metabolism, is the main site for lipogenesis. Subacute cadmium Chloride stress significantly elevated the total lipid, triglyceride and cholesterol content of liver and so the liver weight. Cadmium concomitantly inhibits the protein synthesis by the production of free radicals (Saxena *et al.*, 2009). Inhibition of protein synthesis in liver leads to depression of lipoprotein synthesis and may be considered as probable reason for elevated lipid content of liver (Hamid, 2006).

The increase in the serum concentration of cholesterol may also result from Cadmium's ability to decrease its uptake by macrophages that play an important role in the processing of cholesterol (Remirez and Giemenz, 2002). Moreover, Cadmium may contribute to the development of hyper-cholesterolemia via increasing the production of inflammatory cytokines such as tumor necrosis factor α (TNF-α) and interleukin1β (IN-1β) (Harstad *et al., 2004*). Several studies have also shown that cytokines are involved in the increase in serum triglyceride levels by stimulating hepatic lipogenesis and suppressing fatty acid oxidation (Memon et al.,1993; Nachippan *et al.*, 1994).

Cadmium inside the body first of all binds to hepatic metallotheionin for excretion. When binding capacity is exceeded by cadmium concentration, it starts to create cellular toxicity. The toxicity is mediated by production of free radical. Cadmium exposure has implicated in alterations of enzymes, carbohydrate, proteins and lipid content of liver along with serious histological changes. (Friberg *et al.,* 1986)

Hepatocytes contain a well developed enzymatic system related to metabolism of proteins, fats, carbohydrates and xenobiotics. These enzymes are either present in cytosol or attached with biological membranes *viz.* plasma membrane, mitochondrial membrane and lysosomal membrane. ALT and LDH are cytosolic enzymes, while AST has two isozymes one being cytoplasmic and the other being bound to mitochondrial membrane. ALP is found firmly attached to plasma membrane and ACP is present within lysosomes (Luxton, 1999).

Toxic effect of cadmium on hepatocytes induces oxidative stress producing reactive oxygen species (ROS) (Zwenis *et al.,* 1992). ROS leads to production of free radicals and subsequent depletion of antioxidant cell defence, resulting in imbalanced oxidant/antioxidant in mammalian tissues. It causes the peroxidation of unsaturated fatty acids in bio-membranes (Radhika *et al.,* 2007).

Besides peroxidation, disruption of thiol proteins is also a crucial part of cell injury; it also enhances the lipid peroxidation. Increased lipid peroxidation causes oxidative inactivation of both membranous and soluble proteins. These damages release the enzymes from the membranes joining the biliary canalicules and sinusoidal border of parenchymal cells into the sinusoidal fluid causing the elevation of hepatic enzyme levels (Grey and Micheal, 2002).

Increased acid phosphatase in liver may be due to the metallic nature of cadmium which alters the cell membrane permeability and loss of lysosomal stability (Srivastav *et al.,* 2007). Cadmium reacts with membrane $Na^+ - K^+$ ATPase pump inducing cell-swelling and lysis of hepatocytes, this results in LDH release which is an indicator of hepatocyte death (Levinsky *et al.,* 1970).

Abetment of cadmium toxicity with rebalancing the impaired prooxidant/ antioxidant ratio through supplementation of antioxidant nutrients are still not completely clear. However, evidences suggest significant protective effects of dietary herbal supplementations. *Catharanthus,* chosen in the present study is one such herb.

Cantharanthus roseus is rich in alkaloids, carbohydrates, flavonoids, triterpenoids, tannins, coumarin, quinone and phenolic compounds (Uniyal *et al.,* 2001). HPLC studies revealed that flavonol glycosides (di- and trisaccharides of kaempferol, quercetin and isorhamnetin) are its major constituents, which are found to possess antioxidant property that compensate with oxidative stress induced by cadmium (Ferreres *et al.,*2008;). They are lipid soluble chain-breaking antioxidants, known to protect biological membranes and lipoproteins from oxidative stress. They may arrest oxidative stress at several levels of endogenous antioxidant mechanism, thus preventing serum electrolyte imbalance resulted due to cadmium intoxication. Being lipophilic in nature, they stabilizes hydrophobic interactions in the membrane thus minimizes lipid peroxidation.

Reduction in oxidative stress could be well understood as below:

$$SOOH + metal \longrightarrow SOO^{*} + metal^{(n-1)} + H^{+}$$

$$SOO^{*} + AH \longrightarrow SOOH + A^{*}$$

$$A^{*} + X^{*} \longrightarrow \text{Non radical complex}$$

Where,

S = Substance oxidized

AH = Antioxidant molecule

A^{*} = Antioxidant radical

X^{*} = another radical

Intake of *Catharanthus* reduces the peroxidation injury by Inhibition of ROS. This stabilizes the membrane integrity and reduces membrane fluidity of hepatocyte and glomerular cells. This reduces the leakage of hepatic enzymes, reverts Na^{+}- K^{+} ATPase back at its location, retains negetive charge and slit diaphragm of GFM and recoveres Jxtraglomarular apparatus.

Pretreatment with *Catharanthus* in Cadmium intoxicated rats was shown to be normalizing the elevated levels of serum lipids. This hypolipidemic effect of *Catharanthus* is mainly attributed to anti-lipoperoxidative activity of quercetin present in it, which prevents the oxidation of membrane lipid components and thus preserving the cellular and organeller membranes from the oxidative injury elicited by Cadmium. (Prabhu et al., 2013). In addition, quercetin is reported to exert anti-inflammatory effects (Ferry et al., 1996), thereby, reducing the inflammatory reactions of cytokines, which in turn suppress their influence on lipid metabolism thus regaining the normal level of lipids, cholesterol and triglyceride.

The restoration of oxidant/antioxidant balance is reflected by normalized serum levels of nitrogenous wastes, electrolytes, proteins, lipids and metaboloic enzymes. The findings of present study conclude that cadmium is a highly toxic metal, while *Catharanthus roseus* is found to be a good protective agent against this toxicity. It ameliorates the impaired body functions associated with cadmium toxicity in albino rats offering itself as a novel drug for future and need to be evaluated for further study.

REFERENCES

1. Agency for Toxic Substances and Disease Registry (2008): Toxicological Profile for Cadmium, Draft for Public comment. US Department of Health and Human Services, Atlanta, US.

2. Anetor J.I. (2002): Serum Uric Acid and Standardized Urinary Protein: Reliable Bioindicators of Leads Nephropathy in Nigerian Lead Workers. *African J Biomed Res,* 5: 19-24.
3. Babson, A.L. and Babson S. R. (1973): Kinetic Colorimetric Measurement of Serum Lactate Dehydrogenase Activity. *Clin. Chem.,* 19: 766-769.
4. Bassir, O. (1971): Handbook of Practical Biochemistry. Ibadan University Press, Ibadan, Nigeria. pp: 53-54.
5. Bessey, O.A., Lowery O.H. and Brock M.J. (1946): A Method for Determination of Alkaline Phosphatase with 5 mm^3 of Serum. J. Biol. Chem., 164: 321-329.
6. Cherian M.G., O2 Heany J., Kusiak R.A. (1985): Health Effects of Cadmium and its Inorganic Compounds, Ontario Ministry of Labour, Toronto.
7. Choudhary H., Harvey T, Thayer W.C., Lockwood T.F., Stitelor W.M., Goodrum P.E., Hasset J.M., Diamond G.L. (2001): Urinary Cadmium Elimination as a Biomarker of Exposure for Evaluating a Cadmium Dietary Exposure – Biokinetics Model. *J Toxicol Environ Health,* 63: 221-250.
8. Cole, T.G., Klotzsch S.G. and Mc Namara J.R. (1997): Measurement of Triglyceride Concentration. In: Hand Book of Lipoprotein Testing. AACC Press. Washington D C, pp: 115.
9. Congui, L.M., Chicca A., Pilastro A., Turchetto M. and Tallandini L. (2000): Effects of Chronic Dietary Cadmium on Hepatic Glutathione Levels and Glutathione Peroxidase Activity in Starlings. *Archives of Environmental Contamination and Toxicology,* 38: 357-361.
10. Denham M.J., Hodkinson H.M., Fisher M. (1975): Glomerular Filtration Rate in Sick Elderly Patients. *Oxford J,* 4 (1): 32-36.
11. Dioka, C.E., Orisakwe O.E., Adeniyi F.A. and Meludu S.C. (2004): Liver and Renal Function Tests in Artisans Occupationally Exposed to Lead in Mechanic Village in Nnewi, Nigeria. *Int J Environ Res Public Health,* 1 (1): 21-25.
12. Dumas, B.T., Peters T.J. and Biomonle G.T. (1975): Protiens (Total Protiens) in Serum, Urine and Cerebrospinal Fluid. In: Selected Methods of Clinical Chemistry. Vol. 9 (W.R. Foulkner and S. Meits, eds.) Washington DC, pp: 822-828.
13. E.L.B. Novelli, Marques S.F.G., Almeida J.A., Diniz Y.S., Faine L.A. and Ribas B.O. (2000): Toxic Mechanism of Cadmium Exposure on Cardiac Tissue. *Toxic Substance Mechanisms*, 19(4): 207-217.
14. Ellison D.H. (2008): Atlas of Kidney Diseases. Colorado: Blackwell Publishing, 2008.
15. E-Waste Guide (2008): http://www.ewaste.in.
16. Ferreres F., Pereira D.M., Valentão P., Andrade P.B., Seabra R.M. and Sottomayor M. (2008): New Phenolic Compounds and Antioxidant Potential of *Catharanthus roseus. J Agric Food Chem,* 56(21): 9967-9974.
17. Ferry, D.R., Smith A., Malkhandi J., fyee D.W., Detakats P.G. and Anderson D. (1996): Phase I Clinical Trial of the Flavonoid Quercetin: Pharmacokinetics and Evidence for *in vivo* Tyrosine Kinase Inhibition. *Clin Cancer Res,* 2: 659-668.
18. Finney D.J. (1971): Probit Analysis, 3rded, Cambridge University Press, Cambridge, pp: 8-80.
19. Folch, J., Less M. and Stanley G.H.S. (1957): A Simple Method for Isolation and Purification of Total Lipids from Animal Tissues. *J. Biol. Chem.*, 226(1): 497-509.
20. Friberg L., Elinder C.G., Kjellstrom T. and Nordberg G.F. (1986): General Summary and Conclusions and Some Aspects of Diagnosis and Treatment of Chronic Cadmium Poisoning. *Cadmium and Health,* 2: 247-255.

21. Glant, S.A (1992): Primer of Biostatistics, 3rd ed, McGraw Hill, New York, pp: 24-56.
22. Gray, M.W. and Michael. J.I. (2002): Toxicology Pathology. 2nd ed. Elsevier. London, pp: 41.
23. Hamid, A.N.M. (2006): Diphenyl dimethyl bicarboxylate as an Effective Treatment for Chemical Induced Fatty Liver in Rats. African J. Biomed. Res, 9(2): 77-81.
24. Hillman, G.J. (1971): Continous Photometric Measurement of Prostate Acid Phosphatase Activity. *Clin. Chem. Clin. Biochem,* 9: 273-277.
25. Hollis L., Hogstrand C. and Wood C. M. (2001): Tissue Specific Cadmium Accumulation, Metallothionein Induction and Tissue Zinc and Copper Levels during Chronic Sublethal Cadmium Exposure in Juvenile Rainbow Trout. *Arch Environ Contam Toxicol,* 41: 468-474.
26. Hussain, H.E.M.A. (2002): Hypoglycemic, Hypolipidemic and Antioxidant Properties of Combination of *curcumin* from *Curcuma longa*, Linn. and Partially Purified Product from *Abroma augusta*, Linn. In Streptozotocin Induced Diabetes. *Indian J. Clin. Biochem.*, 17 (2): 33-43.
27. Institoris, L., Siroki O., Undeger U., Desi I. and Nagymajtenyi L. (1999): Immunotoxicological Effects of Repeated Combined Exposure by Cypermethrin and the Heavy Metals Lead and Cadmium in Rats. *Intern. J. of Immunopharmacol.,* 21: 735-743.
28. Itokawa Y., Abe T., Tabei R. and Tanaka S. (1974): Renal and Skeletal Lesions in Experimental Cadmium Poisoning: Histological and Biological Approaches. *Arch Environ Health.* 28: 149-154.
29. Klassen, C.D. (1996): Heavy Metals and Heavy Metal Antagonists. In: *Goodman and Gilman's The Pharmacological Basis of Therapeutics,* (Hardman J. G., Gilman A. G. and Limbird L. E., eds) McGraw – Hill, New York, pp: 1649-1672.
30. Levinsky, W.J., Smalley R.V., Villyer A.N. and Shindler R.L. (1970): Arsine Hemolysis. *Arch Environ. Health*, 20: 436-440.
31. Longe, L.J. (2005): Cadmium Poisoning. In: The Gale Encyclopedia of Alternative Medicine. 1(2): 342-372.
32. Luxton. R. (1999): BMS Explained Clinical Biochemistry. Butterworth – Heinemann Press. Oxford, pp: 228-240.
33. Marya, R.K., (2003): The Kidney. In: Medical Physiology. CBS Publishers and Distributors, New Delhi, pp: 534-559.
34. Mata, P., Alonso R., Lopez-fare A., orders J. M., Lahore C., Caramel C., Codices R., Blanquez E. and Deova M. (1996): Effect of Dietary Fat Saturation on LDL Oxidation and Monocyte Adhesion to Human Endothelial Cells *in vitro. Arterioscler. Thromb. Vasc. Biol.,* 16: 1347-1355.
35. Memon R.A., Grunfeld C., Moser A.H., Feingold K.R. (1993): Tumor Necrosis Factor Mediates the Effects of Endotoxin on Cholesterol and Triacylglycerol Metabolism in Mice. *Endocrinology* , 132: 2246-2253.
36. Nachiappan V., Curtiss D., Corkey, B. E. and Kilpatrick L. (1994): Cytokines Inhibit Fatty Acid Oxidation in Isolated Rat Hepatocytes: Synergy Among TNF, IL-6 and IL-1. Shock, 1: 123-129.
37. Navas-Acien, A., Selvin, E., Sharrett, A. R., Calderon-Aranda, E., Silbergeld E. and Guallar E. (2004): Lead, Cadmium, Smoking, and Increased Risk of Peripheral Arterial Disease. *Circulation,* 109: 3196-1201.
38. Newman, D.J. and Price C.P. (1999): Renal Functions and Nitrogen Metabolism. In: Tietz Textbook of Clinical Chemistry, 3rd Edition. (Burtis, C.A. and E.R. AshwoodS eds.) WB Saunders, Philladelphia. pp: 1024-1264.

39. Patra R.C., Swarup D. and Senapat S.K., (1999): Effects of Cadmium on Lipid Peroxides and Superoxide Dismutasein Hepatic, Renal and Testicular Tissue of Rats. *Veterinary and Human Toxicology*. 41(2): 65-67.
40. Prabhu, S.M., Muthuamani M. and Shagirtha K. (2013): Quercetin Potentially Attenuates Cadmium Induced Oxidative Stress Mediated Cardiotoxicity and Dyslipidemia in Rats. *European Review for Medical and Pharmacological Sciences*, 17: 582-595.
41. Radhika R., Geetha S., Lakshmi R. and Kannan M. (2007): Antioxidants are Boon to Life. *Agrobios Newletter,* VI (6): 11-12.
42. Ramesh Babu B., Parande A.K. and Ahmed Basha C. (2007): Electrical and Electronic Waste: A Global Environmental Problem. *Waste Manag Res.*, 25: 307-18.
43. Ramirez D.C. and Gimenez M.S. (2002): Lipid Modification in Mouse Peritoneal Macrophages after Chronic Cadmium Exposure. *Toxicology,* 2: 172: 1-12.
44. Reitman S. and Frankel S. (1957): A Colorimetric Method for the Determination of Serum gglutamic Oxaloacetate and Pyruvate Transaminases. *American J. Clin. Pathol.,* 28: 56-63.
45. Rhoads R.A. and Tdnner G.A., (1995): Medical Physiology. Lippincort William and Wilkins, Philadelphia.
46. Roeschlau, P., Bernt E. and Gruber W.J. (1974): Enzymatic Determination of Total Cholesterol in Serum. *Clin. Chem. Clin. Biochem.,* 25(1): 226.
47. Saxena, P.N., Bajaj P., Saxena N. and Anand S. (2009): Hepatoprotective Role of *Curcuma aromatica* Leaf Extract Following Arsenic Trioxide Intoxication in Albino Rat *Rattus norvegicus* (Berkenhout), *Proc. Nat. Acad. Sci. India, Sec. B*, 79(III) : 50-55.
48. Schnellmann R.G. and Kelly K.J. (2008): Atlas of Kidney Diseases, Blackwell Publishers, Colorado.
49. Shaikh Z.A., Vu T.T. and Zaman K. (1999): Oxidative Stress as a Mechanism of Chronic Cadmium-induced Hepatotoxicity and Renal Toxicity and Protection by Antioxidants. *Toxicol Appl Pharmacol,* 154: 256-263.
50. Siddhu, P., Garg M.L. and Dhawan D.K. (2004): Protective Effects of Zinc on Oxidative Stress Enzymes in Liver of Protein Deficient Rats. *Nutr. Hosp.,* 19(6): 341-347.
51. Skeggs, L.T. and Hochstresser H.C. (1964): Thiocyanate Method (Colorimetri Method) of Chloride Estimation. *Clin. Chem.,* 10: 918-920.
52. Soisungwan S., Muneko N., Pailin U., Yuvaree V., Jason R. B. and Michael R. M. (2004): Effects of Chronic Exposure to Low-level Cadmium on Renal Tubular Function and CYP2A6-mediated Coumarin Metabolism in Healthy Human Subjects. *Toxicol Let,* 148: 187-197.
53. Srivastava, S., Jadon A. and Shukla S. (2007): Effect of Tiron and it's Combination with Nutritional Supplements Against Vanadium Intoxication in Female Albino Rats. *J. Toxicol. Sci.*, 32(2): 185-192.
54. Sutoo, D.K.A. and Shunichiro, I. (1990): A Mechanism of Cadmium Poisoning: The Cross Effect of Calcium and Cadmium in the Calmodulin-dependent System. *Archives of Toxicology* 64: 161-164.
55. T. Wang and Giebisch G. (1996): Effects of Angiotensin II on Electrolyte Transport in the Early and Late Distal Tubule in Rat Kidney. *Am. J. Physiol. Ren. Flu. Elect. Physiol.* 39: 211 -219.
56. Tietz, N.W., Prude E.L. and Sirgard-Anderson O. (1994): Tietz Textbook of Clinical Chemstry (Burtis, C.A. and E.R. Ashwood, eds.) WB Saunders Company, London, pp: 1345-1374.

57. Uniyal G.C., Bala S., Mathur A.K. and Kulkarni R.N. (2001): Symmetry C18 Column: A Better Choice for the Analysis of Indole Alkaloids of *Cathranthus roseus. Phytoche Anal.,* 12: 206-210.

58. Verbeke M., Van De Voorde J., Lameire N. (1996): Prevention of Experimental Acute Tubular Necrosis: Current Clinical Applications and Perspectives. *Adv Nephrol,* 25: 177-216.

59. Zwennis W.C. and Franssen A. C. (1992): Assessment of Occupational Exposure to Cadmium in the Netherlands, 1980-1989. *Am J Ind Med,* 21: 793-805.

WASTE DISPOSAL AND MANAGEMENT *Pages:* 31-49
Edited by: Dr. Pawan Kumar 'Bharti'; Dr. B. Tabassum; and Dr. Priya Bajaj
ISBN: 978-93-5056-729-6
Edition: 2015
Published by: Discovery Publishing House Pvt. Ltd., New Delhi (India)

3

Waste Generation, Management and Utilization in University of Nigeria, Nsukka *A Model Approach*

Okenmuo, F.C., Igwe, C.A. and **Ezeaku, P.I**

ABSTRACT

The paper presents a study undertaken to improve the waste management approach of the University of Nigeria in its bid to achieve a world class standard. The study is based on strategies to suggest alternative uses of waste generated in the institution while maintaining environmental quality. The research develops a model known as CTTU model. The acronym models for *Collection, Transportation, Transformation and Utilization.* The model adopts an ambitious goal of 'Zero Waste' or 'All utilizable'. Wastes are broadly classified into biodegradable and non-biodegradable. The biodegradable can be transformed into fertilizers which can go back into the soil or used as fuel plus other uses. The non-biodegradable can be reused, recycled or converted to energy WtE. The model starts from the point where wastes become 'waste' to its further utilization. The conceptual structure challenges researchers and practitioners, encourages innovation. It starts with a picture of a man with waste in his hands asking himself, "What can I still do with this". The CTTU model is novel and requires further research, development and application.

INTRODUCTION

Society's concern for environmental quality has forced waste generators to seek non-polluting, but still affordable ways of disposing of waste

Department of Soil Science, University of Nigeria, Nsukka, Nigeria.

materials. Although, once seen as mere waste products to be flushed in to rivers and out to sea, these materials are increasingly seen as sources of nutrients and organic matter that can be used beneficially to promote soil productivity in agriculture, forestry and disturbed land reclamation (Brady and Well, 2002).

The soil is a primary recipient, by design or accident, of a myriad of waste products and chemicals used in modern society. It has been convenient to "throw things away". Every year, millions of tons of products from a variety of sources – industrial, domestic and agricultural, find their way into the world's soil, they become part of biological cycles that affect all forms of life (Brady and Well, 2002). The major problem caused by waste to the environment is pollution (Adewole, 2009).

In the past 20 years, there have been suggestions for a new type of soil science: a soil science that is more holistic, part of a network of society, geared towards soil care approach or in relation with the society. Hence, the interest of the soil scientist is to maintain environmental quality through waste utilization.

Whereas soils tell us about the history of every human settlement, and give us information about the social structure of our modern society; waste is an unavoidable by-product of human activities, economic development, urbanization and improved living standards. In Nigeria, there are twenty-seven federal universities (www.nuc.org) and several polytechnics, college of educations and secondary schools that receive funding from the federal government and have resident staff quarters and students' hostels. The University of Nigeria is amongst them. Since the formal opening of the university on 7 October 1960, there has been steady increase in students' enrolment, growing infrastructural development and observed marginal improvement in the standard of living of University workers resulting from relatively enhanced emoluments and also increased commercial activities within the campus. The increase in population and living standard has been equated to waste generation (although there are other factors).

Presently, the firm responsible for collecting wastes from the students' hostels and staff quarters is Sonafem agency, while Total Facility Company is responsible for clearing lawns, fields, collecting the bigger bins and transporting to landfills located at Ofulonu, Odenigbo Road, Nsukka. However, no further treatment or management is carried out. Adverse environmental impact of this kind of practice has been reported to include: wind-blown litter, attraction of vermin, generation of liquid leachate, greenhouse gases, odour and killing vegetation (Okeniyi and Anwan, 2012). Wastes are comprised of biodegradable and non- biodegradable fractions-organic matter and recyclables, alternative methods are being sought for their utilization. The present system is observed to be inefficient and incapable of maintaining environmental quality. More so, the waste collection from storage bin is not adequate- around the institution: either the bin storage capacity is not large enough or that the collection schedule of the contracting firm is irregular. The effect of these anomalies is the overflow of bins, indiscriminate dumping and littered environment. Also, behind the students hostels (precisely Mbanefo Hostel), there are noticeable and unhealthy sights of broken sewage lines where farmers grow crops.

Mbagwu (2003) classified improperly disposed urban and sewage wastes as agents of soil degradation. One common waste in the University of Nigeria is water sachet. It is made of low density polyethylene (LDPE), and is usually littered on campus. The situation is worsened by the non-biodegradable nature of the sachet and the unavailability of recycling technology in Nigeria.

The CTTU model for waste utilization is therefore proposed as a convenient method of waste collection, transportation, transformation and utilization. It proposes ethical waste management options for conserving natural resources in order to ensure that wastes are put to alternative uses for wealth creation. Agunwamba *et al.* (1998) observed that the core of solid waste management in Nigeria is the absence of policies, enabling legislation and an environmentally stimulated and enlightened public. The CTTU model is expected to aid in that respect.

The aim of this paper is therefore to improve understanding of the mechanisms of waste generation at the University of Nigeria, to stimulate waste utilization concept through awareness of the adverse consequences of present practices, to assist in waste quantifying in order to predict potentialities for utilization, and to develop a working model for waste utilization –known as the CTTU model.

BRIEF DESCRIPTION OF THE UNIVERSITY OF NIGERIA

The University of Nigeria, Nsukka established in 1960 lies on the North-West corner of the Eastern Region of Nigeria at a distance of about seventy kilometres from Enugu, the then regional capital, but now the capital of one of the states that make up the region. The University is located in Nsukka Local Government on latitude 6° 51′ 24″N and longitude 7° 23′ 45″E and 400m above sea level. The mean annual rainfall is 1,614. The maximum and minimum mean monthly temperatures range from 26°C to 33°c and 19°c to 22°c respectively. The vegetation is derived savanna. The soil belongs to Nsukka and Mpologwu series classified as Ultisol.

The population of the two-campus University has grown from 220 students at inception as (Obechina *et al.*, 1986) to student enrolment at present, of about 30000 - 35000 annually. Statistics from the Academic Planning Unit show that in the 2006/2007 academic year the overall students' enrolment in both campuses was about 31,159 out of which 20,688 enrolled at the Nsukka campus. Furthermore, there are about 21 resident students' hostels with an estimated 2,220 rooms at the Nsukka campus of the university as at the 2007/2008 academic session. In addition, there are twelve faculties, sixty-two departments and several public and academic buildings in the Nsukka Campus.The University also has about 642 senior staff housing units of various grades (flats, bungalows and duplexes) and 92 junior staff housing units.

Information from the Students Affairs Unit of the University indicates a growing number of the population of officially recognized resident students over the years which now stands, on average, of about 9720 students/year. The University community is indeed a mini-township (Unachukwu, 2010).

The University receives funding from the Federal Government through the National Universities Commission. However, due to continuing adjustments in government's economic policies, coupled with high students' enrolment, growing infrastructural development, and demand for better conditions of service etc, financial releases from government are no longer sufficient to meet the growing needs of the University. The administration under Prof. Barth Okolo has a vision of making the university a world class University. These cannot be achieved through infrastructural development alone but also through enhanced waste utilization, sustainable resource conservation and atitudinal change. The CTTU model of waste utilization will help the institution positively contribute to growing environmental concerns such as climate change, environmental quality and managing wastes to reduce pollution while creating wealth. The model will help the institution attain a world class standard through the 'zero waste' principle.

BACKGROUND STUDIES OF WASTE GENERATION

Waste is an unavoidable by-product of human activities. Development, urbanization and improved living standard in cities increase the quantity and complexity of generated municipal soild waste (WSW) (Hrebicek and Soukopova, 2010)

Leton and Omotosho (2004) defined solid wastes as non liquid and non-gaseous products of human activities regarded as useless. It could take the form of refuse garbage and sludge.

Adewole (2009) defined waste as any liquid or gaseous substances being scrap or being super flows, refuse or reject is disposed as unwanted.

Waste generation scenario in Nigeria has been of great concern both locally and globally. Of the categories of wastes generated, solid waste posed a hydra - headed problem beyond the cope of various solid waste management systems in Nigeria (Geoffrey, 2005).

Sada (1984) observed in 1980, on average balance of 100metric tons of solid waste are piled up in Benin City. This is because while about 350 metric tons of solid wastes are generated daily the maximum rate of evacuation achievable was only 250 metric tons daily. Uwadiegwu and Chukwu (2013) remarked that studies by Uchegbu in 1988 reported that big cities like Enugu, Lagos, Kano etc. in Nigeria produced on the average 46 kg of solid waste per person, per day and as living standard rise people consume more and generate more waste.

The causes of waste problem is not the volume produced but in the degree of effectiveness of soild waste management. One cannot say that the developing countries produce more solid wastes than the developed. However, it is the management that makes the difference (Omuta, 1988).

Waste disposal services in developing countries there are three options to getting rid of waste; landfilling, incineration or recycling. Landfilling is the cheapest alternative but can become problematic in terms of shortage of land and pollution/harzardous waste spreading from the dumpsites.

Incineration is not really suitable for developing countries since their waste often contain high level of organic material (Nas and Jaffe, 2004). Ogwueleka (2003) also observed that wastes in developing countries contain so much moisture that fuel has to be added to maintain combustion, low calorific value and low combustible components of solid waste in Nigeria make incineration uneconomical.

The most environmentally friendly and cost effective alternative of waste disposal is recycling. Efficient recycling and composting could save 18.6% in waste management cost 57.7% in land full cost (Agunwamba, 1998).

Wastes can be classified by a multitude of schemes according to White *et al.* (1995) by:

- Physical states - solid, liquid or gaseous;
- Original use - packaging waste, food waste etc;
- Material type - glass, paper etc;
- Physical properties - combustible, compostable, recyclable;
- Origin - domestic, commercial, institutional, agricultural, industrial etc;
- Safety level - hazardous and non- hazardous.

Waste compositions in developing countries are similar. Bandara *et al.* (2007) in a study in Moratuwa, Sri Lanka observed that the average amount of waste per capita per day in the area was 374g of organic waste, 18.9g of paper, 14.1g of plastic, 66.9g of glass and 29.7g of metal. He therefore called for a focus on managing biodegradable organic waste (having about 90% of the total waste), considering the fraction and potential to impact the quality of leachate and gas generation if deposited in a sanitary landfill.

A study by Alaci and Ezeaku (2008) in Bole sub-city of Addis Ababa reveals rate of waste generation to amount to 293,611 kg with 267,920 kg biodegradable content and is expected to increase if the current moderate of economic growth in the national economy is sustained. The study further reveals that at individual level, an average of 0.19 kg solid waste per day is generated in Ureal, while around Airline village, the rate is 1.70 kg per day. The clear difference between quantities of waste generated between the two sub-cities is a pointer to the socio-economic variation within the two locations. The scenario is that an area of higher socio-economic status generates more wastes.

The quantity and rate of solid waste generation in various states in Nigeria depends on the population, level of industrialization, socio-economic status of the citizens and kinds of commercial activities being predominant (Babayemi and Dauda, 2009). Nigeria having a population of 120 million (Sridhar and Adeoye, 2003) generated 0.58kg, solid waste per person per day. This is similar to Ogwueleka (2009) whose figures range from 280kg/m^3- 370kg/m^3 and waste generation rates ranging from 0.44 - 0.66kg/capita/day in Nigeria.

In a study in Covenant University Ota in Nigeria using a generator-based study with a population of about 8,141 population, waste materials were sorted into materials types which include paper/cardboard, plastic food pack, plastic bottles, metal cans, food wastes, polythene bags, polystyrene food pack and combustible miscellaneous waste materials over a period of 10 weeks (Okeniyi and Anwan, 2012). Fig 1 shows the waste percentage generated from the University.

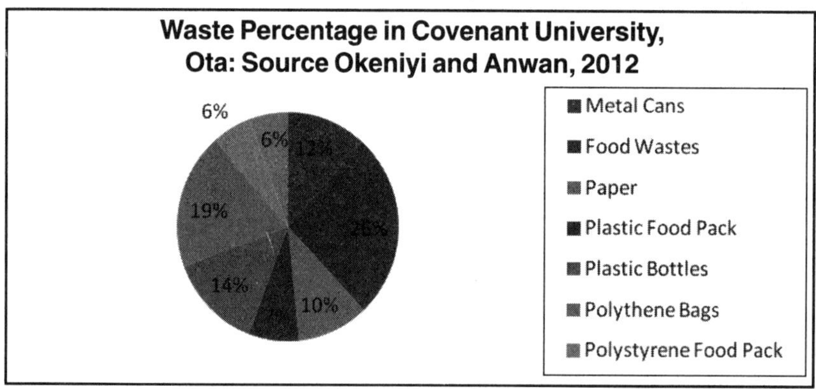

Fig. 3.1: **Waste Percentage in Covenant University, Ota: Source Okeniyi and Anwan (2012)**

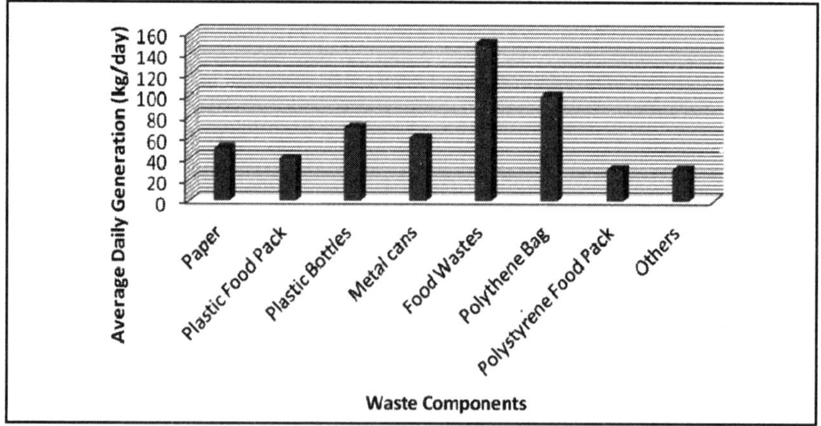

Fig. 3.2: **Waste Generated Daily showng their Components: Source Okeniyi and Anwan (2012)**

The sources of waste generation in university of Nigeria include; offices, lecture halls, residential quarters, hostels, farm and agricultural areas, hospital, business units including canteens, laboratories. Others include construction and demolition areas, sport complexes, churches etc.

The wastes include papers, food wastes, plastics, bottles, crop residues, garden wastes, chemicals, concrete, asphalt, wood, water satchet, ICT waste, soil, sludge, metal etc. Generally, they can be classified using diagram below (Fig. 3.3) into biodegradable and non-biodegradable.

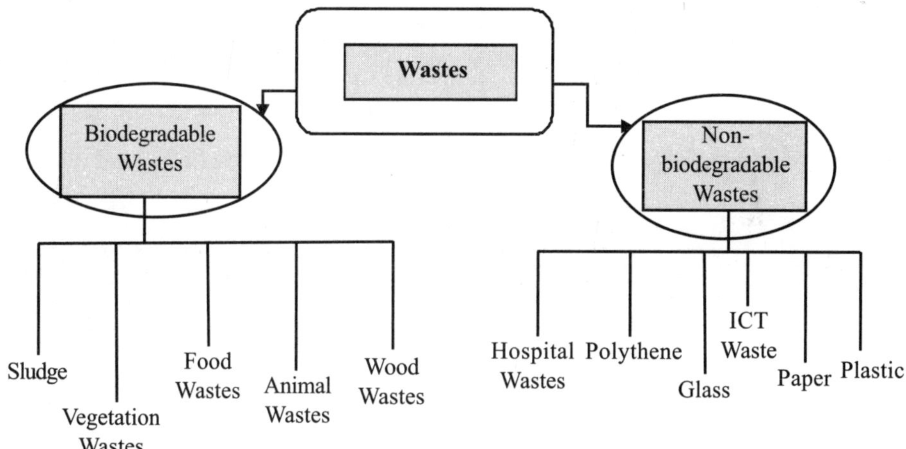

• *Fig. 3.3:* **Classification of some Wastes Generated in University of Nigeria based on their Ablities to Decompose**

PRESENT WASTE MANAGEMENT STRATEGY

Presently, our waste management programmes involve simply moving waste from one place to another and not really managing it. Smaller bins are placed in offices and rooms the generator disposes the bin to the outer small bins located in the corridors, laboratories and mainly under shades. These categories are handled by the Sonafem agency which they daily empty into the larger bin, handled by the Total facility agency that also control the overgrown lawn. Larger bins are located in common areas near buildings and campus grounds. The volume of the bin is about 3m^3.Fig 4 shows a photo of the larger bin.

The bin are evacuated into vehicle for landfill to remote outskirts precisely Ofulonu, Odenigbo road within Nsukka town. It is instructive to warn that these locations considered 'remote' today may become settlement sites tomorrow, considering population growth and scarce land resources, meaning that we are currently burying time bombs that may explode tomorrow to consume millions of human beings.

Fig. 3.4: **One of the Larger Bins Between Odili and Nkrumah Hostels, UNN**

Behind the hostels are sewage lines which have been broken or blocked by waste materials and waste water. Crops like maize, vegetables, potatoes etc. studies have shown that waste water percolates the soil system and enriches the toxicity levels of heavy metals and become victims of its hazardous effects by consuming crops grown on the contaminated soil (Onweremadu, 2008).

A walk around the institution clearly shows that waste generation rate and collection and management has a missing link as most bin overflow and indiscriminate littering especially of water sachets. A profile dug at the hind part of the students hostels indicated that water sachets were found even at the B-horizon of the soil profile. The negative environmental consequence of these condition include; soil-water imbalance, reduction of soil aeration, runoff and increasing susceptibility to flood events and erosion by blocking canals and impeding drainage. In Nigeria, solid waste management is characterized by inefficient collection methods, insufficient coverage of the collecting system and improper disposal (Ogwueleka, 2009).

THE C.T.T.U. MODEL AND ASSUMPTIONS

The CTTU model is a waste utilization model that aims to achieve the zero waste targets through waste resource utilization. This will lead to conservation of resources e.g. petroleum resource which is projected to be depleting, creating wealth through alternative use of resources while reducing the negative impact climate change, soil pollution and health hazards associated with inadequate waste management practices.

Fig. 3.5: **Shows a Profile where Polythene can cause Soil Pollution Near Farm at the Mbanefo Hostel**

Fig. 3.6: **Is a Bin located near Nkrumah Hostel Overflowing**

Life-cycle assessment (LCA) can help to decide whether it is sustainable either to reuse or recycle waste streams or to recover the energy only. LCA is a comparative methodology used to determine the environmental impact and energy or resource composition of products and services over their whole life cycles (extraction of raw materials, production of the product itself, use of their product and treatment after disposal as waste). Any utilization strategy that consumes more resources and energy or has a greater negative environmental impact than the initial production from primary raw materials is considered "non- sustainable" (Recycling Research and Technology, nd)

The CTTU model for waste utilization agrees with LCA waste hierarchy as we say in Nigeria- "prevention is better than cure. (Fig. 3.6) shows the waste hierarchy.

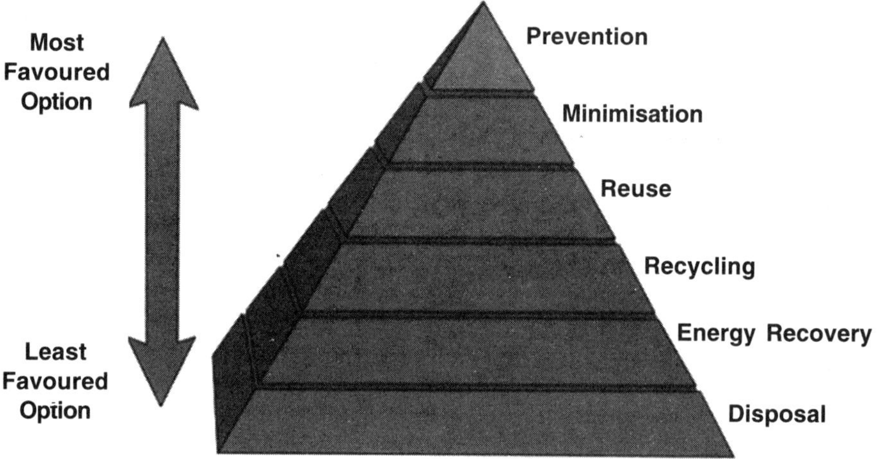

However, most goods and services must be provided in order to meet man's needs. The disposal will take the model of collection, transportation, transformation and utilization. The model involves the waste generator (who sorts out his waste into biodegradable and non- biodegradable using containers clearly labeled). The waste is carried by firm responsible for cleaning and disposed in outer two containers labeled and provided with facilities to suit the kind of waste e.g. organic wastes must have been tightly tied (by waste generator) or outer container should have a lid. The firm responsible for evacuating the waste carries it off to transformation sites for further sorting, processing and possible utilization.

A major challenge in the CTTU model is the attitude of individuals involved and presence of facilities to achieve effective utilization of material. The factor affecting resurce utilization is shown in Fig. 3.7.

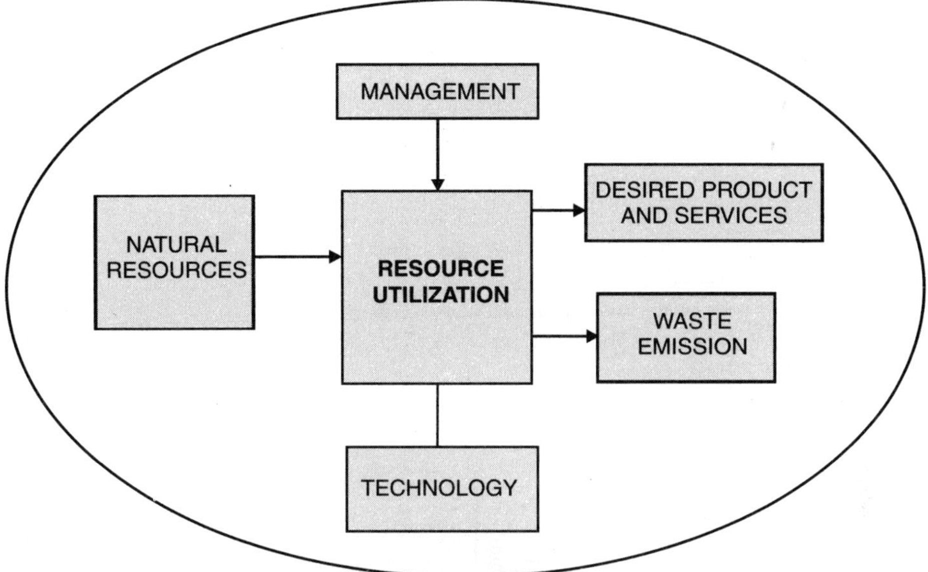

Fig. 3.7: **Factors Affecting Waste Resource Utilization**

Assumptions of the CTTU Model

The population of the University was assumed to be stable excluding other persons and activities which contribute to the waste generation. If the average number of students residing in the 21 hostels are 9,720 and staff residing in the residential quarters be 15persons for each of the 12 faculties. With little or no outside interfere.

Therefore; 15 staff × 12 faculties =180 staff

180 staff + 9,720 students = 9,900 people

If the average waste generated per person (per capita) per day is 0.58kg solid waste/ capita/day.

Therefore; 0.58 × 365 days = 211.7kg/capita/year

In one year, one person in University of Nigeria, Nsukka will generate 211.7kg/capita/year of solid waste. And waste generation for 9,900 people per year will be

211.7 × 9,900 = 2,095,830 kg per year.

Another assumption is that the models need two refuse bin to be maintained.The model is shown below (Fig. 3.8).

WASTE UTILIZATION

Food Wastes

Food wastes have been observed to be high in most studies in triopical Africa (Bandara et al, 2007; Okeniyi and Anwan, 2012). Food waste is biodegradable and its disposal using landfill system constitutes environmental harzards (especially if adequate provisions are not made).

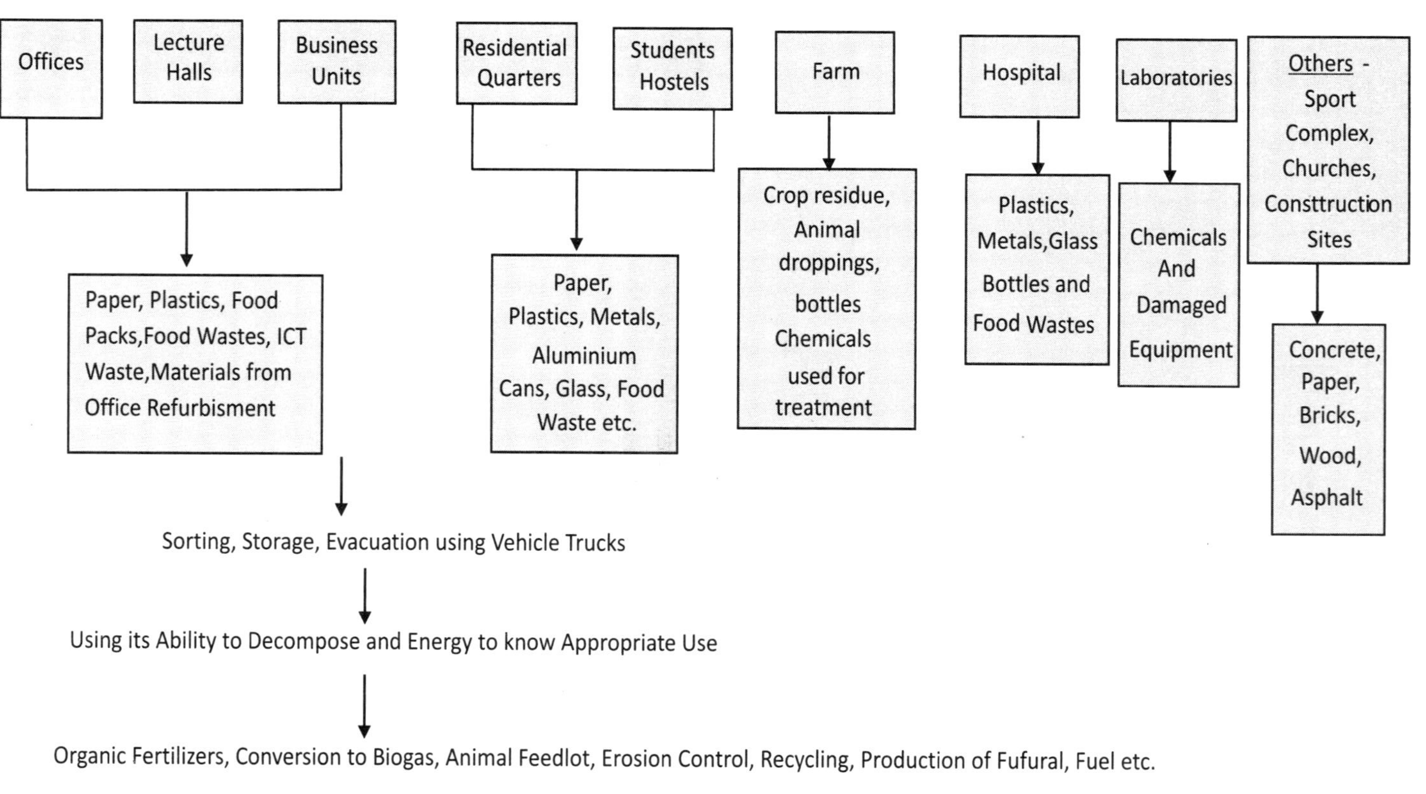

***Fig. 3.8*: The CTTU model for Waste Utilization**

Examples of such environmental harzard include emission of potent greenhouse gases like methane and leakages of leachate which could contaminate water streams.

A more friendly approach is the inclusion of a bio- gasification scheme in the system of handling food wastes. Dual benefits accruable from the scheme include the generation of biogas as recoverable energy from waste and usage of the degraded residue from the digester as composts for agricultural land conditioning (Mendes et al., 2003; Mor et al., 2006). Composted materials could be used as fertilizers. Composting is the process of aerobic biological decomposition of organic materials under controlled condition of temperature, humidity and pH. In the past, international Non-Governmental Organizations (NGOs) have sponsored small scale composting in Nigeria but the practice has not had significant impact in Nigeria (UNEP-IETC, 1996).

Utilization of Maize Cobs for the Production of Furfural and Active Carbon

Maize is planted almost everywhere in the university environs but mainly grown in the Crop Science Research farm. The consumption rate has been observed to be high. However, after consumption, cob is disposed off and becomes a serious environmental concern. It is easy to find it littered all over the campus probably due to low awareness of its utilization and partly due to attitude.

In Pakistan, Latif and Chughtai (2002) reported that furfural finds wide range of application as a solvent in liquor and polymer industry. It can also be used as motor fuel and as a preservative for biological specimen due to its germicidal character. It can also find some use as substitute for turpentine in varnish manufacture. Active carbon prepared by activating the carbonaceous raw materials with activating agents at high temperature is a versatile chemical in almost every industry. It is used as aclarifying and decolorizing liquid; in benzol recovery plants for the extraction of hydrogen sulphide from coal and coke oven gases; production of sulphur dichloride; the removal or fuel oil from alcohol; for assisting the production of high vacuum; the removal of odour from water; the removal of disagreeable fumes from processes and the recovery of vapors. The procedure for the preparation of good quality furfural and active carbon using H_2SO_4 or HCl is reported by Latif and Chughtai (2002).

Sommers (2010) observed that historically, corncobs has been viewed as waste materials, but presently, scientific research has made it a raw material and a valuable resource. Corn cobs and corn shocks plowed into the soil enhances the soil properties. He also expounded the nutrient composition to incude; hemicelluloses that upon splitting with acid produce appreciable quantities of xylose and arabinose with lesser quantities of glucose and galactose fermentable sugars. This makes them suitable starting materials for manufacturing organic compounds. The 5-member ring-furfural, OC_4H_3CHO is formed by hydrolysis through the destructive reflux distillation of chopped corncobs with dilute acid (often H_2SO_4 and small quantity of NaCl). It is used to manufacture resins for brakes or fiberglass, an important solvent in lubricating oil refining and also ethanol.

This is a good area where the institution can take steps in line of alternative fuel generation considering the exhausting and in adequate crude oil supply.

Agricultural Wastes

This is the outcome of crop, animal and research activities in the area. Such wastes include animal droppings, crop residue after harvest, fruit dropping or weeding, wastes from herbicides and pesticide application and animal treatments.

Much research has been carried out in the area of crop residue and animal wastes. Oil palm is a common tree crop in the University of Nigeria. It has a great potential of reducing fertilizer expenses by recycling the oil palm bunch waste (Awanlemhan and Ojeniyi, 2012). In their study, Oil palm bunch ash (OPBA) in combinations with NPK. The OPBA, NPK and their combinations increased soil organic matter, nitrogen, phosphorus, potassium, calcium, magnesium and effective cation exchangeable capacity over the control. They proposed that OPBA should serve as liming materials as it was found to increase soil pH singly and in combination. Also, palm kernel cake can serve as animal meal.

Studies carried out on waste materials cassava peels, prunnings of *Panicum maximum* (Elephant grass), Chromoleana odorata (Siam weed), Tithonia diversifolia (Mexican sunflower) and poultry manure. Shokalu *et al.*(2012) observed that after composting Tithonia had highest nitrogen content of 1.59% followed by Chromoleana and P. maximum (0.62%). Phosphorus was highest for poultry manure followed by Chromoleana and P. maximum. Cassava peels had the highest potassium content. Magnesium, Iron and Zinc content of Chromoleana was higher than other organic materials. Due to different compositions, researchers decided to obtain a compost mix from five organic materials. They found out that different compost mixes especially of Tithonia, cassava peels and Chromoleana contained adequate levels of some macro elements which make them ideal as organic fertilizers. Shokalu *et al.* (2010) had earlier reported that tithonia and cassava composts could be used horticulturally for melon, okra, celosia and other vegetables. Therefore, weeds can be returned to the soil after composting.

Chughtai *et al.* (1991) used khabble grass (Cynodon dactylon) for the production of furfural and active carbon

Utilization of Sewage Sludge

The University of Nigeria has a central sewage treatment unit and the wastes move down to the area by gravity. However, some openings exist in the collecting lines and waste water from kitchen, bathroom sometimes mixes with the sewage. The situation is further compounded with the absence of any futher treatment and farmers applying the wastes directly to crops. In order to reduce heavy metal contents, pathogens and increase recycling rates of nutrients, septic tanks should be fitted from other contaminants and technology to change liquid to solid encouraged (Shimming, 2002).

Shimming (2002) reported that the nutrient contained in the liquid produced from biogas tanks and toilets are used directly as basal application and top dressing for crops. The liquid from biogas fermentation can also be used for seed treatment, leaf application, fish production and pig production. The gas from biogas fermentation can be used for cooking, temperature control in green houses and animal houses. The solid part from biogas tanks can be used for basal or top application and for edible mushroom and earthworm production. Water discharged from the treatment plant can be used directly for field irrigation, if it meets the standard. Sludge can be used to make compound fertilizers, if heavy metals meet the standard. Spreading machines can be used here.

Construction, Demolition and Excavation Wastes

Construction, demolition and excavation waste (CDEW) materials consists of debris generated during construction, renovation, demolition of buildings, roads etc. they are often heavy materials such as concrete, wood, metals, glass, salvaged building components, soil, rock and dredged materials. CDEW has accounted for the largest proportion of the waste stream in England. In 2009, this was approximately 67% of the total waste produced in UK (DEFRA, 2009).

In the University of Nigeria in its bid to achieve a world class standard, much infrastructural projects are going on (and are expected to continue) involving ; construction (roads, buildings etc), demolition of old and unplanned structures, excavations in order to maintain drainage line, sewage lines and bore holes.

The wastes generated here can be manipulated from an engineering point of view to maintain areas like the Franco student's hostel area and other places where erosion of various degrees are occurring. It will also be useful as land reclamation and restoration agent.

Sawdust which can be obtained from CDEW has been studied along with wood ash as a potential soil amendment (Folorunso and Ojeniyi, 2003). They observed sawdust and wood ash gave better crop yield than control plots in addition to enhanced soil properties. Osemwota *et al.* (2012) in his study observed that using three rates of sawdust (0, 4 and 8t/ha), that at 4t/ha sawdust in combination with 6,360litres/ha abattoir resulted in optimum maize yield of 4.04t/ha while yield of 2.89t/ha was obtained from the control.

CDEW wastes such as unwanted wood, funiture, tables- whch are very common.Eg. wood wastes when pooled together, can be used in the production of charcoal for electricity generation which will serve as an alternative to both hydro-electricity and thermal electricity generation. Studies in this regard has been carried out by Aina (2006)

Utilization of Used Water Sachet and Polythene Packages

Catalytic degradation of water sachet waste over HPA/KIT-6 has been observed as a method obtaining clean fuel and intermediates for the chemical and petrochemical industries (Usman *et al*, 2012). This technique been harnessed to re-use water sachet waste which causes blockage of drains and resultant flooding. This way, environmental problems arising from water sachet waste can be reduced drastically while yielding useful products in the fuel oil range. Owolabi and Amosa (2010) reported a new technology in Fountain University where low density polyethylene (LDPE) becomes softer when subjected to heat, flows when subjected to pressure and solidifies when cooled to room temperature. As used water sachet were used super wax production with k25 serving as vehicle or solvent which dissolves the polythene wax. Super waxes are used in Nigeria in the manufacture of candles for religious and decorative purposes, and in polishes, matches, waxed paper, and cosmetics. Waxes are also generally used in the manufacture of rust preventives, rubber antioxidants, electrical insulators, paper coatings, printing inks, textile finishes, leather dressings. This range of products requires waxes of different melting points, as well as of different gloss, hardness, tensile strength, and ductility.

Yinusa and Stephen (2010) observed that used pure water sachet can save quantity of bitumen required in the production of asphaltic pavement mixes. The dissolved pure water sachet modified asphalt are equally effective to carry heavy traffic and still liberate the environment from the health hazards of the pure water waste sachets.

Hazardous Wastes

Hazardous wastes are wastes that contain one or more substances which might be dangerous to the environment or life. It may be present in waste stream including municipal solid, commercial and industrial; construction, demolition and excavation waste streams.

According to UK Environmental Agency (2005) waste is hazardous if they have one or more of the following hazardous properties:

- Explosive
- Oxidizing
- Highly flammable
- Irritant
- Harmful (if ingested or inhaled)
- Toxic
- Carcinogenic
- Corrosive
- Infectious
- Teratogenic
- Mutagenic (may induce/ increase hereditary genetic defects)
- Ecotoxic (may present immediate or delayed risks to the environment)

Although, it is ideal to say that waste is hazardous to the environment some have greater negative impact than others. For instance, in Germany, used batteries are carefully packaged and returned to supplying company for recycling. It is advised that wastes which have the above qualities should be sent to supplying company at agreed prices for recycling. ICT waste should also be recycled.

Hospital Wastes

Medical wastes could be converted to energy through incineration with appropriate technologies to convert to energy. The toxic fumes are controlled and toxic ash residue disposed off. Bottles from the area can be reused in the laboratories or sent to the supplying company for recycling.

CONCLUSION

Given that solid waste is not always collected properly, households collect and dump waste in what is called "anyhow and anywhere dumping style." This syndrome largely accounts for the dumping of wastes in open spaces and this negates the aim of environmental management that aims at effective and efficient waste management.

Resources are depleting while waste generation continues to rise and environment is polluted. There is need to urgently find alternative sources of energy, fuel and land conditioners; before the unexpected happens. In utilizing waste to achieve further value, it is important to understand, quantify and model waste usage associated with the collection, sorting/separation, processing and utilization of waste.

The CTTU model is efficient, novel and flexible. It starts from the point where wastes becomes 'waste' to and follows through until utilization. The utilization may further generate another waste but this time minimized in size, toxicity and minimal area for disposal (biomass reduction). Any model that ensures sustainable management of soil resources and maintaining environmental quality is strongly advocated.

REFERENCES

Adewole, A.T. (2009) Waste Management Towards Sustainable Development in Nigeria: A Case study of Lagos State. *International NGO Journal* vol 4(4) pp. 173-179.

Agunwamba, J.C. (1998) Analysis of Scavengers Activities and Recycling in some Cities in Nigeria. Environmental Management. 32(1):116-127.

Aina, O.M.(2006) Wood Waste Utilization For Energy Generation. Proceedings of the International Conference on Renewable Energy for Developing Countries - 2006.

Babayemi, J.O. and Dauda, K.T. (2009) Evaluation of Solid Waste Generation, Categories and Disposal Options in Developing Countries: A Case Study of Nigeria. J. Appl. Sci 3(2) 83-88. www.bioline.org.br/ja.

Bandara, N.J. G.J., Hettiaratchi, J.P.A , Wirasinghe, S.C., Pilapiya, S. (2007) Relation of Waste Generation and Composition to Socio-economic Factors: A Case Study. Environ monit Assess 135:31-39.

Brady, N.C and Weil, R.R. 2002. The Nature and Properties of Soils. 13th edtn, New dehli, India Pearson Education Inc.

Copeland, B.R. (1989) International Trade in Waste Products in the Presence of Illegal Disposal. *Journal of Environmental Economics and Management.* 20, 143-162.

DEFRA (2009) http://archive.defra.gov.uk/environment/waste/topics/documents/commercial-industral-waste-aims-actions-091013.pdf

Environmental Agency (2005) Full list of Harzardous Properties. http://www.environmentalagency.gov.uk/static/documents/GEH00506BKTR-e-e.pdf

Alaci Davidson and Ezeaku Peter (2008). Solid Waste Management: Practice and Economic Potential in Addis-Ababa. pp. 132-145. In M.P Van Dijk and J. Fransen (Eds) Managing Ethiopian Cities in an Era of Rapid Urbanisation. Published by Institute for Housing and Urban Development Studies (IHS) and Eburon Academic Publishers, Delft, The Netherlands (info@eburon.nl/www.eburon.nl)

Folorunso, O.O. and Ojeniyi, S.O (2003) Effects of Sole and Amended Plant Residue on Soil Nutrient and Yield of Okra. *International J of Agric Sc., Environ. And Technology,* Vol. 3: 4.

Geoffrey, I.N. (2005) The Urban Informal Sector in Nigeria Towards Economic Development, Environmental Health and Social Harmony. Global Urban Development Magazine 1 (1).

Hrebicek, J. and Soukopova, J. (2010) Integrated Model of Municipal Waste Management of the Czech Republic. http://www.iemss.org.

Igwe, C.A. (nd) Land Reclamation Including Waste Management (Lecture note).

Latif, S. and Chughtai, F.A. (2002) Utilization of Corn Cobs for the Production of Furfural and Active Carbon. Parkistan Agri Sci, vol. 39(2) 146-148.

Lenton, T.G. and Omotosho, O. (2004) Landfill Operations in the Niger Delta Region of Nigeria. Engineering Geology 73(1-2)171-177.

Mandes, M.R., Aramakito, T. and Hanakic, K. (2003) Waste Management 23, 403-409.

Mbagwu, J.S.C. (2003) Aggregete Stabiltity and Soil Degradation in the Tropics. Lecture given at The College of Soil Physics Trieste, 3-21.

Mor, S., Ravindra, K., De Visscher, A., Dahiya, R.P. and Chandra, A. (2006) A Science of Total Environment. 371, 1-10 Management.

Nas, P.J.M and Jaffe, R. (2003) Informal Waste Management, Shifting the Focus from Problem to Potential, Environment, Development and Sustainabilty 6. 337-353.

Obechina, E., Chukwuemeka, I. and Umeh, J.A. (1960) University of Nigeria. An Experiment in Higher Education.

Ogwueleka, T.C. (2009) Municipal Solid Waste Characteristics and Management in Nigeria. *Iran .J. Environ.Health Sci. Eng*, 6(3) pp. 173-180.

Okeniyi, J.O and Anwan, E.U. (2012) Solid Waste Generation in Covenant University Ota, Nigeria: Characterization and Implication for Sustainable Management. *J. Environ Sci* 3(2): 419-424.

Omuta, G.E.D. (1988) Urban Solid Waste Generation and Management; Towards an Environmental Sanitation Policy. In P.O. Sada and F.O. Odemerho(eds). Environmental Issues and Management in Nigeria Development. Evans Brothers Ltd. (pub), Ibadan.

Onweremadu, E.U. (2008) Physico-chemical Characterization of Farmland Affected by Waste Water in Relation to Heavy Metals. Journal of Zhejiang University Science. 3: 366-372.

Osemwota ,I.O. Isitekhale, H.H.E and Bakare, A (2012) Effects of Abattoir Effluents and Sawdust on Yield and Yield Components of Maize (Zea mays). Nig. J. Soil Sci. 22(2) 58-63.

Owolabi, R.U and Amosa, M.K.(2010) Laboratory Conversion of Used Water Sachet(Polyethylene) To Superwax/ Gloss Like Material. International Journal of Chemical Engineering and Applications, Vol. 1, No. 1, June.

Recycling, Research Technolgy (nd) Earth Engineering Center Colombia University.

Sada, P.O. (1984) Urbanization and Living Conditions in Nigerian Cities, Research Triangle Institute.

Summers, V. (2010) Practical uses of corn cobs- yahoo voices. www.voices.yahoo.com

Umoh, S.D. and Etim, E.E. (2013) Determination of Heavy Metal Contents from Dumpsites within Ikot Ekpene, Akwa Ibom State, Nigeria. *The IJES* 2(2) 123-129.

Unachukwu, G.O. (2010) Energy Saving Opportunities at the University of Nigeria, Nsukka. Journal of Energy in South Africa. Vol. 21(1) pp. 2-10.

UNEP-IETC (1996) Inertional Source Book on Environmentally Sound Technologies for Municipal Solid Management. Osaka/Shiga, UNEP International Environmental Technology Centre.

Usman, M.A. Alaje,T.O. Ekwueme,V.I. Adekoya,T.E. (2012) Catalytic Degradation of Water Sachet Waste (Lpde) Using Mesoporous Silica Kit-6 Modified With 12-Tungstophosphoric Acid. Petroleum & Coal 54 (2) 85-90 www.vurup.sk/petroleum-coal.

Uwadiegwu, B.O and Chukwu, K.E. (2013) Strategies for Effective Urban Solid Waste Management in Nigeria. *European Scientific Journal* 9(8)185.

White, P.R., Franke, M., Hindle, P. (1995) Integrated Solid Waste Management: A Lifecycle Inventory, Chapman and Hall, London.

www.nuc.org.

Yinusa A.J and Stephen S.K.(2011) Dissolved Pure Water Sachet as a Modifier of Optimum Binder Content in Asphalt Mixes. *Epistemics in Science, Engineering and Technology*, 1(4): 176-184.

Pages: 50-57

WASTE DISPOSAL AND MANAGEMENT

Edited by: **Dr. Pawan Kumar 'Bharti'; Dr. B. Tabassum;** and **Dr. Priya Bajaj**

ISBN: 978-93-5056-729-6

Edition: **2015**

Published by: **Discovery Publishing House Pvt. Ltd., New Delhi (India)**

4

Biotechnology
Dominant Technology in Waste Treatment

Priya Bajaj*, B. Tabassum* and **Alina Javed****

ABSTRACT

Biotechnology is used increasingly as the Environmentally Sound Technology (EST) of choice in many applications, particularly pollution clean-up. It also offers enormous promise in tackling many more environmental problems. New applications are expected to include water treatment, treatment of solid wastes (including biodegradable plastics), biomining, agriculture (creating plants resistant to the most adverse weather conditions), combating desertification, and even to form the basis for cleaner production.

"The future of sustainable development rests largely in local and national hands. Commitment to an eco-revolution will be bottom up, if at all."

Key Words: Biotechnology, Sustainable Development, Waste Management.

INTRODUCTION

Biotechnology broadly defined as any technique that uses living organisms to make or modify a product, improve plant or animals, or develop micro-organisms for specific use, is not new per se. Advanced biotechnologies are moving rapidly from research into commercial production – opening up new frontiers in areas from manufacturing to health care to pollution clean-

* Department of Zoology, Govt. Raza PG College, Rampur (UP), (India).

** Department of Biotechnology, Jamia Millia Islamia, New Delhi, (India).

up. Already, biotechnological techniques are making an important – in some cases, essential – contribution to the protection and clean-up of the environment. They rely on the ability of natural processes to degrade organic molecules. Microbes play a pivotal role digesting and degrading organic compounds to their mineral components,to the point where they can mineralize most organic substances. There are several ways in which biotechnology can prevent or reduce environmental damage, including:

- **Added-value processes**, which convert a waste stream into useful products.
- **End-of-pipe processes,** which purify the waste stream to the point where products can be released without harm into the environment.
- **Development of new biomaterials,** leading to the manufacture of materials with reduced environmental impact.
- **New biological production processes,** that generate less, or more manageable, waste.

Biotechnology is already the dominant technology for waste treatment. Biological treatment can cope with a wide range of effluents more effectively than chemical or physical methods, and is particularly suitable for treating waste containing the more common organic pollutants. Since then, both aerobic and anaerobic processes have been developed.

- Aerobic treatment has become the established technology for low- and medium-strength wastes, and also for toxic and recalcitrant molecules.
- Anaerobic processes are more effective for highly organic wastes, such as food processing wastewaters, municipal sludges and animal husbandry slurries.

BIOTECHNOLOGICAL METHODS FOR WASTE MANAGEMENT

These methods are widely used to remove nitrate, phosphate, heavy metal ions, chlorinated organic compounds and toxic substances. The main aim of waste treatment is to reduce organic matter generally. Nowadays cleaning up industrial pollutants is becoming critically important and this is leading to the development of biological processes for removing specific pollutants. Traditional off-gas treatment methods – incineration, dispersion, catalytic oxidation, scrubbing and adsorption – are best suited to handling large volumes of well-defined waste gases. Malodour problems from waste plants in particular are usually caused by varying mixtures at very low concentrations. Biological control offers a simpler alternative to chemical oxidation, leaves no chemical residues and uses less energy. The biotechnological processes used in air/off-gas treatment are primarily:

- ***Biofiltration:*** Immobilized micro- organisms, sticking to an organic matrix such as compost or bark, degrade the gas pollutants. Biofiltration is relatively cheap, but cannot treat all types and concentrations of pollutants.

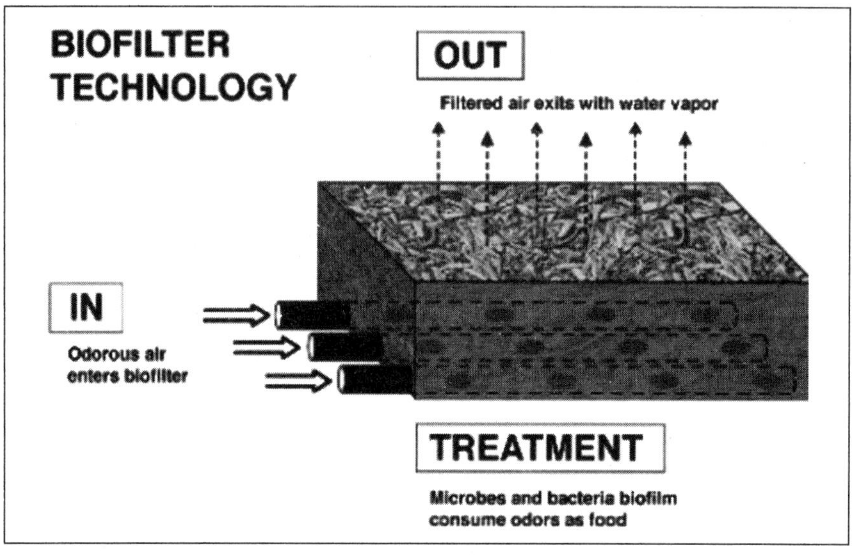

Fig. 4.1

- ***Bioscrubbing:*** The pollutants are washed out using a cell suspension, which is regenerated by microbial activity in an aerated tank. Bioscrubbers can clean highly contaminated off-gases, but require larger investment and have bigger running costs.

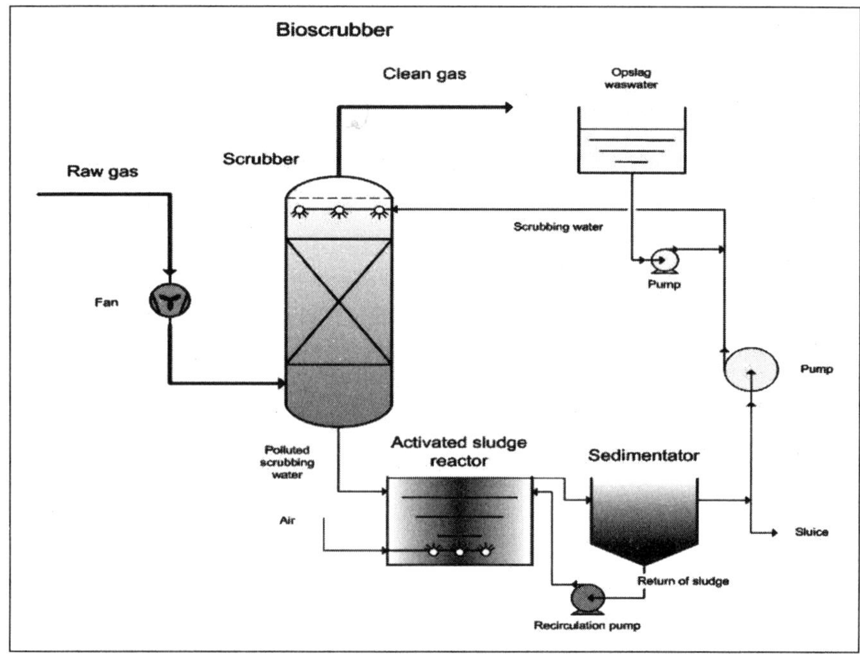

Fig. 4.2

- ***Biotrickling filtration:*** Immobilized micro-organisms sticking to an inert matrix degrade the pollutants while they are suspended in a water film and supplied with inorganic nutrients by a medium trickling through the device.

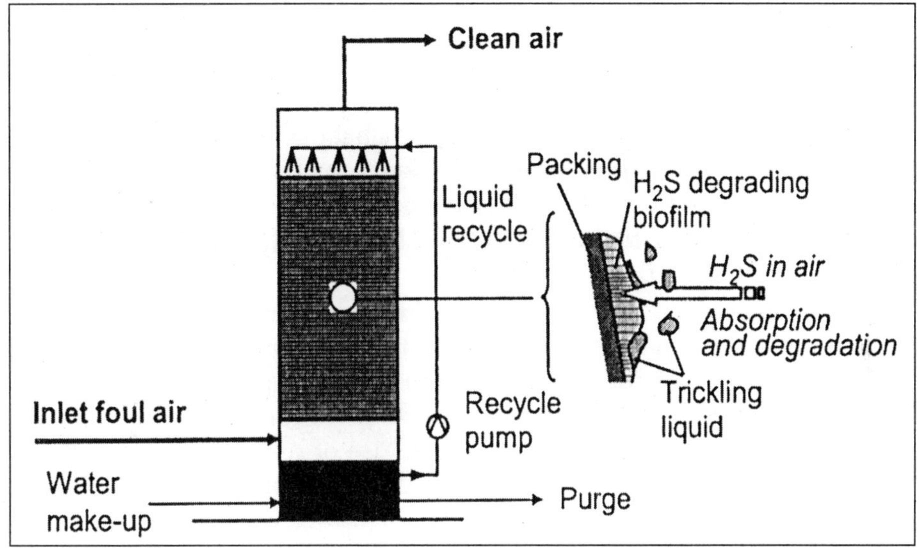

Fig. 4.3

Biofilters have also been used to remove easily biodegradable compounds emitted by oil cracking or off-gases from the petrochemical industry, and the feed and food. Biofilters replace physical or chemical air treatment techniques.

ADVANTAGES OF BIOTECHNOLOGICAL SYSTEMS

- Bio- scrubbers and biotrickling filtration systems have been introduced successfully in sectors such as food, brewing, some chemical processes, wastewater treatment units and agriculture.
- Overall, biological treatment of air/off-gas problems competes favourably with other techniques in terms of energy consumption, materials balance and cost.
- A major advantage is that pollutants are totally converted into harmless substances, without the accumulation of toxic residues or side products.
- Moreover, biotreatment technologies remove gaseous air pollutants from industrial units located in the centres of heavily populated industrial zones.

USING MICROORGANISMS AGAINST INDUSTRIAL POLLUTION

Industries established long ago in the rural areas are now creating serious pollution problems for new communities that have developed nearby. In Monterey, United States – which has a cluster of industries including glass, cement, steel, chemical, paper and brewing – one company, producing rayon fibre and cellophane film, had to cope with serious sulphur gaseous emissions from two facilities close to houses built 20 years after the factories. It was decided to explore the use of micro-organisms, since both contaminants contained sulphur and theoretically were easily degradable by naturally occurring bacteria. Biological treatment was compared with four other methods – chemical scrubbing, carbon adsorption, catalytic and thermal incineration, and chemical and photochemical oxidation – and was chosen because biological reactors were easy and cheaper to install, maintenance was low, and the company had experience of biological processes for wastewater treatment.

SPECIFIC USE OF ENVIRONMENTAL BIOTECHNOLOGY: DECONTAMINATING POLLUTED WATER

Environmental Biotechnology (EB), plays extremely important role in water pollution management, is the multidisciplinary integration of sciences and engineering in order to utilize the huge biochemical potential of microorganisms, plants and parts thereof for the restoration and preservation of the environment and for the sustainable use of resources. Environmental Biotechnology is utilized to develop advanced technologies based on biological systems to improve efficiency and reduce or utilize waste to benefit a wide range of industries and the environment. As Environmental Biotechnology, houses all of the Ecology offices and laboratory facilities, therefore it is highly useful and focuses on research in real-time direct environmental assessment and biological treatment, bioremediation, and natural attenuation.

Fig. 4.4

Basic Research Areas of Environmental Biotechnology

Co-metabolism: Environmental Biotechnology has emonstrated that co- metabolism is a dominant process for the degradation of PAHs, chlorinated solvents, and fuel oxygenates. Co-metabolic processes are difficult to study and require novel experimental approaches. One approach under development is the use of genetic probes to identify the presence of metabolic pathways implicated in co- metabolic processes. In this research, physiological responses are being linked to gene probe signatures to develop methods for identifying co-metabolic potential in environmental samples. The second approach uses a kinetic evaluation of partial transformation reactions to compare and characterize bacterial enzyme systems implicated in co-metabolism. Co- metabolic processes are competitive enzyme reactions and can be tested and modeled as such. Both these approaches are yielding unique and valuable advances in our understanding and application of co-metabolic and partial transformations.

Biotreatability: Environmental Biotechnology does a number of types of treatability tests for contaminants in soil and water, using soil columns, respirometers, bioreactors, and field respiration tests. Real-time direct biogeochemical techniques are being developed to provide the most direct possible methods to measure the rates of biodegradation and the effect stimulants and environmental conditions have on both the functional microbial components and the biogeochemistry of the environment being studied. For example, mixed waste biotreatment includes both the engineering of bioreactors for the treatment of high strength waste streams and understanding how natural attenuation or active bioremediation can be applied to mitigate the impact of the weapons legacy.

Biotransformation Kinetics: Environmental Biotechnology is linking engineering and microbiology in an integrated programme to examine biotransformation kinetic for pollutant clean-up and microbial product formation. The kinetic programme examines microbial response and activity as a function of substrate concentrations and time. The results of kinetic studies are being used in reactor design and operations analysis.

Modeling: Environmental Biotechnology currently does not have a modelling programme, but is developing collaboration with modeling groups within ESD.

Enzyme Engineering for Improved Biodegradation

The ever-increasing information regarding the structure and function of enzymes and pathways involved in biodegradation of recalcitrant pollutants offers opportunities for improving enzymes or entire pathways by genetic engineering. Control mechanism and enzyme properties can be tailored by site directed mutagenesis, which is often guided by computer assisted modeling of the three-dimensional (3-D) protein structures. For example, site directed approaches have been applied to enlarge the binding pocket of haloalkane dehalogenase, resulting in several-fold faster dechlorination of dichlorohexane. Perhaps the use of computational methods to predict subtle and distal changes in the protein backbone without perturbing the overall protein structure could be used to further improve enzyme function and stability.

Evolutionary and Genomic Approaches to Biodegradation

Evolutionary approaches are extremely useful for optimization of an entire biodegradation pathway comparing to step by-step modifications offered by rational design. This was recently demonstrated by the modification of an arsenic resistance operon using DNA shuffling. Cells expressing the optimized operon grew up to 0.5M arsenate, a 40-fold increase in resistance.Moreover, a 12-fold increase in the activity of one of the gene products (arsC) was observed in the absence of any physical modification to the gene itself. The authors speculate that modifications to other genes in the operon affect the function of the arsC gene product. Such unexpected but exciting results are more likely to be realized using irrational approaches.

RESEARCH PROJECTS PRODUCE RESULTS IN THE UNITED STATES

The Environmental Protection Agency (EPA) in the United States is leading a major effort by government scientists, private industry and the academic community to find new ways to use naturally occurring micro-organisms to clean up environmental contaminants.

- In one study, EPA scientists applied white rot fungus to samples contaminated with pentachlorophenol and other toxic compounds: preliminary results showed that pentachlorophenol concentrations of up to 1,000 parts per million were reduced by 85-90 per cent.
- At another site, petrochemical wastes were treated with a process which involved injecting air into the liquid to encourage aerobic degradation, adding nutrients, using centrifugal pumps to emulsify the waste, and mixing the subsoil in with a hydraulic dredge. Within 120 days, volatile organic compounds in the waste were reduced from 3,400 to 150 parts per million, benzene concentrations from 300 to 12 parts per million, and vinyl chloride levels from 600 to 17 parts per million.
- Treating ground water contaminated with benzene, toluene and xylene from an aviation fuel spill by adding hydrogen peroxide as an oxygen source to stimulate indigenous microbes, brought the water within EPA's drinking water standards within six months.

These results demonstrated that while bioremediation is a slow process, it is less costly than alternative clean-up methods. By converting toxic chemicals to other materials, it actually removes the toxic elements from the environment, rather than just separating them for disposal later on.

"Sustainability is our Responsibility"

REFERENCES

1. Angenent L T, Karim1 K, Al-Dahhan1 M H, Wrenn B H, Domy´_guez-Espinosa R (2004), "Production of Bioenergy and Biochemicals from Industrial and Agricultural Wastewater", Trends. Biotechnol., Vol. 22, pp. 477-482.
2. Bae W, Chen W, Mulchandani A, Mehra R (2000), "Enhanced Bioaccumulation of Heavy Metals by Bacterial Cells Displaying Synthetic Phytochelatins", Biotechnol. Bioeng., Vol. 70, pp. 518-524.
3. Bae W, Mehra R, Mulchandani A, Chen W (2001), "Genetic Engineering of Escherichia coli for Enhanced Uptake and Bioaccumulation of Mercury", Appl. Environ. Microbiol. Vol. 67, pp. 5335-5338.
4. Bae W, Wu C, Kostal J, Mulchandai A, Chen W (2003), Enhanced Mercury Biosorption by Bacterial Cells with Surface-Displayed Mer R.", Appl. Environ. Microbiol., Vol. 69, pp. 3176-3180. Int. J. LifeSc. Bt & Pharm. Res. 2012 A K Chauhan et al., 2012.
5. Bailey J E (1991), "Toward a Science of Metabolic Engineering", Science, Vol. 252, pp. 1668-1691.
6. Bang S W, Clark D S, Keasling J D (2000), "Engineering Hydrogen Sulfide Production and Cadmium Removal by Expression of the Thiosulfate Reductase Gene (phsABC) from Salmonella Enterica Serovar Typhimurium in Escherichia coli", Appl. Environ Microbiol., Vol. 66, pp. 3939-3944.
7. Bontidean I, Berggren C, Johansson G, Csorgi E, Mattiasson B, Lloyd JR, Jakeman K J and Brown N L (1998), "Detection of Heavy Metal Ions at Femtomolar Levels Using Protein-Based Biosensors", Anal. Chem., Vol. 70, pp. 4162-4169.
8. Bru¨hlmann F and Chen W (1999), "Tuning Biphenyl Dioxygenase For Extended Substrate Specificity", Biotechnol Bioeng., Vol. 63, pp. 544-551.
9. Canada K A, Iwashita S, Shim H and Wood T K (2002), "Directed Evolution of Toluene Ortho Monooxygenase for Enhanced 1-naphthol Synthesis and Chlorinated Ethene Degradation", J. Bacteriol., Vol. 184, pp. 344-349.
10. Cho CM-H, Mulchandani A and Chen W (2002), "Bacterial Cell Surface Display of Organophosphorus Hydrolase for Selective Screening of Improved Hydrolysis of Organophosphate Nerve Agents", Appl. Environ. Microbiol., Vol. 68, pp. 2026-2030.

WASTE DISPOSAL AND MANAGEMENT *Pages:* 58-72
Edited by: **Dr. Pawan Kumar 'Bharti'; Dr. B. Tabassum;** and **Dr. Priya Bajaj**
ISBN: 978-93-5056-729-6
Edition: **2015**
Published by: **Discovery Publishing House Pvt. Ltd., New Delhi (India)**

5

Animal and Farm Waste Management Through Vermibiotechnology and Mechanical Cow Composting Machine

Ran Vir Singh

INTRODUCTION

In recent time, environmental degradation is a major threat for existence of living being in the world. The safe disposal of animal, farm and solid waste are the major problem at national and international level. It may contribute to environmental risk like emission of green house gases which increase global warming, ground and surface water pollution, poor hygiene in villages and urban areas which is hazardous for animal and human health.

Due to invention of hybrid varieties of various crops in last five decades, the demand of chemical fertilizer, pesticide, insecticide and weedicides has been increased rapidly in most of the countries of world to increase grain, vegetable, fruit, flower, milk, meat and egg production to meet out the requirement of increasing trend of population. Due to this reason fertility and soil health are deteriorating continuously because the death of earthworms and beneficial micro organism and depletion of micro plant nutrients.

Earthworms are ecosystem engineers as they are subdivided in two functional group based on their feeding habit and vermicast shape: (1) Garbage processing species, which harbor and feed on animal and agro-waste and excrete granular from of vermicast; (2) soil processing species, which live and feed on mineral soil and excrete microaggregate form of

Animal Genetics Division, Indian Veterinary Research Institute, Izatnagar – 243 122 (UP), (India).

vermicast. Earthworm gut are ideal laboratory to multiply beneficial soil and decomposition microorganism. By stimulating the decomposition of plant material earthworms can increase the availability of plant nutrients. Beside this well known positive effect on soil fertility. It is also often suggested that earthworms induce long term stabilization of soil labile carbon (C) by protecting C in microaggregates formed in large macroaggregate. This has led to repeated suggestions that earthworms promote soil C storage and hence reduce net CO_2 emission. This possible contribution of earthworms to long term C stabilization seems to be in sharp contrast with the short-term earthworm induced emission of CO_2 and N_2O.

Earthworms can be used as source of animal feed protein for fish, chicken and suckling pigs. Wound healing ointment prepared by earth worms is having very good potential in healing of wounds.

Organic farming is a natural method of farming system which primarily aims at cultivating the land and raising crops in such a way as to keep the soil alive and in good health by use of organic waste (crop, animal and solid wastes) and other biological materials along with beneficial microbes (biofertilizer) to release nutrients to crops for increased sustainable pollution free environment. Organic agriculture should be based on living ecological systems and cycles. Excessive application of chemical fertilizer is hazardous for soil health and costlier for crop production. Hence, we may shift to practices which are cheap, eco-friendly, meets the more nutrient requirements, sustain quality of food and fodder production. In this direction in nature's laboratory, microorganism and earthworms which harbor on animal and agro waste are important biological organism helping nature to maintain nutrient flow from one system to another and to minimize environmental degradation. Traditional methods of recycling of animal and farm waste takes 6 months duration and inferior quality farm yard manure. Farmers need a improved method of recycling of animal and farm waste which will take short duration and good quality of manure. Keeping in view of above cited facts, IVRI, Izatnagar had conceived a research project in area of recycling of animal and farm waste through vermibiotechnology and mechanical cow composting system. The recycling technologies developed under this project will be discussed in this paper.

ANIMAL AND FARM WASTE GENERATION

Livestock and crop production business generate huge amount of biodegradable waste. Higher economic growth and rapid urbanization of population in general are usually accompanied with generation of enormous amount of biosolid. India generate about 300 carore tones of animal and farm waste. By using of optimum recycling eco technology viz. vermibiotechnology and mechanical cow composting machine, this huge amount of biodegradable waste can be converted in value added organic products viz. vermicompost, nutriwash, vermiculture and compost.

VERMIBIOTECHNOLOGY

It is a simple biotechnological process of composting in which animal and farm waste harbour species of earthworms and microorganisms which are used to enhance and accelerate the process of waste conversion into value added organic products viz. vermicompost, nutriwash and high quality of animal protein. The multiplication of earthworms and favorable microorganisms (using earthworm as bioreactors) in organic waste is called vermiculture. The liquid extract from vermibiomanure and wash of earthworms are termed as nutriwash.

Principle of production of vermicompost and value added organic products:

1. Air circulation in the beds of animal and agro-waste is increased due to movement of earthworms which enhance the process of aerobic fermentation.
2. Earthworms eat biodegradable waste. These worms grind big particles into small particles by gizzard. This process increase surface area of decomposed feed. Earthworm's gut microorganism and enzymes help in processing of biodegradable feed.
3. Earthworms act as versatile natural bioreactor to increase the population of beneficial microorganism of soil fertility and garbage processing. The gut of earthworm is having optimum temperature and moisture to increase the population of microorganism. It is appropriate to mention that earthworms promote microbial population either by virtue of their own intestinal mechanism or by their casts, serving as 'Culture Plate' for development and multiplication of several strains of bacteria. These bacteria are beneficial for decomposition process as well as converting nutrients into available form of plants nutrients.
4. Mucoprotien in gut is mixed in digested substrate through biochemical process. This process help in breakdown of plants nutrients from biodegradable substances into available form for plants.
5. Earthworms eat garbage more than their body weight in one day and excrete about 33% in form of vermicast to consumed amount of feed. Animal and agro-waste harbour microorganism eat in amount of thousands time more than their body weight in one day. Earthworms and microorganism are used to enhance and accelerate the process of waste conversion in value added organic products viz. vermicompost, nutriwash, growth promoters and proteinaceous worm biomass. This is principle of nutrition that the animal which are more in smaller body weight but they eat many times more than higher body weight animals.

EARTHWORM SPECIES SEED BANK WHICH HARBOUR ON ANIMAL AND FARM WASTE

There are four garbage processing earthworm species available in Earthworm Seed Bank of IVRI, Izatnagar. Out of these, *Eisenea foetida*

(Fig. 5.1) and *Eudrilus eugeniae* (Fig. 5.2) are exotic *Lampito mauritii* (Fig. 5.3) and *Perionyx ceylensis* (Fig. 5.4) designated a "Jai Gopal" are the Indian earthworm species.

Fig. 5.1: Eisenea foetida

Fig. 5.2: Eudrilus eugeniae

Fig. 5.3: Lampito mauritii

Fig. 5.4: Perionyx ceylensis **designated "Jai Gopal"**

STUDY ON SUITABILITY OF EARTHWORM FOR RECYCLING OF ANIMAL AND FARM WASTE

Studies on suitability for garbage processing earthworm species were carried out at IVRI, Izatnagar under project "Recycling of animal and farm waste and application of value added organic products in sustainable crop production and animal husbandry" during 2006 to 2008. In the initial studies various indigenous earthworm species were examined to identify by the suitable species on the basis of the following characteristics:

1. Inhabiting capability on animal and farm waste.
2. Heat and cold tolerance ability (0 to 45°C).
3. High prolificacy and various feeding ability.
4. Superior quality of vermicast.
5. Smallest period of interval from hatching to maturity.
6. Long life span.
7. Very rich in protein.
8. Multiplication of beneficial soil and fermentation micro-organism.

The studies indicated that *Perionyx ceylensis* designated as "Jai Gopal" (Fig. 5.4) was the most suitable earthworm species till reported in the world. This earthworm species is very much suitable for vermi composting and garbage processing. This is the first report of India.

IVRI, Izatnagar is presently maintaining four earthworm species viz. *Eisenia foetida, Eudrilus eugenia, Lampito mauritii* and *Perionyx ceylansis* in Seed Bank. Principles of selection and mating plan are followed to develop high prolific, voracious feeder, heat and cold tolerance character's and improve capability of inhabiting on animal and farm waste.

An indigenous earthworm species was collected from 24, South Pargana district of Sunderban region of West Bengal in 2006. This earthworm species was genetically improved through intense selection and mating plan. The sample of earthworm were sent to Zoological Survey of India for identification. They identified this earthworm species as indigenous and its scientific name is *Perionyx ceylansis.*

This is an indigenous earthworm species which has not any threat for biodiversity of Indian earhtoworm in our country based on experiment conducted at IVRI, Izatnagar. Hence, *Perionyx ceylansis* designates as "Jai Gopal" is recommended for vermicomposting in India and tropical countries. It is better from two exotic earthworm *Eisenea foetida and Eudrilus eugeneae.*

Earthworms alone responsible for garbage processing is inappropriate. Microbial decomposition involves a variety of organism and a complicated network of exchanges and feed back which are yet to be fully understood. It is appropriate to mention that earthworms promote microbial population, either by virtue of their own intestinal mechanism or by their casts, serving as 'Culture Plate' for development and multiplication of several strains of bacteria. These bacteria are beneficial for the decomposition process as well as converting nutrients in to available forms for plants. A beneficial consortium of microorganism has been enriched in "Jai Gopal" vermiculture.

DEVELOPMENT OF NEW INDIAN EARTHWORM SPECIES

Indian farmers are using mainly exotic earthworm species viz. *Eisenea fetida* and *Eudrilus eugeniae* for recycling of animal and farm waste because Indian earthworm species were poorer in vermicomposting and fecundity. Keeping in view of this problem in mind, we took initiative to develop a high prolific and voracious feeding of animal and farm waste. We had collected 50 indigenous earthworm species along with their feed from Sunderban Delta of West Bengal which were high organic soil processor and adaptive in hot and humid climatic conditions. We had reared these earthworm in earthen pots and fed them natural habitat feed which was rich in organic soil. These earthworm were maintained on same feed in Earthworm Breeding Laboratory at IVRI, Izatnagar up to one month. We had prepared feed for earthworm species by mixing of three ingredients viz. soil (S), vermicast (V) and cow dung (C). The ratio of three ingredient in ten different feed formulation were W1 (10%V + 10%C + 80%S), W2 (20%V + 20%C + 60%S), W3 (30%V + 30%C + 40%S), W4 (40%V + 40%C + 20%S), W5 (50%V + 50%C), W6 (40%V + 60%C), W7 (30%V + 70%C), W8 (20%V + 80%C), W9 (10%V + 90%C) and W10 (100%C). The high organic soil processing earthworm species were inoculated in W1 feed after one month adaptability at IVRI, Izatnagar. These earthworms were reared on W1 feed till they reproduce cocoon and juvenile of F1 generation. All survived F1 generation cocoon and juvenile were inoculated in W2 feed. F1 generation earthworms were reared on W2 feed till they reproduce cocoon and juvenile of F2 generation. In subsequence way F2, F3, F4, F5, F6, F7 F8 and F9 generation earthworms were inoculated on W3, W4, W5, W6, W7, W8, W9 and W10 feed, respectively. All survived next generation cocoon and juvenile were inoculated in higher content of organic feed. The life cycle of each earthworm species ranged from 45 to 50 days in different seasons. We had followed *inter se mating* plan in production of next filial generation earthworms. After successful *inter se mating* of nine generation earthworm, it was observed that most of earthworms and juvenile of F9 were survived on 100% cow dung feed. The phenotypic characters of newly developed Indian earthworm species viz. number of hatchling per cocoon (no) incubation period (days), weekly cocoon production of one pair earthworm (no.), adult body weight of 100 earthworms (gm), population after 3 months from mating of one pair (no.) and heat tolerance were characterized and compared from two exotic earthworm species. It was observed that newly developed Indian earthworm species "Jai Gopal" is better than *Eisenea fetida* and *Eudrilus eugeniae* in characters of fecundity, heat tolerance, quality of vermicast and cow dung processing. The earthworm breeding stratagies for genetic improvement in this species is continuously followed.

Procedure of recycling through vermibiotechnology: The following steps are involoved in recycling.

Selection of project site:

Farmers and entrepreneurs should consider following criteria in selection of project site.

1. Availability of biodegradable raw material for recycling.
2. The project site should be located at highest place and proper drainage system should also be existed.
3. There should be a market for sale of vermicompost and other value added organic products.

SELECTION OF EARTHWORM SPECIES

The farmers should select garbage processing newly developed Indian earthworm species *Perionyx ceyelensis* whose popular name is designated as "Jai Gopal". This species is well adopted in tropical agro climatic condition. The vermiculture of this earthworm species is available @ 250/kg at IVRI, Izatnagar. The "Jai Gopal" Vermiculture Technology has been commercialized by the Institute @ Rs 22,472 which include technical know how, training and vermiculture of "Jai Gopal" earthworms.

ESSENTIAL REQUIREMENTS FOR MANUFACTURING OF VERMI-COMPOST

Construction of Vermi Tank and Vermi Sheds

Farmers and entrepreneurs should construct vermi tank and vermi shed as per design recommended by IVRI, Izatnagar (Fig. 5.5). There are four methods for production of vermicompost viz. tank, pit, heap and ring method. Out of these vermi tank is one of the best method for recycling of animal and farm waste because it provide aerobic environment for microorganism and earthworm species. There is also minimum loss of plant nutrients in this method.

The dimension of vermi tank is strictly followed as 30cm height, 90 cm width and length as per requirement of farmers. If height is increased more than 30 cm, there will an anaerobic fermentation which decrease the growth of earthworm and aerobic decomposition. If width of wall of vermi tank is increased more than 90 cm farmers/workers will feel inconvenient in turning of solid waste and harvesting of finished product. The 60 cm or as per width of wheel barrow space should be kept vacant between two vermi tanks for movement and various operations. The well of vermi tank should constructed in half brick in 1:7 ratio of cement and sand. The floor of tank should constructed by brick on face side (37 bricks in one square meter). The gap between brick should be filled by plaster of cement and sand in ratio of 1:12. Vermi sheds should be established on 15° clock wise direction of latitude from equatorial line so that these sheds will remain more cool in summer and more warm in winter season. Throughout year foliage trees should be planted at distance of 5 feet from wall of shed in western and southern side. The height of wall of sheds should constructed 3 feet and above this wall 4 feet height iron woven net should be fixed so that birds can not enter inside the sheds. Asbestos sheet or thatch bamboo can be used in ceiling of vermi sheds. The height in centre of shed is kept 10 to 11 feet with 3 to 4 feet slope towards wall. The gate can be fabricated of iron wire and rode with size of 7 feet height and 4 feet wide. There should be proper ventilation in side vermi sheds.

Fig. 5.5: **Vermicompost Sieving Machine**

AVAILABILITY OF OPTIMUM FEED FOR EARTHWORMS

Earthworms do not eat green leaves and fresh dung. They eat only decomposed biodegradable solid waste. Firstly green crops residues and leaves of plants should be dried and followed by shredded in 2 to 4 cm size. Afterward dried biodegradable waste should be mixed with bioinnoculam fresh cow dung properly. Windrows up to one meter height are made by mixed waste and allow for decomposition for 10 to 15 days in summer and 4 to 5 days in winter seasons. In first week the temperature will rise up to 60 to 65°C. After wards the temperature of heap will decline up to 30 to 35°C in summer. Turning of heap after one week in desirable followed by sprinkling of water. Forty percent moisture are maintained in heap. The feed is not prepared in deep pit to avoid anaerobic fermentation because the worms do not like to eat it. Proper ventilation are maintained in heap. Due to optimum moisture (40%) high temperature and aerobic micro organism will enhance fermentation of lignin, cellulose and hemicelluloses of crop residues and cow dung. After pre fermentation up to 12 to 15 days in summer and 4 to 5 days in winter. The feed is ready for feeding of worms. The optimum temperature for vermiculture production is 20 to 25°C. During winter season when temperature decline below 15°C in this situation to increase temperature of vermi bed 3 to 4 days old fermented biodegradable waste can be feed to earthworm.

List of suitable biodegradable waste for production of vermiculture and vermicompost production.

Sl. No.	Source Feed Ingredient	Suitable Biodegradable Solid Waste for Products of Vermicompost
1.	Animal dung	Cow, buffalo, goat, sheep, horse, ass, wild animal's dung biogas slurry mixed with dry leaves. Poultry dropping and pig feasces can be mixed @ 10% in cow dung for feeding of worms.
2.	Agriculture waste	Plants stubble, paddy straw, weeds, dry leaves fruit rind, vegetable and fruit waste.
3.	Urban Solid Waste	Kitchen waste from household and restaurants waste from market yards and places of worship.
4.	Agro industries	Peel, rind and unused pulp of fruits and vegetables from food processing unit Pressmud and seed husk from vegetable oil refineries fine baggase and boiler ash from sugar factories spent wash, barley waste yeast sludge from breweries and distillery unit, coir of fruits, paper and date expired seeds from seed production units, stem, leaves and flowers after extraction of oil from aromatic oil extraction industry and coir pith from coir industry.

OPTIMUM VENTILATION

Optimum ventilation is essential for supply of oxygen to earthworms and aerobic microorganism. Earthworms respire from his whole body in presence of optimum moisture. The oxygen is very essential for microbial and biochemical process in the gut. The vermibed should not filled by feed with pressure. The 2/3 portion of vermibed should filled by new feed and 1/3 portion should be kept for finished product of vermicompost.

Before harvesting finished product. It is kept in 1/3 portion of bed up to 10 to 12 days more so that extra water can be evaporated and all earthworms will move towards new feed and all cocoon will hatch so that hatchling will also move toward new feed. The height of vermi tank should not kept more than 30 cm to check anaerobic fermentation. Proper and optimum ventilation in vermi bed is only possible when height of tank is kept up to 30°C.

OPTIMUM MOISTURE

The whole body/skin of earthworm act as respiratory system to exchange gases. Therefore, it is very much essential to moist the whole body of earthworm. For more activity and more enhancement of recycling ability of earthworms, it is also essential to maintain 40 to 50 percent moisture in feed. There should be proper drainage of excess water from vermibeds and flooring of bed is constructed through brick on face. The gap between two bricks should be filled by 1:12 ratio of cement and sand so that extra water can easily seepage in ground. Farmer can test excess water in feed by making shape of ball when ball is pressed by hands than water is seepage. It mean excess moisture. When ball is not properly formed by pressing with hands. It mean below moisture level than 40% in feed. If ball is properly formed. It means feed contain optimum moisture 40 to 50% level. Vermi tank should not filled by water. To maintain optimum level of moisture in feed sprinkling is followed by putting sprinkler on pipe. Always avoid sprinkling on finished product. Never use saline water for sprinkling on vermi beds.

OPTIMUM TEMPERATURE

The 20 to 30°C ambient temperature is always good and optimum for vermiculture and vermicompost production. The *Eudrilus eugeniae* will not survive more than 35°C and below than 10°C ambient temperature. However *Eisenia foetida* will survive between 5° to 40°C temperature. The newly developed Indian earthworm species "Jai Gopal" is having ability to survive between 0 to 42°C ambient temperature. For management of optimum temperature in vermi beds. We should allow pre fermentation of biodegradable material in one meter height windrows up to 10 to 15 days during summer in sheds. The moisture level in feed is maintained between 40 to 50° percent only. If it increase more than 50 percent in vermi bed or in heap. The dung fly will lay eggs followed by maggots in feed emerged. We should follow prevention to create this situation in summer. In northern state of our country 15th November on wards the ambient temperature starts decline. Therefore we can feed earthworms directly after 3 to 4 days pre fermentation of feed so that temperature of vermibed will be increased. It enhance the process of recycling. In situation of less ventilation and high moisture in vermitank, temperature of feed in bed is increased which is harmful for recycling process. Turning of feed is desirable to maintain optimum moisture and temperature in the bed, when it is required.

OPTIMUM pH AND REMOVAL OF TOXIC MATERIAL FROM FEED

Seven pH of earthworm feed is optimum for faster growth when ever pH level increase or decrease in the feed, it has significant effect on recycling processing. Saline water is not suitable for vermiculture production. Salt and toxic feed material have also harmful effect on growth of earthworms and microorganisms. Always neutral pH feed and water should be used.

MULCHING ON VERMIBEDS

There is wide variation in climatic parameters in different agro climatic zone of our country. When temperature of bed starts declining below 10°C temp. In that season, mulching using old jute begs, paddy straw and dry leaves is desirable on structure of beds. When temperature starts increase more than 15°C in vermibeds under closed shed, mulching should be removed from surface of beds. Mulching can also be done. In open area to protect worms from high temperature, check evaporation and protect worms from birds.

PROTECTION OF EARTHWORMS FROM THEIR PREDATOR

Due to 67% protein in earthworms become best food for birds, mole, frog, mongoose and mountain rat. Surroundings of vermi sheds should be properly cleaned so that these predators can not hidden. Iron wire net should be used in shed to enter birds inside sheds. Frog should be catch with hand and through away from side. Mountain rat can be killed using rat kill biscuit in shed. Mole can be traped by keeping a tub in shed with dimension of 30 to 40 cm depth filled with indigenous cow urine. As per behavior, mole attracts toward dirty smelly things in house holds. Indigenous cow urine is having foully smell. Therefore, mole is attracted towards a cow urine tub where it will fall in the cow urine filled and traped. A lime of ash around vermished can protect to enter red ants inside the beds. The vermiculture production site is made free from termites. An anti termite treatment is performed at site of the project. The feed of earthworms should not carry any termite. It should be checked properly before feeding to earthworms.

HARVESTING AND SIEVING OF VERMICOMPOST

When biodegradable solid waste are digested by earthworms and microorganism. They excrete in the form of vermicast. After 20 day of inoculation of earthworms, we start to harvest vermicast and make heap in vermibeds to evaporate moisture and moving of hatchling and earthworms towards feed in bed. This process is repeated at every 15 days. Harvested finished vermicompost should be sieved by vermicompost sieving machine (Fig. 5.6). About 30 to 40% moisture in finished vermicompost should be maintained for beneficial microorganism.

Benefits of vermiculture and vermicompost production:

1. Generation of self employment for rural youth, women and farmers.
2. Cheap and eco-friendly technology and base for sustainable agriculture and animal husbandry.
3. Application of vermicompost and other value added organic products will improve the nutritive quality of food products.
4. Enhancement in disease resistance in human and animals by consuming organic food and feed.
5. Helpful in maintaining clean environment of village and cities.
6. Helpful in reducing production of green house gases.
7. Helpful in conservation of soil, water forest, animal and human.

8. Availability of raw material in each village and city for production of vermicompost and organic manure.
9. vermicompost and other value added organic products can be manufacture in each village.
10. Availability of all plant nutrients and beneficial soil organism in vermicompost.
11. Vermicompost can be applied in any crop in different combination based on availability.
12. Vermibiotechnology is a very easy and ecofriendly technology in learning.

MECHANICAL COW COMPOSTING MACHINE

It is also called Rotary Drum Type composting method (Fig. 5.7). It is an excellent composting concept for smaller communities label. There is a rapid and enclosed pathogen kill process in the system. The composting time reduced drastically from 6 month to 1 to 2 weeks.

Fig. 5.6: **Layout of Vermibeds**

PRINCIPLE OF COMPOSTING

There are three reasons why a mechanical cow or a rotary drum composter speeds up the composting process. The first in that the material is constantly in motion, ensuring that all of the organic waste is in constant contact with oxygen and micro organism. The second is that material that is freshly added to the drum is treated with warm ammonia laden air. Inside the drum the tumbling action mixes, agitates and generally moves material through the drum. The third is that thermophilic and mesophilic microorganism are mixed in waste inside the drum which fasten the decomposition rate of lignin, cellulose and hemicelluloses of crop residues. The thermophilic and mesophic micro-organism is grown in media which comprise Indian cow dung + pulse flour + molasses @ 20kg, 2kg and 30kg, respectively in 100 liters water. This medium should be stirred every eight hours for three days. The consortium of these micro organism as bioinnoculam is properly mixed in crop and vegetable residues or with other organic wastes for the initial 30 days for the development of rich microbial consortia inside the drum. Feed stocks are loaded at one end compost is removed at the opposite end with regard to the composting process, the key function of the rotation is to expose the material to air, add oxygen and release heat and gaseous products of decomposition.

Fig. 5.7: **Machenical Cow Composting Machine**

Results of mechanical cow composting machine:

1. Long term monitoring (250 days) suggested that most of the organic waste combinations were composted successfully within 7 to 10 days period.
2. Adequate air supply was provided in the form of exhaust fan in the drum, as the biological degradation process is aerobic in nature, and the drum was maintained at a temperature of approximately 60 °C to 70 °C even in cold weather conditions (Ambient Temperature : 6 °C).
3. Instead of classical mesophilic phase, the incoming material directly enters into thermophilic phase, resulting in rapid decrease in TOC, C/N ratio, CO_2 evolution, BOD, COD.

4. Higher final total nitrogen (2.6 %) and final total phosphorus (6 g/kg) pointed out the high compost quality.
5. It is found that indigenous cow dung is necessary as feeding material with other organic wastes for the initial 30-40 days for the development of rich microbial consortia.
6. Bacteria plays a more important role compared to acetenomycetis and fungi in rotary drum composting.
7. Poultry dropping @ 20% is mixed with organic waste which enhance the nutritive quality of compost.
8. End product of compost through this method is required further maturation for hygienization.
9. Vermicomposting for maturation of primary stabilized composts yield better results during all seasons in term of TN (2.64-3.22%) and total phosphorus (5.2-7.25 g/kg).
10. All biodegradable solid waste used for vermicompost can be recycled in mechanic cow composting machine.

Advantage of mechanical cow:

1. Required less space.
2. No odor problem
3. Capacity of drum is available from 0.2 m^2 to 7.6 m^2
4. Most of the drums especially small sized are movable.
5. Yield very uniform marketable compost.
6. Material is isolated from environment, no leaching or spillage.
7. Extremely versatile, tested with various types of food, straw dust, grass cuttings, animal manure sludge etc.
8. Easy for the design according to the requirements.

Pages: 73-77
WASTE DISPOSAL AND MANAGEMENT
Edited by: Dr. Pawan Kumar 'Bharti'; Dr. B. Tabassum; and Dr. Priya Bajaj
ISBN: 978-93-5056-729-6
Edition: 2015
Published by: Discovery Publishing House Pvt. Ltd., New Delhi (India)

6

The Fundamental Microbiology of Sewage

Alina Javed*, Priya Bajaj and B.Tabassum****

ABSTRACT

The purpose of this module is to provide a fundamental background on the relationship between microbes, wastewater, and wastewater treatment, i.e., why are we concerned about microbes in wastewater, what role do they play in wastewater treatment, and what happens when "clean" water is released into the environment.

Key words: Microbes, Sewage, Wastewater Treatment.

INTRODUCTION

Wastewater, by its nature, is teaming with microbes. Many of these microbes are necessary for the degradation and stabilization of organic matter and thus are beneficial. On the other hand, wastewater may also contain pathogenic or potentially pathogenic microorganisms, which pose a threat to public health. Waterborne and water-related diseases caused by pathogenic microbes are among the most serious threats to public health today. Waterborne diseases whose pathogens are spread by the fecal-oral route can be caused by bacteria, viruses, and parasites (including protozoa, worms, and rotifers). The major bacterial pathogens and their associated diseases are:

* Department of Biotechnology, Jamia Millia Islamia, New Delhi, (India).
** Department of Zoology, Govt. Raza PG College, Rampur (UP), (India).

Bacterial Pathogens	Related Disease
Salmonella	Salmonellosis
S. typhimurium	Typhoid fever
Shigella	Shigellosis
Enterococcus (Fecal Streptococci)	Diarrhea
E. coli (Fecal Coliform)	Diarrhea
Vibro cholera	Cholera
Camplyobacter jejuni	Gastroenteritis

Viruses are defined as genetic elements, containing either DNA or RNA and a protein capsid membrane, which are able to alternate between intracellular and extracellular states, the latter being the infectious state. The major viral pathogens include:

Viral Pathogens	Related Disease
Hepatitis A	Hepatitis
Norwalk-like agents	Gastroenteritis
Virus-like 27 nanometer particles	Gastroenteritis
Rotavirus	Gastroenteritis and polio

Diarrhoea is one of the most common features of waterborne disease. Fecal pollution is one of the primary contributors to diarrhea. Examples of bacteria commonly associated with diarrheal disease are *Shizella dysenteriae* and *Salmonella typhi*.

INDICATORS AND DETECTION

Water quality, and its threat to public health, has inspired development of tests designed to measure its suitability for drinking, bathing, and release back to the environment. Water that looks clear and pure may be contaminated with pathogenic microorganisms. Therefore, even water that appears "pure" must be tested to ensure that it contains no microorganisms that might cause disease. On the other hand there are so many potential pathogens that it is impractical to test for them all. Because of this, tests have been developed for indicator organisms. These are organisms that are present in feces (or sewage), survive as long as pathogenic organisms, and are easy to test for at relatively low cost.

Indicator organisms *indicate* that fecal pollution has occurred and microbial pathogens might be present. Total and fecal coliforms, and the enterococci - fecal streptococci are the indicator organisms currently used in the public health arena. Coliform bacteria include all aerobic and facultative anaerobic, gram-negative, nonspore-forming, rod-shaped bacteria that ferment lactose with gas formation. There are three groupings of coliform bacteria used as standards: Total coliforms (TC), fecal coliforms (FC) and *Escherichia coli*.

Total coliforms are the broadest grouping including *Escherichia, Enterobacter, Klebsiella*, and *Citrobacter*. These are found naturally in the soil, as well as in feces.

Fecal coliforms are the next widest grouping, which includes many species of bacteria commonly found in the human intestinal tract. Usually between 60% and 90% of total coliforms are fecal coliforms.

E. coli are a particular species of bacteria that may or may not be pathogenic but are ubiquitous in the human intestinal tract. Generally more than 90% of the fecal coliform are *Escherichia*.

BIOLOGICAL WASTEWATER TREATMENT

One of the primary goals of biological treatment is the removal of organic material from wastewater so that excessive oxygen consumption won't become a problem when it is released to the environment. Another goal of biological treatment is nitrification/denitrification. Nitrification is an aerobic process in which bacteria oxidize reduced forms of nitrogen. While denitrification is an anaerobic process by which oxidized forms of nitrogen are reduced to gaseous forms which can then escape into the atmosphere. This is important because the release of nitrogen to the aquatic environment can also cause eutrophication. Immobilization of phosphate through bacterial assimilation or precipitation is important for the same reason. Another goal of biological treatment is elimination of pathogenic microorganisms either through predation or out-competition. The oxidation/stabilization of organic sludge is also of importance in biological treatment of wastewater.

BIOCHEMICAL OXYGEN DEMAND (BOD) AND EUTROPHICATION

Organic material in wastewater originates from microorganisms, plants, animals, and synthetic organic compounds. Organic materials enter wastewater in human wastes, paper products, detergents, cosmetics, and foods. They are typically a combination of carbon, hydrogen, oxygen, and nitrogen and may contain other elements. Wastewater may also contain small amounts of synthetic organic molecules (i.e., pesticides and solvents) which may range from simple to complex in structure.

The oxidation of organic materials in the environment can have profound effects on the maintenance of aquatic life and the aesthetic quality of waters. Biochemical oxidation reactions involve the conversion of organic material using oxygen and nutrients into carbon dioxide, water, and new cells. The equation that expresses this is:

Organic material + O_2 + nutrients $\rightarrow$ CO_2 + H_2O + new cells + nutrients + energy.

It can be seen from this equation that organisms use oxygen to breakdown carbon-based materials for assimilation into new cell mass and energy. A common measure of this oxygen use is biochemical oxygen demand (BOD). BOD is the amount of oxygen used in the metabolism of biodegradable organics. If water with a large amount of BOD is discharged into the environment, it can deplete the natural oxygen resources. Heterotrophic bacteria utilize deposited organics and O_2 at rates that exceed the oxygen-transfer rates across the water surface. This can cause anaerobic conditions, which leads to noxious odors. It can also be detrimental to aquatic life by reducing dissolved oxygen concentrations to levels that cause fish to suffocate. The end result is an overall degradation of water quality.

Wastewater often contains large amounts of the nutrients, particularly nitrogen and phosphorous (as phosphate- PO_4^{3-}). Nitrogen and phosphorous are essential for growth of all organisms and are typically limiting in the environment.

The introduction of large concentrations of these nutrients from untreated or improperly treated wastewater can lead to eutrophication. Eutrophication is the process by which bodies of water become rich in mineral and organic nutrients causing plant life, especially algae, to proliferate, then die and decompose thereby reducing the dissolved oxygen content and often killing off other organisms. A specific health problem associated with increased levels of nitrogen is methemoglobinemia or blue-baby syndrome. This disease is a direct result of elevated concentrations of nitrite.

FUNDAMENTALS OF BIOLOGICAL TREATMENT

The basic mechanisms of biological treatment are the same for all treatment processes. Microorganisms, principally bacteria, metabolize organic material and inorganic ions present in wastewater during growth. A bacterial perspective of contaminant removal involves several steps. First, there must be a liquid-phase transport of the contaminant to the cell surface. Next, there must be a sorption of the contaminant to the cell surface. Third, if necessary, extracellular enzymes will hydrolyze the contaminant into subunits, which can then be transported by diffusion to and through the cytoplasmic membrane.

It is important to realize that biological wastewater treatment alone does not result in the regeneration of potable water.

MICROBIOLOGY OF ONSITE SYSTEMS

The septic tank works by a combination of sedimentation and anaerobic (without molecular oxygen) digestion. Anaerobic bacteria are responsible for the digestion. Anaerobic bacteria are non-pathogenic and are present in large numbers in the human intestine. A new supply of these bacteria are regularly added to the septic tank with each flush of human fecal material. Anaerobic digestion represents an incomplete digestion. Methane, hydrogen sulfide, and sulfur dioxide gases are produced, as well as a sludge of high molecular weight hydrocarbons. This sludge will readily decompose further when exposed to oxygen and aerobic bacteria. This further decomposition will take place in the municipal sewage treatment plant or landfill if either of these places is used to dispose of sludge pumped periodically from septic tanks.

REFERENCES

1. M. Fang, J.W.C. Wong, G.X. Li*, M.H. Wong Effect of Coal Ash Residues on the Microbiology of Sewage Sludge Composting.
2. Eric W. Mood Microbiology of Water and Sewage.
3. Michael Wagner, Alexander Loy, Regina Nogueira, Ulrike Purkhold, Natuschka Lee, Holger Daims Microbial Community Composition and Function in Wastewater Treatment Plants.
4. Khopkar, S. M. (2004). *Environmental Pollution Monitoring And Control.* New Delhi: New Age International. p. 299.
5. PUB (Singapore National Water Agency) (2011). “NE Water: History.”
6. Ashton, John; Ubido, Janet (1991). “The Healthy City and the Ecological Idea”. *Journal of the Society for the Social History of Medicine* 4 (1): 173-181. Retrieved 8 July 2013.
7. Lewis Dunbar B. Gordon (1851). *A Short Description of the Plans of Captain James Vetch for the Sewerage of the Metropolis.*
8. H. Stanbridge (1976). *History of Sewage Treatment in Britain.* Institute of Water Pollution Control.
9. P.F. Cooper. “Historical Aspects of Wastewater Treatment”. Retrieved 2013-12-21.
10. Martin V. Melosi (2010). *The Sanitary City: Environmental Services in Urban America from Colonial Times to the Present.* University of Pittsburgh Press. p. 110.
11. Colin A. Russell (2003). *Edward Frankland: Chemistry, Controversy and Conspiracy in Victorian England.* Cambridge University Press. pp. 372-380.
12. Sharma, Sanjay Kumar; Sanghi, Rashmi (2012). *Advances in Water Treatment and Pollution Prevention.* Springer. Retrieved 2013-02-07.
13. Epidemics, Demonstration Effects, and Municipal Investment in Sanitation Capital.
14. Edwin Chadwick and the Engineers, 1842-1854: Systems and Antisystems in the Pipe-and-Brick Sewers War Technology and Culture”. 1992.
15. Tilley, David F. (2011). *Aerobic Wastewater Treatment Processes: History and Development.* IWA Publishing. Retrieved 2013-02-07.

WASTE DISPOSAL AND MANAGEMENT *Pages:* 78-88
Edited by: Dr. Pawan Kumar 'Bharti'; Dr. B. Tabassum; and Dr. Priya Bajaj
ISBN: 978-93-5056-729-6
Edition: 2015
Published by: Discovery Publishing House Pvt. Ltd., New Delhi (India)

7

Electronic Waste Disposal and Societal Response

Faiza Naeem

INTRODUCTION

One of the challenges that the contemporary society and its environment faces is the management of disposal of Electronic waste. As a result of scientific and technological advancements in the present day world, man has acquired a large number of electric and electronic equipments and gadgets that help him solve his day-to-day problems in almost all spheres of his life.

Devices such as mobile phones, batteries of all sorts, television sets, microwaves, grinders, vacuum cleaners, electronic vehicles etc. are just a few examples of electronic and electric items that are in common and daily use of today's man. Most of these devices contain materials that are quite harmful to human health and environment if not properly handled and disposed off.

E-waste can be defined as all electronic and electric goods and products which have lost their life and have been discarded. E-waste can contain hazardous substances and its improper treatment can lead to adverse effects for human health and environment. Substances like lead, cadmium, mercury, etc present in E-waste can cause respiratory and carcinogenic disorders and pose serious threats to environment.

It has been estimated that about 5 million tons of E-waste is produced in the world each year. India generates about 2 million tons of E waste

Department of Zoology, Govt. Raza PG College, Rampur (UP) 244 901, (India).

annually. The Environmental Protection Agency estimates that only 15-20% of E-waste is recycled, rest of these electronics go directly into incinerators and landfills.

A

B

C

Fig. 7.1 (A, B, C): **E-Waste in Land-Fill and Garbage Dumping Ground**

EFFECTS OF CHEMICAL TOXICANTS

E-waste has proved to be highly dangerous to the public health and flora and fauna of the ecosystem. Some of the undesirable effects brought about by some well-known toxicants are considered below.

IMPACT OF E-WASTE ON HUMAN HEALTH

Lead: Lead is present in monitors, circuit boards, glass panels etc. It can cause damage to kidney, reproductive system and central and peripheral nervous systems. Young Children are particularly susceptible. Lead generally affects children more severely than adults. Most of lead poisoning occurs in children. Symptoms of chronic lead poisoning are of three general types:

Neuromuscular effects, collectively called lead palsy includes weakness, fatigue, wrist-drop, palsy, and impairment of muscle metabolism resulting into residual paralysis and muscular atrophy. Central nervous system effects include a panoply of nervous system disorders that may lead to delirium, convulsion, coma and death. Gastrointestinal troubles, include intestine stresses.

Mercury: Mercury is present in fluorescent lamps, batteries, switches etc. It can cause various skin disorders. Mercury is readily absorbed by human body, Ultimately inhibiting Enzymatic activity and Leading to cell damage. Mercury is potent and versatile poison. Methyl mercury vapors cause fatal poisoning. Mercury poisoning was responsible for Minemata disease in epidemic from Minemata Bay of Kyushu in Japan during 1953-1961, and at

Niigata also in Japan in 1965. The cause of death was the fish contaminated with mercury. Mercury also bring about genetic effects causing chromosome breaking, interference with cell division, resulting in polyploidy and abnormal distribution of chromosomes. Toxicity of mercury is much higher than any other substance, about 1,000 times ore potent than colchicines.

Cadmium: Cadmium is Present in photocopying machines, semiconductors batteries, etc. Cadmium is poisonous at very low levels and is known to accumulate in human liver and kidney. It causes hypertension, emphysema and Renal damage. It poses the risk of Irreversible effects on human health. It may turn to be carcinogenic in mammals.

Beryllium: Present in mother boards, can cause lung cancer, beryllicosis and skin diseases such as warts.

Fig. 7.2: **Batteries Containing Cadimum**

IMPACT OF E-WASTE ON ENVIRONMENT

E-waste is continuously degrading the environment and adversely affecting the quality of water, air and soil. Some of serious damages caused by E-waste to the environment are as under.

WATER POLLUTION DUE TO E-WASTE

Large amounts of E-waste are being dumped into landfills without being properly treated. E-wastes that are dumped into landfills, produce contaminated leakages which eventually pollute ground water and other water streams. Due to drinking of contaminated water the lives of not only humans but also of animals are at risk. The elements like mercury that leak into water bodies make fishes unsafe to eat. Mercury poisoning was responsible for Minemata disease in epidemic from Minemata Bay of Kyushu in Japan during 1953-1961, and at Niigata also in Japan in 1965. The cause of death was the consumption of fish contaminated with mercury.

Fig. 7.3: **Mother Boards Cotaining Beryllium**

Fig. 7.4: **Water Pollution due to E-Waste**

AIR POLLUTION DUE TO E-WASTE

Burning of E-waste releases toxic fumes, that adversely affect air quality and make it unfit for living organisms. Incineration is controlled and complete combustion process, in which waste material is burned in specially designed incinerators at high temperature. Incineration of toxic E-waste is taking place without restriction around the world, especially in poorer countries. The amount and toxicity of chemicals released by this activity is quite alarming. Burning of E-waste releases toxic heavy metals such as cadmium, lead, mercury, highly toxic dioxins, furans etc, which are known to cause cancer. At many places open burning of E-waste is carried out. Since open fires burn at relatively low temperature, they release many more pollutants than in controlled incineration.

A

B

Fig. 7.5 (A, B): **Inceneration of E-Waste**

SOIL POLLUTION DUE TO E-WASTE

E-waste has become chief source of soil pollution. Due to improper disposal toxic substances from E- waste cause soil contamination and enter food chain and contribute to several health problems. Chemical toxicants that leach out from E-waste due to improper dumping pollute the soil to the varying extents. These chemical toxicants, particularly heavy metals are not readily degraded in the environment and bring about several undesirable effects on organisms. They can make soil barren.

EMERGING PROBLEMS OF E-WASTE IN SOME MEGA CITIES OF INDIA

E-waste has lead to several un ignorable problems in various parts of the world, that has gained the attention of environmentalist around the globe. India generates about 2 million tons of E-waste annually. The Environmental Protection Agency estimates that only 15-20% of E-waste is recycled, rest of these electronics go directly into incinerators and landfills. Let us have a look at the emerging problems of E-waste in some mega cities of India.

Delhi: India's capital is emerging as the world's dumping capital for e-waste, and likely to generate e-waste to an extent of 50,000 metric tons (MT) per annum by 2015 from the current level 30,000 metric tons per annum growing at a compound annual growth rate (CAGR) of about 25%, according to an ASSOCHAM recent estimate.

Mumbai: Mumbai generates 19,000 tons of E-waste annually. The city does not have any method for its safe handling. In Mumbai, as in the rest of India, there are no set procedures or legislation regulating e-waste. The waste is mostly taken by scrap dealers, either at auctions from large companies or collected from various users, and scavengers. The re-usable parts are sold as spares, while the rest is used to recover various metals. The biggest environmental and health hazards come from the recovery of metals such as gold, silver, copper etc. The residues which contain heavy metals and toxic organic traces are dumped in the open. This metal recovery takes place almost exclusively in the informal sector, without any ecological and environmental precautions being taken.

Banglore: Bangalore produces some 20,000 tons E-waste annually. This figure is rising by 20% per year and could reach 500% by 2020.

MANAGEMENT OF E-WASTE

Since the problem is severe, managing e- waste has become need of an hour. Some management options must be adopted to handle the bulk e wastes. We can manage E-waste by three simple steps: Reduce, Reuse, Recycle.

Reduce

Rethinking what you buy, refusing to buy latest fad and reducing the consumption can have a big impact on your E waste footprints. Choose long lasting, durable products over disposable once. Try to repair old equipments rather than buying something new.

Fig. 7.6: **Shredding of E-waste**

Reuse

When you really need something new, think about who can benefit from your old technology and appliances. Give your old technology and appliances to someone who can use them. Check with your friends, family, relatives and charItable organizations. Many Non Profit Organizations can help you donate your old electronics to those who can't afford to buy their own. This way you can bring smile on many faces.

Recycling

Recycling is defined as assembling, developing, promoting or buying new products which are made from waste material. Through recycling, we can stop hazardous waste going to landfills and save resources which can be used to manufacture new products. In the process of recycling E-waste is collected, sorted, labeled, decontaminated at the recycling centers. Recycling involves several decontamination phases:

- The first phase Consist of Removing the Hazardous Fractions like Cells, batteries, capacitors etc. In second Separation phase E-waste is put through shredder; in this process appliances are opened in order to recover hazardous fractions that have left in first decontamination Phase.
- In second Separation phase E-waste is put through shredder; in this process appliances are opened in order to recover hazardous fractions that have left in first decontamination Phase. Ferrous based waste is retrieved using a cylindrical magnet. Once retrieved iron is returned to

steel industry, where it is used to manufacture new products. Plastic and several metals are separated and are recycled into new products.

SOCIO-ECOLOGICAL CONCERNS

Technological developments have a direct bearing on the development and evolution of human society. Technological development can be considered as a response to the solutions that a society seeks to solve its various problems in the different spheres of human life. Society and technology interact with each other. The technological development brings in its wake not only the solutions of human problems but also brings about certain known and unknown problems. The societal response to the problems created by technological developments is not always adequate enough to deal with such problems as effectively as needed. As a result there is always a gap between the technological development of a society and its moral, social and legal institutions. The failure of the later to keep pace with the former create social and environmental problems.

By its very nature technology aims at providing easy solutions to human problems. Today no area of human life remains isolated and untouched by technological advancement. Be it agriculture, industry, transportation, communication, health and housing, education and entertainment, even religious and spiritual spheres of human life. Everywhere we find that the technology is playing ever increasing role. Because of its proven ability to enhance the comforts of life, technology attracts all and sundry alike. For example electronic gadgets and appliances like cell phones, digital watches, cameras, computers, microwaves, and innumerable such other devices are nowadays increasingly becoming items of common use.

Although people tend to easily adopt these devices for their use, but they quite often fail to adapt themselves to the demand of proper use of such devices. Take for example the use of cell phones while driving motor cars or motor bike involves a lot of risks, yet people seldom care. Although there is a law banning the use of mobile phones while driving, neither the drivers nor the law enforcing agencies care about it.

Likewise Electronic rickshaws and electronic bikes have of late become in common use, but there are no traffic rules specifically meant for regulating the use of these vehicles. Recently after an accident in Delhi involving E-Rickshaw causing death of a child that the High court of Delhi had to intervene and direct the Delhi government to frame necessary rules governing the plying of E-Rickshaws.

These and such other examples prove the point that we adopt the technological devices quite quickly but fail to adapt ourselves to the demands of their proper use. Likewise when it comes to the proper disposal of E-waste we quite often fail to respond in scientifically sound manner.

RESPONSIBILITIES OF GOVERNMENT, INDUSTRIES AND CITIZENS IN E-WASTE MANAGEMENT

Responsibilities of the Government

Government should set up programmes to generate awareness about correct disposal of E-waste. Recycling centers should be established in small towns and cities. Government must encourage the production of less hazardous equipments. New laws should be established regarding E-waste.

Responsibilities of Industries

All involved persons should be properly qualified and trained before handling E- waste in industries. Production of less hazardous products should be encouraged. Companies should adopt waste minimizing techniques..

Responsibilities of the Citizens

While buying electronic products, opting for those that are made with fewer toxic constituents, use recycled content, are energy efficient, are designed for easy upgrading or disassembly, use minimal packaging and offer leasing or take back options. Never give your dry cell batteries, mobile phones, printer cords, fluorescent lamps and other such household articles to unorganized dealers, as they use illegal ways to recycle them, which can cause hazards to health and environment.

CONCLUSION

E-waste is going to be the problem of alarming proportions in today's world. We must take appropriate and necessary steps to grapple with the problem. The government, the industry and the common man must take serious notice and play their respective roles in all seriousness. E-waste should never be disposed with the garbage and other household waste. E-waste should be collected at separate sites and should be sent for various processes like Reuse, recycling and donating. So far as the behaviour of the common man is concerned we find that quite often people tend to ignore the scientific advice and behave quite carelessly to the great disadvantage to themselves and the society at large. Although the scientific knowledge about the hazards and harmful impact of e-waste has increased manifold in recent times, yet the level of awareness among the masses has not increased in the same proportions. There seems a huge gap between knowledge and awareness in society. The government, non governmental organizations educational institutions must come forward to spread knowledge about proper disposal of e-waste among the masses. The threat to society and environment is real and challenging let us accept this challenge before it is too late to remedy the alarming situation that has already started casting its shadow on human society and its environment.

REFERENCES

1. Sharma, P.D 2013 "Ecology Microbiology Animal Behaviour Pollution and Toxicology"
2. Sharma, P.D 2013 "Environmental botany and plant pathology"
3. http://www.prokerala.com/going-green/e-waste-management-and-role-of-government-and-indistries.php
4. http://web1.cnre.vt.edu/lsg/GEOG3104S10Web/Group2/Open%20Waste%20Burning.html
5. http://www.treehugger.com/gadgets/european-e-waste-labeled-second-hand-is-unloaded-in-ghana.html
6. http://www.elaw.org/node/896
7. http://www.atterobay.com/blogs/hazardous-elements-in-e-waste-things-you-should-know/
8. http://www.greencitizen.com/learn-more/harmful-effects/
9. http://shanghaiist.com/2007/04/23/ewaste_recyclin.p
10. http://ewasteguide.info/galleries/e-waste-bu
11. http://is.oregonstate.edu/greening-it/reducing-electronic-waste
12. http://www.cleanair.org/program/waste_and_recycling/electronic_waste
13. http://www.gogreenewaste.com/news.html
14. http://www.learner.org/interactives/garbage/solidsolut.html
15. http://ewasteguide.info/hazardous-substances
16. https://sites.google.com/site/dukeewaste/mercury
17. Sopie Curtis http://www.techweekeurope.co.uk/knowledge/ghana-slum-faces-growing-e-waste-problem-39972
18. http://www.ncbi.nlm.nih.gov/pmc/articles/PMC1247531/

WASTE DISPOSAL AND MANAGEMENT *Pages:* 89-114
Edited by: **Dr. Pawan Kumar 'Bharti'; Dr. B. Tabassum;** and **Dr. Priya Bajaj**
ISBN: 978-93-5056-729-6
Edition: **2015**
Published by: **Discovery Publishing House Pvt. Ltd., New Delhi (India)**

8

Technologies for Biodegradable and Non-Biodegradable Waste Managements

Virendra Kumar

INTRODUCTION

India today is one of the first industrialized countries of the world. Today we have good industrial infrastructure in core industries like metals, chemicals, fertilizers, petroleum; food etc. What has come out of these? Pesticides, detergent, plastic, solvents, fuel, paints, dyes, food additives etc. are examples. Among them few are biodegradable and non biodegradable components. Biodegradable is a type of waste which can be broken down, in a reasonable amount of time, into its base compounds by micro-organisms and other living things. It can be commonly found in municipal solid waste (sometimes called biodegradable municipal waste, or BMW) as green waste, food waste, paper waste, and biodegradable plastics. Other biodegradable wastes include human waste, manure, sewage, and slaughterhouse waste. In the absence of oxygen, much of this waste will decay to methane by anaerobic digestion. Biodegradable waste can be used for composting or a resource for heat, electricity and fuel by means of incineration or anaerobic digestion. While non biodegradable waste means substances that could not be degrade through enzymatic degradation. It is not strong to be degraded by enzymes, or the substances are not made of organic compounds. (Sharma, 1998)

Plant Protection Officer (Plant Pathology), Ministry of Agriculture & Co-operation, Directorate of Plant Protection, Quarantine and Storage, Regional Pesticide Testing Laboratory, T-2, Ratan Lal Nagar, Kanpur - 208 022

As we become more technologically advanced, we produce materials that can withstand extreme temperatures, are durable and easy to use. Plastic bags, synthetics, plastic bottles, tin cans, and computer hardware - these are some of the things that make life easy for us. But what we forget is that these advanced products do not break down naturally. When we dispose them in a garbage pile, the air, moisture, climate, or soil cannot break them down naturally to be dissolved with the surrounding land. They are not biodegradable. However natural waste and products made from nature break down easily when they are disposed as waste. One of the most common household wastes is polythene - mostly used as polythene bags for shopping and carrying light things. Since they are cheap, they are used by almost everyone- from the local vegetable seller to the supermarket bread shelf. Apart from solid natural waste, there are other types of man-made wastes that are more hazardous to the environment. Cell phone, for instances are made of lead, mercury, plastic and so many millions of them get thrown as garbage. This kind of electronic garbage creates environmental problems. Electronic waste is also fast becoming a big threat to our environment. Batteries are an environmental hazard. The acid leaches not only into the soil but also goes into the ground water. Disposing of them also creates their own problems as the lead is likely to remain in the ash and be released in the air.

KINDS OF WASTES COMPONENTS OF SOLID WASTE MANAGEMENT

The municipal solid waste industry has four components: recycling, composting, land filling and waste-to-energy via incineration. The primary steps are generation, collection, sorting and separation, transfer, and disposal. Activities in which materials are identified as no longer being of value and are either thrown out or gathered together for disposal. (The Hindu, 2013)

COLLECTION

The functional element of collection includes not only the gathering of solid waste and recyclable materials, but also the transport of these materials, after collection, to the location where the collection vehicle is emptied. This location may be materials processing facility, a transfer station or a landfill disposal site.

WASTE HANDLING AND SEPARATION, STORAGE AND PROCESSING AT THE SOURCE

Waste handling and separation involves activities associated with waste management until the waste is placed in storage containers for collection. Handling also encompasses the movement of loaded containers to the point of collection. Separating different types of waste components is an important step in the handling and storage of solid waste at the source.

SEPARATION AND PROCESSING AND TRANSFORMATION OF SOLID WASTES

The types of means and facilities that are now used for the recovery of waste materials that have been separated at the source include curbside collection, drop off and buy back centers. The separation and processing of wastes that have been separated at the source and the separation of commingled wastes usually occur at a materials recovery facility, transfer stations, combustion facilities and disposal sites.

TRANSFER AND TRANSPORT

This element involves two main steps. First, the waste is transferred from a smaller collection vehicle to larger transport equipment. The waste is then transported, usually over long distances, to a processing or disposal site.

DISPOSAL

Today, the disposal of wastes by land filling or land spreading is the ultimate fate of all solid wastes, whether they are residential wastes collected and transported directly to a landfill site, residual materials from materials recovery facilities (MRFs), residue from the combustion of solid waste, compost, or other substances from various solid waste processing facilities. A modern sanitary landfill is not a dump; it is an engineered facility used for disposing of solid wastes on land without creating nuisances or hazards to public health or safety, such as the breeding of insects and the contamination of ground water.

ENERGY GENERATION

Municipal solid waste can be used to generate energy. Several technologies have been developed that make the processing of MSW for energy generation cleaner and more economical than ever before, including landfill gas capture, combustion, pyrolysis, gasification, and plasma arc gasification. While older waste incineration plants emitted high levels of pollutants, recent regulatory changes and new technologies have significantly reduced this concern. United States Environmental Protection Agency (EPA) regulations in 1995 and 2000 under the Clean Air Act have succeeded in reducing emissions of dioxins from waste-to-energy facilities by more than 99 percent below 1990 levels, while mercury emissions have been by over 90 percent. The EPA noted these improvements in 2003, citing waste-to-energy as a power source "with less environmental impact than almost any other source of electricity."

The rapid urbanization and change in life style has increased the waste load and thereby pollution loads on the urban environment to unmanageable and alarming proportions. The existing waste dumping sites are full beyond capacity and under unsanitary conditions leading to pollution of water sources, proliferation of vectors of communicable diseases, foul smell and odors, release of toxic metabolites, unaesthetic ambiance and eye sore etc. It is difficult to get new dumping yards and open dumping is prohibited by law. This is particularly true for India, with severe constraints of land availability, dense population, environmental fragility and expectation for management of solid wastes relies on an overly centralized approach. In earlier days, municipal wastes, comprised mainly of biodegradable matter, did not create much problem to the community as the quantity of wastes generated was either recycled/reused directly as manure or was within the assimilative capacity of the local environment. The biodegradable waste of the urban centers was accepted by the suburban rural areas for composting in the agricultural fields. With increasing content of plastics and non-biodegradable packaging materials, municipal wastes became increasingly unacceptable to cultivators. As a result, the excessive accumulation of non biodegradable wastes in the urban environment poses serious threat. Similar scenario is now emerging in rural areas as well due to the urban-rural continuum, typical to different metro cities of India.

SOLID WASTES

It is domestic, commercial and industrial wastes especially common as co-disposal of wastes. The examples are described below:

EXAMPLES:

1. **Plastics***:* A plastic material is any of a wide range of synthetic or semi-synthetic organic solids that are moldable. Plastics are typically organic polymers of high molecular mass, but they often contain other substances. They are usually synthetic, most commonly derived from petrochemicals, but many are partially natural. Thermoplastics can be re-melted and reused, and thermo set plastics can be ground up and used as filler, although the purity of the material tends to degrade with each reuse cycle. There are methods by which plastics can be broken back down to a feedstock state. Pure plastics have low toxicity due to their insolubility in water and because they are biochemically inert, due to a large molecular weight. Plastic products contain a variety of additives, some of which can be toxic. For example, the World Health Organization's International Agency for Research on Cancer (IARC) has recognized vinyl chloride, the precursor to PVC, as a human carcinogen.
2. **Styrofoam containers***:* A foam food container is a disposable container for various foods, including beverages. Food types may be processed (instant noodles), raw (meat from supermarkets), or cooked (delicatessen).The containers are commonly used to serve takeout food from restaurants, and are also available by request for diners who wish to take the remainder of their meal home.
3. **Bottles:** Plastic bottles were first used commercially in 1947, but remained relatively expensive until the early 1960s when high-density polyethylene was introduced. They quickly became popular with both manufacturers and customers due to their light weight nature and relatively low production and transportation costs compared with glass

bottles. Except for wine and beer, the food industry has almost completely replaced glass with plastic bottles. A plastic bottle is a bottle constructed of plastic. Plastic bottles are typically used to store liquids such as water, soft drinks, motor oil, cooking oil, medicine, shampoo, milk, and ink. The size ranges from very small sample bottles to large carboys.

Fig. 8.1: **Styrofoam Container having Food**

4. **Cans:** A tin can, tin (especially in British English, Australian English and Canadian English), steel can, steel packaging or a can, is a container for the distribution or storage of goods, composed of thin metal. Many cans require opening by cutting the "end" open; others have removable covers. Cans hold diverse contents, foods, beverages, oil, chemicals, etc. Metal cans are not used as shipping containers. Steel cans are made of tinplate (tin-coated steel) or of tin-free steel. In some locations, even aluminium cans are called "tin cans". Steel from cans and other sources is the most recycled packaging material. Around 65% of steel cans are recycled. In the United States, 63% of steel cans are recycled, compared to 52% of aluminium cans.
5. **Papers:** Paper is a thin material produced by pressing together moist fibers, typically cellulose pulp derived from wood, rags or grasses, and drying them into flexible sheets.Paper is a versatile material with many uses. Whilst the most common is for writing and printing upon, it is also widely used as a packaging material, in many cleaning products, in a number of industrial and construction processes, and even as a food ingredient – particularly in Asian cultures.
6. **Scrap iron:** Scrap consists of recyclable materials left over from product manufacturing and consumption, such as parts of vehicles, building

supplies, and surplus materials. Unlike waste, scrap can have significant monetary value. Great potential exists in the scrap metal industry for accidents in which a hazardous material, which is present in scrap, causes death, injury, or environmental damage.

7. **Other trash:** Trash may refer to in garbage: Municipal solid waste, unwanted or undesired waste material, Litter and Waste container, or "Trash can".

LIQUID WASTES: WASTES IN LIQUID FORM

Examples: *Domestic washings, Chemicals, Oils, waste water from ponds, manufacturing industries* and *other sources.*

SOURCES OF WASTES

The following pictures are showing sources of Wastage that may arise from agriculture, house hold, commerce, industries and fisheries.

Fig. 8.2(A): **Source of Wastage from Agricultural Field**

Fig. 8.2(B): **Mixed Domestic Waste**

Fig. 8.3: **Source of Wastage from Household and Commerce and Industry**

CLASSIFICATION OF WASTES ACCORDING TO THEIR DEGRADATION

(A) Bio-degradable:

Which can be degraded (paper, wood, fruits and others).

(B) Non-biodegradable:

Which cannot be degraded (plastics, bottles, old machines, cans, Styrofoam containers etc).

CLASSIFICATION OF WASTES ACCORDING TO THEIR EFFECTS ON HUMAN HEALTH AND THE ENVIRONMENT

A. Hazardous wastes

Substances unsafe to use commercially, industrially, agriculturally, or economically that are shipped, transported to or brought from the country of origin for dumping or disposal in, or in transit through, any part of the territory of the India.

B. Non-hazardous

Substances safe to use commercially, industrially, agriculturally, or economically that are shipped, transported to or brought from the country of origin for dumping or disposal in, or in transit through, any part of the territory of the India.

Characteristics of Biodegradable Waste

- Biodegradable waste is a type of waste which can be broken down, in a reasonable amount of time, into its base compounds by micro-organisms and other living things, regardless of what those compounds may be.
- Biodegradable waste can be commonly found in municipal solid waste (sometimes called biodegradable municipal waste, or BMW) as green waste, food waste, paper waste, and biodegradable plastics.
- Other biodegradable wastes include human waste, manure, sewage and slaughterhouse waste.
- In the absence of oxygen, much of this waste will decay to methane by anaerobic digestion.

Fig. 8.4(A): **Biodegradable Waste Material**

Fig. 8.4(B): **Non-biodegradable Waste Material**

How to Recycle Biodegradable Waste

- Biodegradable waste is animal or plant matter that breaks down naturally with exposure to microorganisms, heat and oxygen.
- Recycling biodegradable waste into a nutrient-rich, usable material is often called "composting." Composting requires that you follow guidelines to create a substance that can later be added to soil to make it better for gardening or other plant growth.
- It is important to determine the best way to recycle this type of waste according to your home or business needs, where you live and your lifestyle. You can recycle biodegradable waste at home, using a service or through a community organization.

MANAGEMENT OF BIODEGRADABLE WASTAGE

Biodegradable wastage can be recycles through Vermitechnology (vermiculture), Vermiculture & Vermicomposting. *Vermiculture* is the culture of earthworms, while Vermicomposting is using earthworms and microorganisms to convert organic waste into black, earthy-smelling, nutrient-rich humus. (Sakthivel, 2013)

Vermicomposting

- Vermicomposting is a technology of composting various forms of biodegradable wastes with the help of earthworms.
- This compost is perfectly balanced and good in plants nutrients.

Vermiculture

It is Composting with red worms (*Eisenia foetida*):

- To improve the soil quality & house plants
- To get rid of kitchen wastes
- Fishing worms
- Save money and the environment

Fig. 8.5: **Process of Vermicomposting**

REQUIREMENTS OF VERMICULTURE

A. Earthworms:

The following three important species of earthworm is beneficial or vermiculture:

- ***Eisenia foetida:*** It is epigeic earthworm and generally occurs upon the earth surface. It is also called as litter and surface dwelling species. *E. foetida* known under various common names such as red worm, brandling worm, tiger worm and red wiggler worm. These worm thrive in rotting vegetation, compost and manure.
- ***Eudrilus eugeniae:*** It is a species of earthworm native to tropical west Africa and now widespread in warm regions, both wild and under vermiculture, also called the african night crawler. Fecundity, growth, maturation and biomass production were all significantly greater at 25°C than 15°, 20°or 30°. {25°C = 77°F}. The growth of individual earthworms increased the lower the population density, but the greatest

overall earthworm biomass production occurs at the highest population density. The greatest number of cocoons per week and the number of hatchlings per cocoon are obtained at 25°C. Cocoons of *E. eugeniae* hatched in only 12 days at 25°C, the earthworms at these temperatures reached sexual maturity in as little as 35 days after hatching.

Fig. 8.6: Eisenia foetida

Fig. 8.7: Eudrilus eugeniae

- ***Perionyx excavates:*** It is a commercially produced Earthworm. They are also known as "blues" or "Indian blues". They belong to the *Perionyx* genus. Their origins may be the Himalayan mountains. This species is particularly good for vermicomposting in tropical and subtropical regions.

Fig. 8.8: Perionyx excavates

Biology of Earthworm: (Jordan & Verma 1997)

1.	Growth rate:	12 mm/day
2.	Body weight:	4-30 mg
3.	Maturity:	40 days
4.	Laying of Cocoons:	4 cocoons/3 times
5.	Life span:	2-3 years
6.	Cocoon incubation period:	16-17 days

B. Pre digested or decomposed organic wastes

Fig 8.9: **Pre Digested or Decomposed Organic Wastes**
(Photographs from National Institute of Plant Health Management (NIPHM) Hyderabad)

C. Source of water

D. Buckets and water sprayer

E. Concrete floor under shade

F. Worm bin: It must be:

- Convenient
- Easily accessible
- In a well-ventilated location
- Covered and protected from wind, sun, and animals

Method of Production of vermicompost: Vermicompost can be produced by any of the following methods:

1. Pit Method:

- **Preparation of Tank:** A tank (10′Length × 3′Height × 3′ Width) may be constructed with brick and mortar with proper water outlets, or a plastic crate (600 mm × 300 mm × 300 mm) with holes drilled at the bottom. Vermibed (vermes = earthworms; bed = bedding) of about 15 to 20 cm thick should be laid with the following layers:
  - Broken bricks (4cm) at the bottom
  - Coarse sand (3 cm)
  - Fine sand (3cm)
  - Red soil (5 cm) at the top

The vermibed should always be kept moist, but should never be flooded.

- Inoculate earthworm @ 1000 worms per square meter area or 10 kg earthworm in 100 kg of organic matter.
- Spray water on the bed and gunny bag. Maintain 50-60% moisture of the pit by periodical water spraying.

Fig. 8.10: **Pit Method of vermicomposting**
(Photographs from National Institute of Plant Health Management (NIPHM) Hyderabad)

2. **Windrow Method:** This method is widely used for large scale production of vermicompost. You may please follow these steps:
   - Load the organic wastes in the form of bed (preferably 10 feet L × 3 feet W × 1.5 feet H). Size of bed may vary as per availability of organic waste.
   - After loading, the fresh bed should be covered with jute mate or dry agriculture wastes such as rice-bran, banana-leaf, maize residue etc.

Fig. 8.11: **Preparation of Vermicompost by Windrow Method**
(Photographs from National Institute of Plant Health Management (NIPHM) Hyderabad)

   - Sprinkle water over the covered vermibed to maintain 40% moisture in bed.
   - Moisture percent can be checked by forming lump of organic waste using hand. it should easily form lump.
   - Bed should be mixed thoroughly to prevent it from becoming compact.
   - The first lot of vermicompost is ready for harvesting after 2-21/2 months and the subsequent lots can be harvested after every six weeks of loading.

- Watering of bed should be stopped for at least 2-3 days before harvesting. Earthworms go down in the moist soil and the compost is collected from the top without disturbing the lower layers of vermibed having earthworm. Vermicompost harvested will be of dark brown colour and free flowing.
- The harvested compost should be stored in dark and cold place.

Fig. 8.12: **Women Farmers Unit Collecting Vermicompost by Windrow Method**

3. Tray Method:

Plastic trays of 45 × 15 × 30 cm dimension can be used for culturing of earthworms. At the bottom of the tray one hole was made to drain the excess water in the medium. Then the tray is filled with cow dung (4kg) and watering was done regularly twice in a day. Once the bed is ready cocoons or worms may be released.

Compositing process: It is an aerobic, here bio-oxidation, non-thermophilic, microbial activity are involve.

Food stocks: The following food stocks are required for vermicomposting:

- Fruit & vegetable scraps
- Banana peels
- Grains & cereals, pasta

Fig. 8.13: **Preparation of Vermicompost by Tray Method**

- Tea bags & leaves
- Cooked eggs & shells
- Coffee grounds & filters
- Onions & potatoes
- Pancakess
- Banana bread, cake
- Leaves
- Plant cuttings

Doses of vermicompost:

- The doses of vermicompost application depend upon the type of crop grown in the field/nursery. For fruit crops, it is applied in the tree basin.
- Vermicompost should be used as a component of integrated nutrient supply system.
- **Crops Dose/rate:**
  - Field crops 5-6t/ha
  - Fruit crops 3-5kg/plant
  - Pots 100-200 g/pot

Advantages of Vermiculture:

- Multiplies of more number earthworm
- Recycles domestic waste
- Compost can be profitably utilized
- Reduces pollution
- Easy way to recycle waste
- Simple and easy to adopt
- Reduce the urban Pests Problem
- Improves public health

- Prevents foul odour of garbage
- Produces high nutritive value compost
- Eco-friendly

Vermicompost is a nutrient rich compost which:

- Helps better plant growth and crop yield.
- Improves physical structure of soil.
- Enriches soil with micro-organisms.
- Attracts deep-burrowing earthworms already present in the soil which indirectly improves fertility of soil.
- Increase water holding capacity of soil.
- Enhances germination, plant growth, and crop yield.
- Improves root growth of plants.
- Enriches soil with plant hormones such as auxins and gibberellic acid.
- It is helpful in elimination of bio-wastes .

NUTRIENT PROFILE OF VERMICOMPOST

Vermicompost contains: 1.6% Nitrogen; 0.7% Phosphorus; 0.8% Potash; 0.5% Calcium; 0.2% Magnesium; 175 ppm Iron; 96.5 ppm Manganese; 24.5 ppm Zinc and 15.5 C:N ratio.

Non-Biodegradable Waste

- Non-biodegradable substances means substances that could not be degraded through enzymatic degradation. It is not biodegradable because the substances have chemical bonds too strong to be degraded by enzymes, or the substances are not made of organic compounds.
- It is not biodegradable because man has manipulated it in such a way to create a product that is too strong to be broken down by the organisms and natural weathering present on earth.
- Characteristics of items that would make them non-biodegradable are pretty much dependent on the chances that it would be create by nature itself.
- For example, many plastics are non-biodegradable based on the fact that they do not occur in nature.
- Lastly, non-biodegradable really refers to an object that does not degrade within a reasonable amount of time in comparison to the human life. Certain items may take 10 million years to degrade, so they are degradable just...not within a relative time span.

Present Scenario

- In India, the system of primary collection of waste is practically non existent, as the:
  - system of storage of waste at source is yet to be developed.
- Doorstep collection of waste from households, shops and establishments is insignificant and wherever it is introduced through private sweepers

or departmentally, the system does not synchronize further with the facility of Waste Storage Depots and Transportation of Waste.

- The waste so stored is deposited on the streets or on the ground outside the dustbin. Thus streets are generally treated as receptacles of waste and the primary collection of waste is done, by and large, through street sweeping.
- An appropriate system of primary collection of waste is to be so designed by the urban local bodies that it synchronizes with storage of waste at source as well as waste storage depots facility ensuring that the waste once collected reaches the processing or disposal site through a containerized system.

Table 8.1: List of Non- biodegradable substances

Plastic	Metal	Others
Polyethylene Nylon Rayon Polyester Lexan PVC (polyvinyl chloride) and dacron	Iron Platinum Steel Tin Aluminum Lead Silver Gold Arsenic Bismuth and Chromium etc.	Ceramics Carbon fiber Fiberglass, Kevlar Foams (cups, coolers), Glasses, Circuit Boards/Silicon based materials, Noble gases and Diamond

POLYTHENE WASTE DISPOSAL

History

- Polythenes are frequently used in Uganda as a packing materials and they are locally called "Kaveera". Polythenes were introduced in Uganda as a subsitute to the paper bags which were initially used for packing especially the light commondities.
- Polythene bags can best be defined as a nonbiodegradable substance that is used by the majority of Ugandans as packing materials. Despite the fact that they are cheap as well as light.

Effect on Waste Disposal

Few facts which create hazardous in the following ways:

- Hard to dispose.
- Act as breeding places for many of the disease germs which, sooner than later cause an epidemic in the surrounding people.
- Loss of soil fertility.
- Spread of diseases, for example *Cholera*

- Death of domestic animals specially the cows and the goats after eating the polythene bags. This clearly show that waste if mismanaged can be very dangerous to the environment.
- Blockage of water systems.
- Unpleasant scenery. etc.

Non-biodegradable Waste Management

- Non-biodegradable waste made up roughly one-third of the municipal solid waste produced in the U.S. in 2009.
- The U.S. Environmental Protection Agency recommends recycling whenever possible, and disposing of your trash at a combustion facility or in a landfill only when recycling is not possible.
- Hazardous waste should be handled separately by your local sanitation department or by private companies that specialize in safe disposal of toxins. Separate glass, plastic and metal from other non-biodegradable waste for recycling. Many urban and suburban areas have curbside recycling programmes; if such a programme is not available, take recyclable materials to the nearest collection facility for processing. Recycling saves space in landfills and reduces the amount of virgin materials that must be mined or manufactured to make new products, saving energy and reducing global climate change in the process.
- Some non-biodegradable waste like used rubber tires and plastic can be burned at combustion facilities. Most of these facilities use the heat generated by incineration to make energy in the form of steam or electricity, which reduces their demand for other nonrenewable resources, including coal and petroleum.
- Landfills provide long-term storage for non-biodegradable waste. Ideally, landfills are carefully situated to prevent contamination from entering surrounding soil and water, and managed to reduce odor and pests as much as possible.

Hazardous Waste Disposal

- Some products like motor oil, pesticides, batteries and paint are potentially hazardous to sanitation workers and the general population as a whole.
- They are also more dangerous to the environment than inert materials like plastic or rubber.
- Many communities offer special collection and disposal programmes to deal with household hazardous waste as safely as possible. In areas with no such programmes, it's legal to dispose of household hazardous waste in the trash.

Follow any special disposal instructions listed on the original container. Before doing so, however, contact the manufacturer or retailer of the material you need to dispose of to ask if they accept old materials for reuse or recycling.

Five modes of waste disposal:

- **Incineration** - it includes burning of waste Incineration is controlled and complete combustion process, in which waste material is burned in specially designed incinerators at high temperature.
- **Sewage Treatment** - it includes treating the waste material and then discarding it in rivers or using treated water for irrigation etc.:
- Sewage treatment is the process of removing contaminants from waste water and household sewage ,both runoff (effluents , domestic, commercial and institutional.
- It includes physical, chemical, and biological processes to remove physical, chemical and biological contaminants.
- Its objective is to produce an environmentally safe fluid waste stream (or treated effluent) and a solid waste (or treated sludge) suitable for disposal or reuse (usually as farm fertilizer).

Fig. 8.14: **Process of Incineration**

- **Landfill -** The waste material is dumped under the ground is known as landfills.
- Landfills provide long-term storage for non-biodegradable waste. Ideally, landfills are carefully situated to prevent contamination from entering surrounding soil and water, and managed to reduce odor and pests as much as possible.

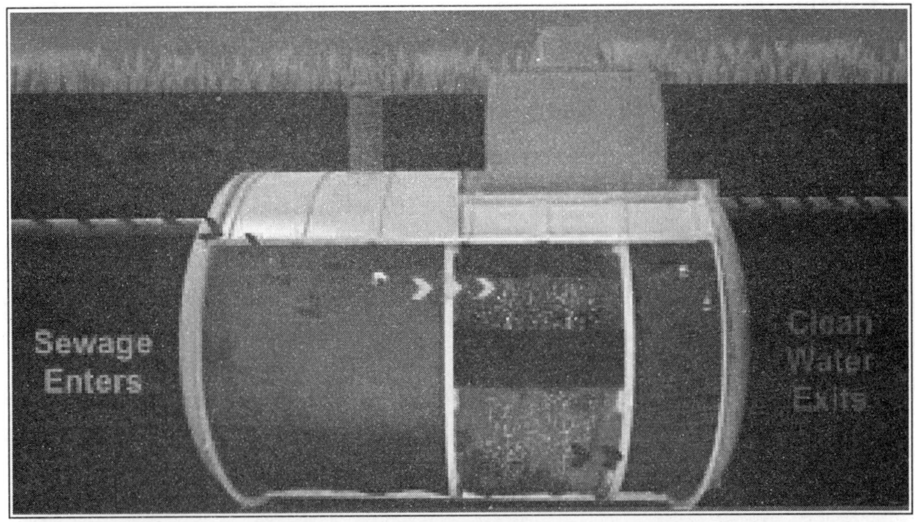

Fig. 8.15: **Process of Sewage Treatments**

Fig. 8.16: **Waste Material are using in Landfilling**

- **Recycle**

- **Combustion**
  - Some non-biodegradable waste like used rubber tires and plastic can be burned at combustion facilities. Most of these facilities use the heat generated by incineration to make energy in the form of steam or electricity, which reduces their demand for other nonrenewable resources, including coal and petroleum.

Fig. 8.17: **Combution**

  - In 2009, combustion facilities burned 3.1 million tons of solid waste, mostly used tires. Combustion of municipal waste also reduces the volume of trash that ends up in landfills.

Steps to be Taken

- Urban local bodies may arrange for the collection of domestic, trade and institutional food/biodegradable waste from the doorstep or from the community bin on a daily basis.
- Local bodies may also arrange through NGOs collection of recyclable waste material/non bio-degradable waste other than toxic and hazardous waste from the source of waste generation at the frequency and in the manner, notified by local bodies from time to time in consultation with the NGOs/Resident Associations, etc.
- Domestic hazardous/toxic waste material deposited by the waste producers in special bins (provided by the local body at various places in the city) may be collected at regular intervals after ascertaining the quantities of such waste deposited in special bins.

METHODS OF PRIMARY COLLECTION OF WASTE

1. Door Step Collection through Containerized Handcarts

A bell may be addixed to the hand cart given to the sweeper or a whistle may be provided to the sweeperin lieu of abell. Each sweeper may be given a fixed area or beat for sweeping plus a fixed number or stretch of houses for collection of waste. The local bodies may, based on local conditions, fix the work norms as they deem appropriate.

2. **Role of Sweeper**

The sweeper should ring the bell or blow the whistle indicating his arrival at the place of his work and start sweeping the street. The people may be directed through adequate publicity campaign that on hearing the bell or whistle they should deposit their domestic biodegradable waste into the handcart of the sweeper or hand over the waste to him/her.

3. **Collection through Motorized Vehicles**

Local bodies as an alternative to doorstep collection through containerized handcarts may deploy motorized vehicles having unconventional/sound horn for doorstep collection of waste. Driver of the vehicle should intermittently blow the horn announcing his arrival in different residential localities and on hearing this, the householder should deposit their domestic waste directly into such vehicle without loss of time.

4. **Primary Collection of Waste from societies/complexes**

In private societies, complexes and multi storied buildings, normally no sweepers are provided by local bodies; hence private sweepers are generally engaged. It may therefore be made compulsory for the management of the societies,complexex and multistoried builders, to keep community bins or containers in which dry and wetwaste may be separately stored by there residents. Such bins may be placed at easily approachable locations to facilitate convenient collection bythe municipal staff or the contractor engaged by the local body.

5. **Collection of Waste from Slums**

Local bodies should collect waste from slums by bell ringing/ whistle system along their main access –lanes. Residents should bring their waste from their houses to hand carts. where slums residents prefer community bins, they should bring their biodegradable waste to these bins only an hour or two before the time of clearance.

6. **Collection-at-the Doorstep in Posh Residential Areas**

In posh residential area where the residents as a whole might not be willing to bring their waste to the municipal hand cart/tricycle, system of collection from the door step on full cost recovery basis may be introduced. This service can be contracted out by the local body of NGOs or contractors' registeredwith the local body may be encouraged to provide such service in area where it is found economically viable to introduce door to door waste collection service. This service mat not be provided to isolated houses, shops and establishments.

Use of Biodegradble Products

There are so many products are available in the market of daily use. We can use it instead of non biodegradable materials. The few biodegradable picture have been showing as follows:

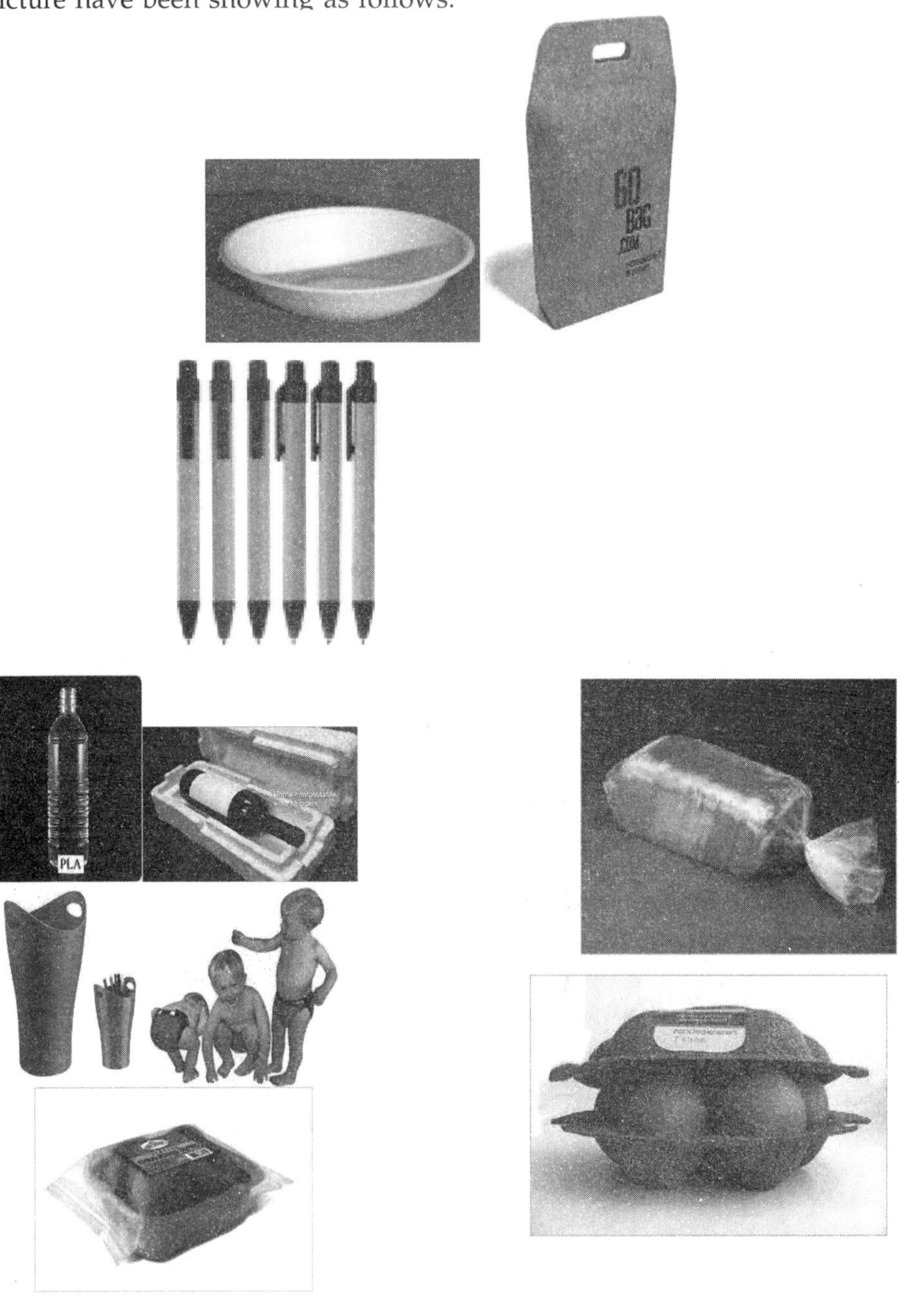

Fig. 8.18: **Different Biodegradable Packaging Materials**

7. **Collection of Duly Segregated Recyclable/Non-biodegradable Waste from households**

Recycle waste has a value. Several rag pickers in the urban areas, therefore, move from street, bin to bin and go to the dump yard to pick up recyclable waste. These rag pickers exposed to health risk as they put their bare hands in contaminated waste. They sell contaminated waste to the waste purchasers stored in slums creating unhygienic conditions. Quite often they spread the waste at the dust bin site to pick up recyclable. This system can be improved by introducing system of collecting recyclable waste from the doorsteps changing the roll of rag pickers to that of waste collectors.

CONCLUSION

An analysis of various technological options, their salient features, environmental implications, cost norms and suitability to the biophysical environment of India has been carried out. It indicates that windrow-composting, vermi-composting and is the most appropriate techniques as far as India is concerned. It is pointed out that the efficiency of the above methods depends on the characteristics of waste, such as, vermicomposting to near-homogenous fruit and vegetable wastes, biogas to slaughter house and fish-market wastes and windrow to heterogeneous wastes from any source. In the case of thermal conversion processes, of course, one has to be very careful to make sure that Safe and effective management of biodegradable and non biodegradable waste is not only a legal necessity but also a social responsibility. Proper collection and segregation of wastage and try to reduce the waste generation. Individual awareness and participation. Use recycle products. Label with agent, concentration and hazard warnings. Communicate about work place hazards. All of them have merits and demerits. Therefore, the choice of this technology has to be done judiciously.

REFERENCES

1. Energy Generation from Municipal Solid Waste "The Hindu" (12.06.2013) pp. 16.
2. http://www.ask.com/question/what-is-non-biodegradable-waste.
3. http://www.en.wikipedia.org/wiki/Biodegradable_waste. Jordan E.L. and P.S. Verma (1997)" Invertebrate Zoology" fourteenth enlarge revised addition book pp. 537-563.
4. http://www.*en.wikipedia.org/wiki/Bottle*
5. http://www.en.wikipedia.org/wiki/Foam_food_container
6. http://www.en.wikipedia.org/wiki/Paper.
7. http://www.en.wikipedia.org/wiki/Plastic
8. http://www.en.wikipedia.org/wiki/Plastic_pollution.
9. http://www.en.wikipedia.org/wiki/Scrap.
10. http://www.en.wikipedia.org/wiki/Tin_can
11. http://www.*localbodies.up.nic.in/swm/chap10.pdf.*
12. National Institute of Plant Health Management (NIPHM) Hyderabad, (A.P.)

13. Picture of Pit and Windrow Methods taken From National Institute of Plant Health Management (NIPHM) Hyderabad, (A.P.)
14. Sakthivel P. (2013) "Earthworm Culture" A Training Manual 2013: Integrated Soil Nutrient and Weed Management (Induction Training Course Vol. I) at National Institute of Plant Health Management (NIPHM) Hyderabad, (A.P.) pp. 103-113.
15. Sharma P.D. (1998) Ecology and Environment, Seventeenth Edition Book, pp. 415-489.
16. www.ask.com/question/examples-of-non-biodegradable-products
17. www.plastics.ca/_files/file.php?filename=file_files/model.
18. www.scribd.com/Polythene-Control-Historical-and-Scientific-Background

Pages: 115-137
WASTE DISPOSAL AND MANAGEMENT
Edited by: **Dr. Pawan Kumar 'Bharti'; Dr. B. Tabassum;** and **Dr. Priya Bajaj**
ISBN: 978-93-5056-729-6
Edition: **2015**
Published by: **Discovery Publishing House Pvt. Ltd., New Delhi (India)**

9

Industrial Waste Management
Problems and Prospects

Faiza Naeem

INTRODUCTION

The Industrial Revolution began in the late 1700s, with the invention of huge machines. These machines could produce large amounts of products cheaply and quickly. In its wake, industrial revolution also gave way to the huge amount of Industrial waste. *Industrial waste is defined as the waste generated by industries during various industrial processes.* There are so many kinds of industrial waste, including dirt and gravel, scrap metals, trash, chemicals, weed grass and trees, wood and scrap lumber, garbage, solvents and similar leftovers.

Industrial waste mentioned above spark concern of both human health and environmental issues. It is estimated that more than 70,000 different chemicals are added each year which is a great number in comparison with the amount of industrial waste disposed off annually. The impact on human health and environmental from these chemicals are still yet to be fully discovered. People who directly work with toxic contaminants such as gas workers or miners have gradually faced with weak health and severe diseases. Waste from manufacturing and laboratory operations when get mixed with water causes water pollution that can kill millions of people using such contaminated water. It also damages the beautiful images of lakes and river systems in the world.

Department of Zoology, Govt. Raza PG College, Rampur (UP) 244 901, (India).

TYPES OF INDUSTRIES

To understand more closely different industries and waste produced by them, let us devide industries into three broad categories:

1. Primary or extreactive industries;
2. Secondary or basic industries; and
3. Tertiary or manufacturing industries.

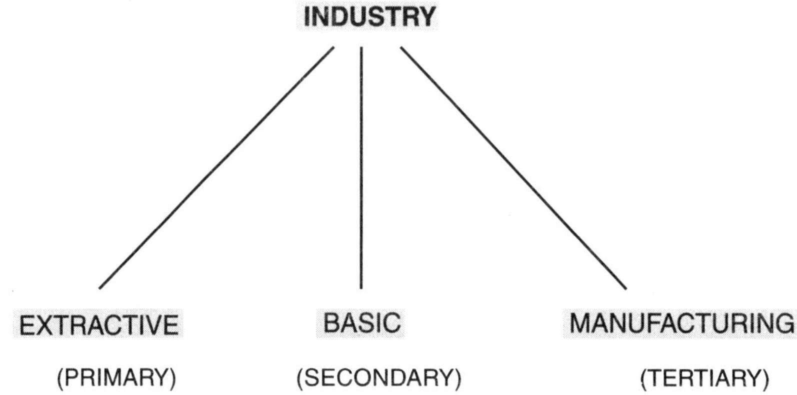

1. EXTRACTIVE INDUSTRIES (PRIMARY INDUSTRIES)

Extraction is a processes that involve the extraction of raw materials from the earth to be used by consumers. The extractive industry consists of any operations that remove metals, mineral and aggregates from the earth. Examples of extractive processes include oil and gas extraction, mining and quarrying. Some examples of such industries are as following:

(i) Mining Industry

Mining is the foundation of industrial civilization. It is the process of extracting minerals like gold, silver, copper, nickel and uranium (metallic) and salt, potash, coal that concentrate naturally in the earth. Mining produce largest amount of the industrial waste. Waste from extractive operations (i.e. waste from extraction and processing of mineral resources) is one of the largest waste streams. It involves materials that must be removed to gain access to the mineral resource, such as topsoil, overburden and waste rock, as well as tailings remaining after minerals have been largely extracted from the ore.

Some of these wastes are inert and hence not likely to represent a significant pollutant threat to the environment save. However, other fractions, in particular those generated by the non-ferrous metal mining industry, may contain large quantities of dangerous substances, such as heavy metals. Through the extraction and subsequent mineral processing, metals and metal compounds tend to become chemically more available, which can result in the generation of acid or alkaline drainage. Moreover, the management of tailings is an intrinsically risky activity, often involving residual processing chemicals and elevated levels of metals. In many cases tailings are stored on heaps or in large ponds, where they are retained by means of dams. The collapse of dams or heaps may have serious impacts on environment and human health and safety. Examples of this are the accidents in Aberfan (Wales, 1966), Stava (Italy, 1985), Aznalcóllar (Spain, 1998), Baia Mare and Baia Borsa (Romania, 2000). Other likely significant impacts relate to the physical footprints of waste disposal facilities and resulting loss of land productivity, effects on ecosystems, dust and erosion. These impacts can have lasting environmental and socio-economic consequences and be extremely difficult and costly to address through remedial measures.

Fig. 9.1: **Mining Waste**

(ii) Quarrying Industry

Quarry wastes are a largely unavoidable by-product of the extraction and processing of aggregates. They are defined as wastes because no market currently exists for them, but unlike many other wastes they are generally inert and non-hazardous. Materials that may be classified as quarry wastes include *overburden* (although this is frequently used in restoration) and *interburden* (material of limited value that occurs above or between layers of economic aggregate material) and processing wastes (non-marketable, mostly fine-grained material from screening, crushing and other processing activities). The type and amount of waste depends on the nature of the operation. Most sand and gravel workings do not produce much, if any, permanent waste. Some produce significant volumes of clay and silt, which could be dug from settling ponds and used during restoration; although most is left in situ and is typically removed to free up space for more plant washings. Hard rock quarries produce variable amounts of quarry waste. Some produce small amounts of overburden while others may have large amounts of overburden and interburden that is not of sufficient quality for the desired product. Any waste that cannot be used immediately is stored in bunds or tips within the boundaries of the aggregate operation. the potential impacts of quarry waste can be summarized as:

(a) **Visual intrusion:** Quarry waste tips and quarry fines stockpiles can be a significant visual intrusion, mainly when waste is dumped off-site or above the skyline (especially when it is not landscaped or vegetated). Although it is often used as a visual or noise screen, it can be considered an eyesore.

(b) **Water:** Run-off from quarry waste tips or quarry fines stockpiles can cause erosion and contaminate local watercourses. Suspended solids (and acid drainage) may harm freshwater ecosystems and impact on other water users. Waste may also create problems if dumped on flood plains where it may exacerbate flooding. Settled silt and clay can also be washed out and displaced from settling ponds and lagoons during storm events.

(c) **Dust:** Large quarry waste tips or quarry fines stockpiles can be a source of airborne dust, which can be exacerbated if they are elevated above the original ground level. Dust may also originate from air filtration units/stacks, haulage trucks, conveyors and transfer points. The effects of dust, suspended solids and disposal have been used to define potential impacts on air, water quality, land quality, fauna and flora, human health and local communities/ other stakeholders

(iii) Logging Industry

Forest slash or logging residues are the portions of the trees that remain on the forest floor or on the land after logging operations have taken place. Forest slash consists mostly of tree branches, top of trunks, stumps, branches, and leaves. Various types of forest slash are listed below:

- *Logging Tops:* This is the unmerchantable upper portion of the stem. The top is typically a stick about 16-18 feet in length with a diameter of 7 inches at the base.
- *Culls:* Culls are that portion of each year's growth of saw timber harvest that is classified as defective and cut and left in the woods. The cull tree does not contain at least 25 percent sound wood in a merchantable saw log now or prospectively because of defect or rot.
- *Precommercial Thinning*: This residue material comes from timber stand improvement and is generally round, densely stocked stands.

(iv) Other Forest Wood Residue

Other wood sources are stand improvements such as culling trees, removing rotten, dead trees, or undersized trees, noncommercial tree species removed from woodlots, and trees from thinning performed on growing stock. In general it may be said that of a typical tree, less than two-third is taken from the forest for further processing, the remainder being either left, burnt or collected as fuel wood by the local inhabitants. After processing, only 28 percent of the original tree becomes lumber, the remainder being residues. It is estimated that traditional logging procedures leave in the wood some 30 to 40% of the original weight of the tree or about ton of the debris per 1000 board feet of log harvested As a solid waste problem this material is scattered over the wide area, is unsightly, constitute fire hazard to the forest, may be a reservoir of destroying disease and insect and represent wastage of natural resource. The negative environmental consequences vary in the severity, irreversibility and significance depending on the form of forest utilization. The impacts might be felt at the local level or may have global significance.

Fig. 9.2: **Logging Waste Heap**

(v) Farming Industry

Like any other industry agricultural practices produces a huge amount of waste, some of which include:

- empty pesticide containers;
- old silage wrap;
- out of date medicines and wormers;
- used tires;
- surplus milk.

It is important that farm waste is kept to a minimum because of the risk of pollution and the need to reduce the amount of waste being buried in landfill sites. concern over pollution resulting from intensive livestock and poultry production—in which large numbers of animals are held in confined production facilities—has increased in recent years. Nationwide, about 130 times more animal waste is produced than human waste—roughly 5 tons for every U.S. citizen—and some operations with hundreds of thousands of animals producing as much waste as a good sized city.

Agricultural waste is one of the largest segments of the nationwide waste problem. These large volumes of agricultural waste threaten surface water and groundwater quality in the event of waste spills, leakage from waste storage facilities, and runoff from fields on which an excessive amount of waste has been applied as fertilizer.

Furthermore, as animal production is increasingly concentrated in larger operations and in certain regions of the country, commonly used animal waste management practices are proving to no longer adequate for preventing water pollution. Within the agricultural waste sector, manure from a variety of livestock and poultry constitutes the largest problem.

If not managed properly, agricultural waste from farm operations can pollute the environment resulting in impacts to water quality and a general loss of aesthetics. The degradation of water quality can impact adjacent waterways and groundwater both onsite and offsite. This degradation reduces the ability of these resources to support aquatic life and water for human and animal consumption. Nitrates, which are commonly associated with fertilizers and agricultural waste runoff, can seep into groundwater. Well water contaminated with nitrates is hazardous to humans, particularly for infants, as it results in oxygen depletion in the blood. As alluded to above, proper waste management can reduce operating costs associated with fertilizer application if managed properly.

2. BASIC INDUSTRIES (SECONDARY INDUSTRIES)

Basic industries are those that take raw material from extractive industries and produce from them refined material which other industries convert into consumer goods. Product from basic industry include wires, tubes, glass, rubber etc. Some examples are as below:

(i) Metal Industry

The wastes from metallurgical industries include slag and scrap metal. Metallurgical industry discharges of concern are, heavy metals, metals, total and suspended solids. They have seriously degraded the quality of important water bodies. Heavy metals, cyanide, inorganic matters, acids or bases, are the main wastes produced from metallurgical industries that can pose substantial hazards to human health or the environment when improperly managed. Because some of these hazardous wastes may undergo violent chemical reaction with water or other materials generates toxic gas. Some of the impacts of chemicals on human health and environment are shown in the table below:

Table 9.1: Effects of Some Toxic Chemical on Health

Chemical	Effects on Human Health
Arsenic	Vomiting, poisoning, liver etc damage
Cadmium	Tumors, renal dysfunction, hypertension, arterio-sclerosis. Itaiitai disease (weakened bones)
Carbon tetrachloride	Liver damage, heart disorder and failure
Chloroform	Kidney and liver damage
Copper	Gastrointestinal irritant liver damage
Cyanide	Acutely toxic
Lead	Convulsions, anemia, Kidney and brain damage
Mercury	Irritability, depression, kidney and liver damage Minamata disease
Nickel	Gastrointestinal and central nervous system
Iron and its oxides	Causes lungs fibrosis due to inhalation of dusts resulting from raw materials preparation
Carbon Tetra Chloride	Causes sickness, vomit, colic, diarrhoea, frustration for central nerves system which causes dizziness. These effects lead to unconsciousness

Table 9.2: Effects of Chemicals on Environment

Chemical	Effects on Environment
Low oxygen level	Toxic to aquatic organisms, causes reproductive defects in and fish, bioacumulates in aquatic organisms
Arsenic	Birds and toxic legume crops
Benzene	Toxic to some fish and aquatic invertebrates
Bis-(2- ethyl- hexyl) phthalate	Eggshell thinning in birds, toxic to fish
	Toxic to fish and bio-accumulation in aquatic organisms
Carbon tetrachloride	Ozone - depleting effects
Chloroform	Ozone- depleting effects
Copper	Toxic to fish
Cyanide	Kills fish, retards growth and development of fish
Lead	Toxic to domestic plants and animals, biomagnifies in food chain
Mercury	Reproductive failure in fish, inhibits growth of and kills fish, methyl mercury biomagnifies
Nickel	Impairs reproduction of aquatic species
Silver	Toxic to aquatic organisms

(ii) Chemical Industry

The chemical industry includes producers of commodity chemicals such as organic and inorganic chemicals and industrial gases, and specialty chemicals such as pharmaceutical products and essential oils. It also includes mixing, blending, diluting or converting basic chemicals to make chemical products and preparations, e.g. paints, pesticides, inks, detergents and cosmetics. Chemical manufacturing businesses produce waste that can have a harmful impact on the environment, such as process residues, spent catalysts or solvents, effluent treatment sludge and contaminated chemical containers. The chemical industry has been recognized as a very polluting sector and has gained the distrust of society. The general public associates chemical industry with waste disposal, pollution, disease, and danger, depletion of natural resources, landfill, accidents and toxic emission. Many substances discarded from chemical manufacturing are classed as waste, including:

- chemical process residues or spent raw materials, e.g. catalysts and sledges;
- residues or unusable solutions of solvents or other chemicals;
- sub-quality chemical products, e.g. adhesives, cleaning preparations, detergents, inks and paints;
- contaminated chemical containers;
- spent or spilled oil, lubricants and fuel;
- contaminated absorbent materials used on spills;
- used packaging, e.g. metal and plastic straps, and polypropylene.

Global chemical pollution is the serious threat to the sustainable development and livelihoods. The problem has impact on both humanity and ecosystems, and include adverse effect from long term exposure to low or sub-lethal concentrations of single chemicals or to a mixture of chemicals.

A recent study by World Health Organization WHO indicated that 4.9 million death are attributable to environmental exposure to chemicals in 2004. In many regions hazardous waste streams are mixed with municipal and solid waste and then either dumped or burned in open air (UN Habitat 2010).

(iii) Paper Industry

Pulp and paper companies also constitute the largest manufacturing sector, providing thousands of high-paid jobs. Unfortunately, the environment, has suffered because of it. Many toxic chemicals are used in paper making, especially toxic solvents and chlorine compounds used to bleach pulp. Additional toxins are used as biocides to prevent bacterial growth in the pulp and finished paper products. Pulp and paper mills are large sources of standard air pollutants, such as carbon dioxide, nitrous oxides, sulfur dioxides, carbon monoxides and particulates. These contribute to ozone warming, acid rain, global warming and respiratory problems. Many of the mills are large enough to have their own coal-fired power plants, raising additional concerns about mercury, arsenic and radioactive emissions.

Paper-making generally produces a large amount of solid waste. Paper fibers can be recycled only a limited number of times before they become too short or weak to make high quality paper. This means the broken, low-quality fibers are separated out to become waste sludge. All the inks, dyes, coatings, pigments, staples and "stickies" (tape, plastic films, etc.) are also washed off the recycled fibers to join the waste solids. These paper mill sludge consume a large percentage of our local landfill space each year. Worse yet, some of the wastes are land spread on cropland as a disposal technique, raising concerns about trace contaminants building up in soil or running off into area lakes and streams. Some companies burn their sludge in incinerators, contributing to serious air pollution problems, including the release of dioxin.

Fig. 9.3: **Waste from Paper Industry**

(iv) Plastic Industry

Plastic waste also imposes negative environmental externalities. It is usually non-biodegradable and therefore can remain as waste in the environment for a very long time; it may pose risks to human health as well as the environment; and it can be difficult to reuse and or recycle in practice. Substantial quantities of plastic have accumulated in the natural environment and in landfills. Around 10 per cent by weight of the municipal waste stream is plastic.

The manufacturing of plastics involve various chemical processes and utilizes variety of chemical compounds and additives including phenols, amines and esters, antioxidants, UV and light stability improvers, antistatic agents and heat stabilizers that impart the finished product specific characteristics for its intended use.

The finished product that is the plastic itself is environmentally quite stable. However, the additives, their chemical reaction and degradation products incorporated into the polymeric material have the potential to be released into the environment and cause significant health and environmental concerns.

The byproducts of plastic combustion are airborne particulate emission (soot) and solid residue ash (black carbonaceous colour). Several studies have demonstrated that soot and solid residue ash possess a high potential of causing significant health and environmental concerns. The soot when generated is accompanied with volatile organic compounds (VOCs), semi-VOCs, smoke (particulate matter), particulate bound heavy metals, polycyclic aromatic hydrocarbons (PAHs), polychlorinated dibenzofurans (PCDFs) and dioxins and has the ability to travel thousands of kilometers, depending on prevailing atmospheric conditions, before it can drop back on earth and enter into the food chain.

Fig. 9.4: **Industrial Plastic Waste**

(v) Glass Industry

Waste generated in the glass industry can be categorized into the following three groups:

- materials handling waste;

- pollution control equipment waste;
- plant maintenance waste.

Materials handling waste includes the waste generated during the receiving and transfer of raw materials at the facility for storage or processing, including raw materials that are rendered unusable when spilled during receiving and transfer. Emissions control equipment at glass manufacturing plants generates waste residues from pollutants produced or captured during the melting, forming, and finishing steps. These may be hazardous or non-hazardous, depending on the process and type of glass.

Glass plant maintenance wastes include waste oil and solvents generated in the forming process, furnace slag, and refractory wastes. Furnace dust, grinding and polishing sludge, and refractory rubble from the demolition of glass furnaces may contain metals and other unsafe materials [Geiger 1993]. During the forming process, oil is used in the forming machines and often contaminates the water that keeps the machines cool. Water-based glue for packaging is another example.

Table 9.3: Summary of Inputs and Waste Products from Glass Manufacture

Area of Manufacturing	Material Inputs	Potential Waste/Emissions
Materials Handling	Silica sand; soda ash; limestone; cullet; oxides	Unusable raw materials; particulates
Processing and Plant Maintenance	Silica sand; soda ash; limestone; cullet; oxides; arsenic; stannic acid; oil; 1,1,1-trichloroethane (TCA); water-based glue; hydrofluoric acid (HF)	Particulates; nitrogen oxides; sulfur oxides; TCA; furnaceslag (magnesium oxide, sodium sulfate); waste oil; water-based glue (solid andliquid form); cullet; refractorywastes; HF; lime
Processing and Plant Maintenance	Water; sodium carbonate; aqueousmedia; ammonia; furnace gas	Particulates; nitrogen oxides; sulfur oxides; a arsenic; stannicacid; hydrochloric acid; ammonia; ammonium chloride; sulfates (selenium, chromium, cadmium, cobalt, lead,sodium)

(vi) Textile Industry

Textile processing industry is characterized not only by the large volume of water required for various unit operations but also by the variety of chemicals used for various processes. There is a long sequence of wet processing stages requiring inputs of water, chemical and energy and generating wastes at each stage. The other feature of this industry, which is a backbone of fashion garment, is large variation in demand of type, pattern and color combination of fabric resulting into significant fluctuation in waste generation volume and load. Textile processing generates many waste streams, including liquid, gaseous and solid wastes, some of which may be hazardous. The nature of the waste generated depends on the type of textile facility, the processes and technologies being operated, and the types of fibers and chemicals used. The overview on the amounts of waste generated within the textile processes are summarized in Table.

The main environmental problems associated with textile industry are typically those associated with water body pollution caused by the discharge of untreated effluents. Other environmental issues of equal importance are air emission, notably Volatile Organic Compounds (VOC)'s and excessive noise or odor as well as workspace safety. The aquatic toxicity of textile industry wastewater varies considerably among production facilities. The sources of aquatic toxicity can include salt, surfactants, ionic metals and their metal complexes, toxic organic chemicals, biocides and toxic anions. Most textile dyes have low aquatic toxicity. On the other hand, surfactants and related compounds, such as detergents, emulsifiers and dispersants are used in almost each textile process and can be an important contributor to effluent aquatic toxicity, BOD and foaming.

The primary residual wastes generated from the textile industry are non-hazardous. These include scraps of fabric and yarn, off-specification yarn and fabric and packaging waste. There are also wastes associated with the storage and production of yarns and textiles, such as chemical storage drums, cardboard reels for storing fabric and cones used to hold yarns for dyeing and knitting. Cutting room waste generates a high volume of fabric scraps, which can often be reduced by increasing fabric utilization efficiency in cutting and sewing.

***Fig. 9.5*: Solid Waste from Textile Processing and Tannery Units dumped on the Roadside**

Table 9.4: Summary of the Waste Generated during Textiles Manu-facturing

Process	Emission	Wastewater	Solid Wastes
Fiber preparation	Little or none	Little or none	Fiber waste and packaging waste.
Yarn spinning	Little or none	Little or none	Packaging wastes; sized yarn; fiber waste; cleaning and processing waste.
Slashing/sizing	VOCs	BOD; COD; metals	Fiber lint; yarn waste; packaging waste; cleaning waste, size unused starch-based sizes
Weaving	Little or none	Little or none	Packaging waste; yarn and fabric scraps; off-spec fabric; used oil.
Knitting	Little or none	Little or none	Packaging waste yarn and fabric scraps; off-spec fabric
Tufting	Little or none	Little of none	Packaging waste; yarn, fabric scraps; off-spec fabric
Desizing	VOCs from glycol ethers	BOD from sizes lubricants; biocides; anti-static compounds	Packaging waste; fiber lint; yarn waste; cleaning and maintenance materials
Scouring	VOCs from glycol ethers and scouring solvents	Disinfectants, insecticide residues; NaOH; detergents, oils; knitting lubricants; spin finishes; spent solvents	Little or none
Bleaching	Little or none	H_2O_2, stabilisers; high pH	Little or none, even if little, the impact could be considerable
Singeing	Small amounts of exhaust gases from the burners exhaustic which components.	Little or none	Little or none
Mercerising	Little or none	High pH; NaOH	Little or none
Heat setting	Volatilisation of spin finish agents synthetic fiber manufacture	Little or none	Little or none

(Contd…)

Process	Emission	Wastewater	Solid Wastes
Dyeing	VOCs	Metals; salt; surfactants; organic processing assistants; cationic materials; colour; BOD; COD; sulphide; acidity/ alkalinity; spent solvents	Little or none
Printing	Solvents, acetic acid -drying and curing oven emissions combustion; gases	Suspended solids; urea; solvents; colour; metals; heat; BOD; foam	Little or none
Finishing	VOCs; contaminants in purchased chemicals; formaldehyde vapors; combustion gases	COD; suspended solids; toxic materials; spent solvents	Fabric scraps and trimmings; packaging waste

(vii) Rubber Industry

Despite the numerous benefits that are rendered to the modernization of this world by natural rubber, the consequence of natural rubber processing has yet provide a serious problem due to its highly polluted effluents. The rapid growth of this industry generates large quantities of effluents coming from its processing operations which is really a big problem because of its wastewater contains high biological oxygen demand and ammonia. Without proper treatment, discharge of wastewater from rubber processing industry to the environment may cause serious and long lasting consequences.

3. MANUFACTURING INDUSTRIES (TERTIARY INDUSTRIES)

Manufacturing industries are those industries that take raw material from basic industries and convert it to consumer goods. Examples are hardware, packaging, soft goods, construction industry etc. Some examples are as below:

(i) Packaging Industry

Packaging is the largest and most rapidly growing category of solid waste. 3.2m tones of the 26m tones of the household waste produced annually is packaging. 150m tones of packaging waste come from industry and commerce each year. More than 30% of municipal solid waste is from packaging.

Although packaging is important to protect products against being damaged and consequently wasted, it constitutes a significant percentage of the waste stream, especially because most of it is used only once and then disposed of. Because of its large volume, packaging waste tends to be very visible. Approximately 70% of primary packaging is used for food and drink which is often contaminated by residues of the original contents when discarded. Up to 38% of the packaging found in a regular shopping basket cannot be recycled and is either incinerated for the recovery of its energy content or sent to landfill. In 2006, the EU produced 65 million tones of packaging waste and it Increased to 77 million tones by 2008. The UK produced an estimated 10.5 million tones of waste packaging in 2007, of which 6.3 million tones originated from households and the remaining 4.2 million tones from commercial and industrial sources.

The overall environmental impacts of packaging are estimated to make up one to a few percent of the total environmental impacts of the economy. For example, the greenhouse gas emissions related to packaging consumption of the original 15 European Union member states are estimated at around 80 million tones of CO_2 equivalent per year. This is around 2% of total greenhouse gas emissions of the EU15. The share of packaging for other environmental impacts, such as air acidification, fine particles and eutrophication is of a comparable magnitude.

(ii) Paper Products Industry

Paper product industry is involved in production of paper products like tissues, napkins, boxes, books magazines and other items using paper. These industry generate large amount of waste which is generally dumped in landfills. Most of the paper products contain hazardous constituents. For example most product have harmful ink. The composition of inks varies widely. Some inks contain chemicals that would be classified as hazardous; Inks frequently get their color from the metals or hazardous pigments they contain. Inks containing metals and/or those using a solvent carrier are often classified as hazardous.

Dimethyl sulphide is a waste product of the pulp and paper industry along with numerous hazardous chemicals including highly toxic sulfur compounds, called total reduced sulfur compounds (TRS), and volatile organic compounds (VOCs) like methanol gas. Also these industries often uses chlorine bleaching, which produces dioxins, a family of chemicals considered environmental hazards, as a byproduct.

(iii) Hardware Industry

The hardware manufacturing process makes use of hazardous chemicals like lead, mercury etc which if not used and disposed in an environmentally safe manner can lead to contamination of natural resources. Water is an integral part of the manufacturing process and needs to be used in a sustainable manner. The possibility of use of CFCs and other ozone depleters in refrigerants and aerosols used in the manufacturing process. High demands, has led to manufacturing these on a large. The usage of energy in manufacturing and transporting such huge volumes and its indirect impact in terms of release of greenhouse gases must be considered.

(iv) Food Processing Industry

Food processing wastes are those end products of various food processing industries that have not been recycled or used for other purposes. Food industry produces large volumes of wastes, both solids and liquid, resulting from the production, preparation and consumption of food. These wastes pose increasing disposal and potential severe pollution problems and represent a loss of valuable biomass and nutrients. Beside their pollution and hazard aspects, in many cases, food processing wastes might have a potential for conversion into useful products of higher value as by-product, or even as raw material for other industries, or for use as food or feed after biological treatment.

The composition of wastes emerging from food processing factories is extremely varied and depends on both the nature of the product and the production technique employed. For example, wastes from meat processing plants will contain a high fat and protein content, whilst waste from the canning industry will contain high concentrations of sugar and starches. Also, the waste may not only differ from site to site but also vary from one time of the year to another. Furthermore, the volume and concentration of the waste material will not be constant. This may cause some problems in managing a consistent working process due to fluctuations in the nature, composition and quantity of raw materials.

Fig. 9.6: **Waste from Food Processing Industries**

(v) Construction Industry

The construction, demolition and renovation of buildings makes up a third of our region's waste. This is 1.6 million tones each year! In some areas all or part of construction and demolition waste stream is unlawfully deposited on land, or in natural drainages including water, contrary to regulations to protect human health, commerce and the environment. The construction industry is a conspicuous user of resources. Materials are derived from numerous sources and suppliers, and minimization of waste presents particular problem. Although many of the materials in use are common to most sites, the fragmented nature of development constrains the practical extent of recycling. Furthermore, despite the long life of its products, their eventual demolition or redevelopment can produce significant waste for land disposal unless re-used. The mass of resources used in the UK construction industry is dominated by stone and primary aggregates: sand and gravel extraction of these primary resources implies major environmental impact from loss of habitat and ecosystem, damage to the landscape, potential subsidence problems and release of methane. Noise and dust and heavy transport through populated areas confer local nuisance and contribute to restricted award of extraction licenses by local authorities. The same issues arise in the disposal or processing/recycling of waste. Construction also has a major impact on the environment in its consumption of energy, both directly and embodied in the materials that it uses. The large bulk of materials used consumes a great deal of energy for transport. Taking into account both direct use and embodied energy, the construction industry consumes about 4.5% of the national total as a consequence of this energy consumption, construction generates over 40 million tones of carbon dioxide. which contributes to global warming from the greenhouse effect. Acid gases and oxides of nitrogen (NO2) are also produced, contributing to acid rain and photochemical smog production. Throughout the construction cycle, and especially at the end of a structure's life, large quantities of waste are produced. Significant quantities of waste are also generated by the construction process itself. Much of this wastage is avoidable on site, but in attention to design detailing, inappropriate material, dimensions, late variations, over-ordering, etc. also contribute to waste.

INDUSTRIAL WASTE MANAGEMENT

The bloom of modern industries and world population bring out a huge amount of waste to our society. Never before has the question of pollution caused worry in public concern as nowadays. In order to survive in the near future, people have to control the industrial waste at any cost. Waste management is concerned with collecting, transporting, recycling and disposing waste material. It is rather effective in reducing pollution, conserving energy and natural resources and offering more jobs for people. In fact, there are 4 major methods of waste management.

(i) Landfills

The first *method of waste management* is land filling. It is considered the most traditional method which still remains a common practice in almost nations. Land filling is an economical way to bring waste under the dirt and the let them decompose. Nevertheless, as a piece of fact, land filling causes some environment problems, namely groundwater pollution, bad odor and methane. Now, a new kind of landfill is designed to minimize these consequences. Modern landfills often contain a gas extraction system to take out the gas generated during waste decomposing process. Next, this amount of gas will be used to produce electricity. However, fewer and fewer landfills are established each because of their bad odor and consuming many spaces. In fact, no one likes living in the areas of landfills.

(ii) Inceneration

The second *method of waste management* is incineration. It is a disposal technique in which waste is converted into heat, gas, steam and ash. Individuals and organizations can all use this method. Statistics show that incineration can reduce the amount of solid waste to 20-30% of the original volume. That method minimizes the weak points of landfills. It requires fewer spaces than land filling and can be operated in any weather. Unlike landfills, it produces stable odor that is better than the previous methods. However, incineration still has some short comings. It is expensive to build and operate incinerators and in need of skilled personnel and continuous maintenance. And it costs much money to treat the ash generated during incineration.

Fig. 9.7: **Waste Landfill**

(iii) Recycling

The third method of *waste management is recycling*. People consider recycling to be the most effective way to manage waste. It refers to the collection and reuse of waste materials. The materials recycled will be reprocessed into a new product that is available for consumption. The most common recyclable materials are aluminum cans, steel, bottles and papers. PVC and PP are also recyclable. This method contributes to energy conservation and water savings but not all kinds of waste materials are recycled such as medical waste and agricultural waste. Hence, people must find out another method to make good its shortcomings.

One of the major benefit of recycling is to reduce the amount of rubbish, toxic chemicals that are hazardous and harmful to people's health and environment. Each year, people dump more than 100 million tons trash into the landfills. With such a big amount of garbage generated each year, there will no more spaces to dump them in the near future, not to mention the present shortage of spaces for landfills if we don't take part in recycling process. Otherwise, recycling also minimizes toxic trash from industrial and manufacturing operations, soil erosion and water savings when raw materials are processed. Fewer amounts of CO2, SO2 and NO are released each day which leads to the reduction of bad effects on people's health, environmental population and global warning. A nation with the recycling rate of 30% can reduce green house gas emissions as much as taking away 25 million cars from the road.

Next, recycling is very economical. Instead of throwing old things out on the streets or putting them in the reposition, we can recycle them and save money. The money we pay recycled items is twice less than the one we spend on new things. As for the whole society, well – run recycling programmes cost less than any other kinds of industrial waste management such as transferring, collection and land filling.

The other benefits of recycling are conserving energy and water. Manufacturing with recycled materials is more beneficial than producing with raw materials. In fact, recycling aluminum can save 95% less energy than using raw materials. Recycling steel, newspaper, plastics and gas sequent save 60%, 40%, 70% and 40%. It is projected to save the usage of energy of 9 million households annually. By recycling 1 million tons of steel, we can save 1.3 million tons of iron ore, 700.000 tons of coal, etc. We can use the same energy to make a new aluminum can to recycle 20 new cans.

Next, recycling industries offer people many jobs. It is estimated that one job is created by incinerating 10.000 tons of waste, 6 jobs are created by land filling 10.000 tons of waste but 36 jobs are created by recycling the same amount of waste. Annually, the US recycling industries offer 1.1 million jobs, which is certainly helpful to the unemployment and raising people's living standard.

Finally, the extra benefit of recycling is to build a strong economy and community. As we know that the country with large amount of natural resources will have more power in the world than the ones which are dependent on others' nation supply. Recycling saves the energy and creates jobs for people that make the country wealthier. Besides, pursuing recycling programmes, people join hands together, promote the same target. Certainly, their relationship will be improved later.

General speaking, we can't deny the *benefits of recycling* to our society. Better late than never; we should do more to protect our own lives as recycling works best if everyone contributes the shares in the recycling process.

(iv) Reducing Waste Generation

The last important method of waste management is to prevent waste materials being generated which means waste reduction. To activate this method, people are recommended to reuse second hand products, repair broken items and design products using less material. It depends on people's awareness and conscience to make this method effective. People are using these methods coordinately to reduce waste and pollution as much as possible.

RESPONSIBILITY OF THE GOVERNMENT

On E-Waste management is quiet crucial in the industrial waste management and some of the tips that can be suggested on the part of government include:

1. Setting up regulatory agencies in each state or county that are capable of consolidating and coordinating with the regulatory functions of the various government and federal authorities pertaining to electronic waste.
2. If necessary, the government should make stringent laws on the proper disposal and management of industrial waste by both private and public institutions. The existing laws if any on industrial waste must be revamped and revised periodically
3. Public awareness programmes should be conducted at regular intervals in order create a positive attitude among the public on industrial waste management.
4. The governments have also responsibility to encourage Research and Development activities related with industrial Waste Management.
5. Heavy fines should be imposed on those industries or individuals who does not follow the Waste management principles or dump the industrial-waste causing environmental hazards.
6. Governments must in the forefront to have a tie up with manufacturers, retailers, industries in exploring the opportunities in providing recycling services.

RESPONSIBILITY OF THE INDUSTRIES

Industries need to be more responsible for the waste generated by them. Proper management practices should be undertaken by industries. Waste minimizing techniques should be adopted. The waste should be properly handled and disposed off. The employees involved in handling waste should be trained regarding correct handling and disposal of industrial waste. Environmental friendly methods that generate less waste should be used. Companies should consult clients regarding onsite waste management responsibilities.

RESPOSIBILITY OF THE CITIZENS

Citizens are the end users of any product or service manufactured by industries and therefore some of the tips that a citizen must follow for safe and proper disposal of industrial waste include:

1. When buying any product opt for those products that have fewer toxic parts in them.
2. The products after their life cycle must be disposed of properly and comes under the preview of proper disposal of industrial waste.
3. They must buy only those products that are energy efficient.

4. Attending awareness programmes on industrial Waste management being conducted by any institutions either government or private

CONCLUSION

Beginning of the industrial revolution lead to the advancement of human society. With the rapidly developing technology more and more products could be manufactured in much less time and much more efficiently. But along with the increase in production of valuable goods, it also increased the generation of waste and consumption of more resources. Impact of Increased industrialization on environment lead to the air water and soil pollution. With the advancement of industries these problems became more pronounced.

Now most of the pollution on the planet can be traced back to industries. In fact, the issue of industrial pollution has taken on grave importance for agencies trying to fight against environmental degradation. Nations facing sudden and rapid growth of such industries are finding it to be a serious problem which has to be brought under control immediately.

Industrial waste contaminates many sources of drinking water, release unwanted toxins into the air and reduces the quality of soil all over the world. Major environmental disasters have been caused due to industrial mishaps, which have yet to be brought under control. Industrial waste is damaging our lives and planet. Hence there is an urgent need to curb the problem.

Waste management have various advantages. Firstly, waste management ensures the environment protection and human health. Without it, more and more amount of waste will be generated each day. People will live in and around dump of landfills surrounded by rubbish and always in danger of suffering from diseases. Secondly, waste management can improve the shortage of raw materials by recycling, reuse old items and waste. Instead of ending up them in the landfills, we can make use of them to create a new product that is very economical and friendly to our environment. The most popular kinds of waste to recycled are steel, glass, PVP, etc. This is one of the best ways to reduce waste and adverse effects of waste in environments. Last but not least, waste management can lead to the creation of a large number of job of various nature. To some extent, it will deal with the unemployment and improve people's living standard. In brief, industrial waste management is very important and beneficial. People should pay much attention to this issue. Industrial waste management can only be successful if industry, the government and the common people take serious note of the problem and work hand in hand. Existing laws should revised and revamp from time to time. The law enforcement agencies also be strengthened and reoriented to ensure strict enforcement of laws.

REFERENCES

1. Sharma P.D., 2013 Ecology Microbiology Animal Behaviour Pollution and Toxicology.
2. Sharma P.D., 2013 Environmental Botany and Plant Pathology.
3. Weeks, J L. 2011 In *74. Mining and Quarrying*, Armstrong, James R.,Menon, Raji.
4. http://www.ilo.org/oshenc/part-xi/mining-and-quarrying/item/610-health-hazards-of-mining-and-quarrying
5. http://businessimpactenvironment.wordpress.com/2011/10/03/environmental-issues-caused-by-rubber-industry/
6. Chandrappa R and D. Bhushan 2012 Solid Waste Management Principles and Practice.
7. http://www.sustainableaggregates.com/sourcesofaggregates/landbased/waste/waste_introduction.htm
8. http://ec.europa.eu/environment/waste/studies/mining/0204finalreportbrgm.pdf
9. http://wasteindustries.org/benefits-of-recycling/
10. http://wasteindustries.org/the-importance-of-industrial-waste-management/
11. http://www.calrecycle.ca.gov/organics/conversion/agforestrpt/Forest/
12. http://www.ukessays.com/essays/information-technology/environmental-impact-hardware-industry-information-technology-essay.php
13. http://www.brownfieldsnet.org/industrial_waste.html
14. http://www.aquatechnology.net/agriculturalwaste.html
15. http://science.howstuffworks.com/environmental/conservation/issues/waste-industrial-info.htm
16. http://www.indiantextilejournal.com/articles/fadetails.asp?id=2420
17. http://garbagepollution.weebly.com/industrial-revolution.html
18. http://www.toxicsaction.org/problems-and-solutions/waste
19. http://dste.puducherry.gov.in/envisnew/INDUSTRIAL%20SOLID%20WASTE.htm
20. http://www.sopac.org/dsm/public/files/resources/Deep% 20Sea% 20Minerals% 20in%20the%20Pacific%20Islands%20Region%20Brochure%205.pdf
21. http://archive.defra.gov.uk/foodfarm/landmanage/waste/minimising/
22. http://www.learner.org/interactives/garbage/solidsolut.html
23. http://wasteindustries.org/tag/recycling-industries/
24. http://www.cleanwateractioncouncil.org/issues/resource-issues/paper-industry/
25. https://www.gov.uk/hazardous-waste-treatment-and-disposal
26. http://rstb.royalsocietypublishing.org/content/364/1526/2153.full
27. http://www.nibusinessinfo.co.uk/content/waste-responsibilities-chemical-manufacturers
28. http://nora.nerc.ac.uk/15901/1/GoodQuarry_Quarry_Fines_%26_Waste.pdf
29. http://www.hrwc.net/wastemanagement.htm
30. http://www.epa.gov/radiation/tenorm/copper.html
31. http://www.fao.org/docrep/t0269e/t0269e08.htm

WASTE DISPOSAL AND MANAGEMENT *Pages:* 138-151
Edited by: Dr. Pawan Kumar 'Bharti'; Dr. B. Tabassum; and Dr. Priya Bajaj
ISBN: 978-93-5056-729-6
Edition: 2015
Published by: Discovery Publishing House Pvt. Ltd., New Delhi (India)

10

Anaerobic Digestion of Tannery Solid Waste for Biogas Production *A Viable Method for Waste Management*

Dejene Tsegaye; Mekibib Dawit and **Khwairakpam Gajananda**

ABSTRACT

The present study characterized the physical properties, total solids (TS), volatile solids (VS) and Carbon to Nitrogen ratio (C/N ratio) of tannery solid waste (TSW). Five different combinations with or without cow dung (CD) were assessed for their biogas production suitability in triplicate batch digesters (D-1, D-2, D-3, D-4, and D-5) with a total volume of 2.8L. The results showed that TS, VS and C/N ratio of wastes were 56.37%, 76.34% and 29.05%, respectively. The results also suggested that the highest volume of biogas (4,756 mL) with a methane content of 60.37% was produced by the digester containing 75% TSW and 25% CD and the lowest biogas (2,539 mL) with quality of 68.06% was produced by the digester containing 100% CD. The average methane contents of the different digesters were D-1 (100% TSW) 53.23%, D-2 (75% TSW: 25% CD) 60.37%, D-3 (50% TSW: 50% CD) 58.78%, D-4 (25% TSW: 75% CD) 57.66% and D-5 (100% CD) 67.31%. Total and volatile solid removal efficiency of all digesters was in the range of 42.27-76.34% and 47.16-79.23%. The study concluded that TSW is a good feedstock for biogas production by utilizing agro-industrial based organic solid waste for bio-energy production.

Key words: Tannery solid waste, anaerobic digestion, waste-to-energy, tannery waste management, solid waste reduction.

Center for Environmental Science, College of Natural Science, Addis Ababa University, P.O. Box 1176, Addis Ababa, Ethiopia.

INTRODUCTION

Industrialization, urbanization and modernization of agricultural activities have increased solid waste generation, thereby, causing detrimental environmental pollutions and problems. Tanning of leathers is among the oldest industries in the world (Kanagaraj *et al.*, 2006). During prehistoric times, tanning activities were structured to meet the resident needs of leather drums, footwear and musical instruments (Durai and Rajasimman, 2011). With the growth of population, the increasing requirement of leathers and its products led to the establishment of large commercial tanneries (FAO, 2010).

Even though, tanning industries play an environmentally important role by giving an innovative use to the leftovers of the slaughterhouse, the conversion of this by-product is potentially pollution-intensive and it is broadly perceived as a natural resource consumer (Cotance, 2002; Kanagaraj *et al.*, 2006). Moreover, leather industries all over the world have been recognized closely for their negative public image because of the generation of air, liquid and solid pollutions to the environment. Tanning industry is not exception to this, producing considerable amount of solid wastes including hazardous wastes containing chromium and is known for its highest pollution load (Thorstensen, 1993; Anita Singh *et al.*, 2010; Durai and Rajasimman, 2011).

The main sources of Tannery Solid Wastes (TSW) are skin trimming, fleshing, keratin, buffing and chrome shaving wastes, which have high protein content. From 1000 kg of raw hide only 200 kg is converted to leather, whereas a large amount of solid waste (800 kg) is disposed off in the surrounding environment (Buljan *et al.*, 2000; Kanagaraj *et al.*, 2006; UNIDO, 2009). If the solid wastes generated during various tanning operations are not properly utilized or managed, they are likely to cause numerous problems to the environment. Tannery industries are likely to invest massively on solid waste safe disposal mechanisms and management in future (Anita Singh et *al.*, 2010).

Burning and disposing of solid wastes on open landfill, releases greenhouse gases from the decomposition of organic matter, it also produces undesirable odors posing health hazards to the community (Divakaran, 1984). The organic wastes generated by the leather industries undergo biodegradation and emit greenhouse gases, primarily methane, which is 25 times more potent than carbon dioxide and to a lesser degree of Nitrous oxide.

The problem can be managed through adoption of eco-friendly waste-to-energy recycling technologies such as anaerobic digestion (AD), which process solid wastes before their disposal (Vasudevan and Ravindran, 2007).

The AD process also referred to as bio-methanation is a multifaceted process, which involves many different microorganisms (conglomerates). Degradation of biodegradable substrate (feedstock) in an oxygen free environment results in the production of biogas, which is rich in methane (CH_4) (Ciborowski, 2004; Pena-Varo, 2002; Mata-Alvarez, 2003). AD is a promising, mature and recognized technologic solution that has the potential to convert TSW into energy efficiently (biogas), elimination of uncontrolled methane emissions and odor, contributing to lessen environmental problems, safe waste management, giving time to set-up more sustainable treatment and disposal routes (Buren, 1979; Vasudevan and Ravindran, 2007). According to Reijnders and Huijbregts (2007), the potential for waste-derived bio-energy to contribute to the bargain of global warming is substantial. Moreover, AD technology can play a key role in realizing three major international environmental policy objectives: (a) Renewable Energy (b) Water Pollution Control (c) Kyoto Protocol/Global Warming mitigation.

In developing countries, tanning industry contributes significantly towards exports, employment opportunity and plays an important role on the economy. In view of this, the present research is aimed to study the efficiency of AD of TSW for biogas production and waste management.

MATERIALS AND METHODS

Feedstock (Substrates) and its Composition

The feedstock (substrates) used for the biogas production at bench scale were TSW and cow-dung (CD) mixed at different ratios. TSW (skin and trimming) samples were collected from Modjo Tannery Share Company, Modjo Town, which is 70 km from the capital city Addis Ababa. About 10 kg of CD was obtained from a private dairy farm at the vicinity of Sululta town: North Shewa, Oromia, Ethiopia, which is 25 km from Addis Ababa. Approximately, 5000 ml of inoculums was taken from an operating biogas plant at the College of Natural Sciences, Addis Ababa University. All the feedstocks were kept at 4^0C in a refrigerator at the Laboratory of the Center for Environmental Science, until sealed in the digester. To increase the surface area of the substrate (TSW) it was pre-treated (cut into pieces) according to Badger *et al.* (1979).

Biogas production potential and quality of the gas produced were evaluated at five different treatments combinations of TSW and CD using a bench scale digester. The following ratios were the five treatments used in the study; D-1 (100% TSW), D-2 (75% TSW: 25% CD), D-3 (50% TSW: 50% CD), D-4 (25% TSW: 75% CD) and D-5 (100% CD) on the basis of (w/w) %. The amount of total solid (TS) of each treatment was kept constant at 100 g and the amount of water added as recommended by Ituen *et al.* (2007), so that the TS in the digester is 8%. Each treatment was run in triplicate and 100 ml of inoculums were added to kick-start the reaction.

Methods for Determination of Feedstock Physico-chemical Property

Total solids (TS), volatile solid (VS) were estimated using APHA, 1998 and Carbon to Nitrogen ratio (C/N) was determined by Adams *et al.*, 1951.

Bench Scale Anaerobic Digester

Bench-scale anaerobic digesters were prepared in the Research Laboratory of the Center for Environmental Science, Addis Ababa University.

Amber bottles of 2.8 L holding capacity was used as bench scale digesters. To create the anaerobic condition, the bottles were covered with a rubber stopper having two outlets and sealed with a gas kit, so that it is confidently air tight. Two gas pipes of 8 mm internal diameter, with the lengths of 0.5 m and 1 m were immersed in the digesters. The 0.5 m long hose was stretched up to the bottom of solution to measure the pH of the slurry, while the second one above the slurry was used to off-take the gas from the digesters for biogas measurement during the AD processes. The 0.5 m hose was sealed by pipette tip while the 1 m long hose was controlled by a valve. The room temperature fluctuation was regulated by sand-jacketing the digesters, which were placed in the partitioned boxes (Figure 10.1).

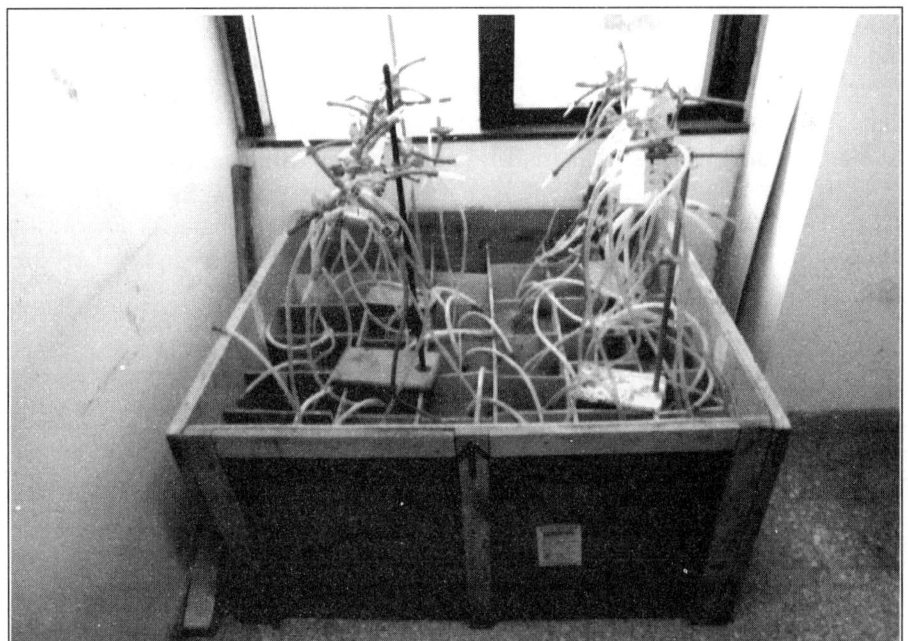

Fig. 10.1: **Bench-Scale Sand-Jacketed Anaerobic Digester Setup Placed in the Partitioned Box**

Biogas and its Quality Determination

The biogas produced was determined by water displacement method, while the quality of the biogas was done by biogas analyzer (Geotechnical instruments (UK) Ltd, S/R: BM 14068). The amount (quantity) of biogas from the digesters was taken to a volumetrically calibrated collector vessel (measuring cylinder) filled with water, which was kept under pressure. When the biogas entered the cylinder filled with water from the top, the pressure of the biogas forced the water into the empty beaker. The volume of the water displaced indicated the total biogas produced. The total biogas produced for each treatment was calculated by deducting the share of inoculums to know the contribution of each digester. The total amount of biogas produced from each digester presented in this paper is the net biogas produced throughout the digestion periods.

The quality of biogas (percentage of methane) was measured weekly using the biogas analyzer, until the gas production ceased. The hose that channeled the gas was directly connected to the calibrated biogas analyzer and the percentage of methane was displayed on the analyzer. Combustibility of the biogas was also seen by connecting the gas line to a Bunsen-burner.

RESULTS AND DISCUSSION

Characterization of Feedstocks for Biogas Production Parameters

The averaged values of TS, VS and C/N ratio of the feedstock are presented in Table 10.1. For CD, the TS obtained in this study are in the range of (15-20%), which is similar with the results of Fulford (1988). The VS as percent of TS for CD is 87.67%, the result come close to the earlier findings of 86.77% reported by Ali *et al.*, (2010) and 86.73% by Li *et al*. (2011). However, the result found in this study is higher than the value reported by Fulford (1998), which was 77%. The VS values for each feedstock in the present study varies from 76.34% - 87.67%, which is within the range of 60% - 87% as reported by Zolar *et al.*, (1998) (Table 10.1).

Table 10.1: Characteristics of the Averaged Feedstock in Terms of Biogas Production Parameters

Parameters / Feedstock	Moisture Content (%)	TS (%)	VS % on basis of TS	Ash % on basis of TS	OC (%)	TN (%)	C/N ratio
TSW	43.63	56.37	76.34	23.66	42.41	1.46	29.05
CD	84.22	15.78	87.67	12.33	49.53	2.74	18.08

The variables given in Table 10.1 are among the main factors that affected the AD processes, the amount and quality of biogas produced. Therefore, these parameters are also an indication of the suitability of the feedstock for biogas production (Ali *et al.*, 2010, Fulford 1988; Li *et al.*, 2011; Pyle, 1978; Zolar *et al.*, 1998).

The C/N ratios of different digesters were 29.05, 21.48, 19.49, 18.6 and 18.14 for digesters D-1, D2, D3, D4 and D-5. The C/N ratio of the digesters decreases as the ratio of TSW decreases from 100% to zero. The C/N ratio of digesters D-1 (29.05) and D-2 (21.48) are in the range of C/N ratio of 20 to 30 as stated by Braun (1982) and Dahlman and Frost (2001), for the digesters to yield optimum biogas. However, the C/N ratio of D-3 (19.49), D-4 (18.6) and D-5 (18.14) are less than the previous study. In another study, Pyle (1978) mentioned that C/N ratio of the feedstock is in the range of 10–30, which complies with the present results (Table 10.1).

The Working Conditions of AD Process

Temperature and pH largely affect biogas production and its quality. These two parameters (Temperature and pH) were given due considerations for better biogas production in this study. The outcomes of these two parameters are given below.

Temperature

The average daily room temperatures during the course of the digestion period was low and it was in the range of 14.5-23.2°C (Figure 10.2). The ambient temperature range during this study was 15-25°C, which can be regarded as temperate climate. The average room temperature was fluctuating initially for about two weeks; afterward it became more or less constant for two months and then it started to increase up to the end of the experiment (Figure 10.2). It is pertinent to note here that the experiment was started at the end of the winter season, where colder temperatures were experienced before noon. Therefore, the temperature trend showed low average room temperatures during the first two weeks of the study.

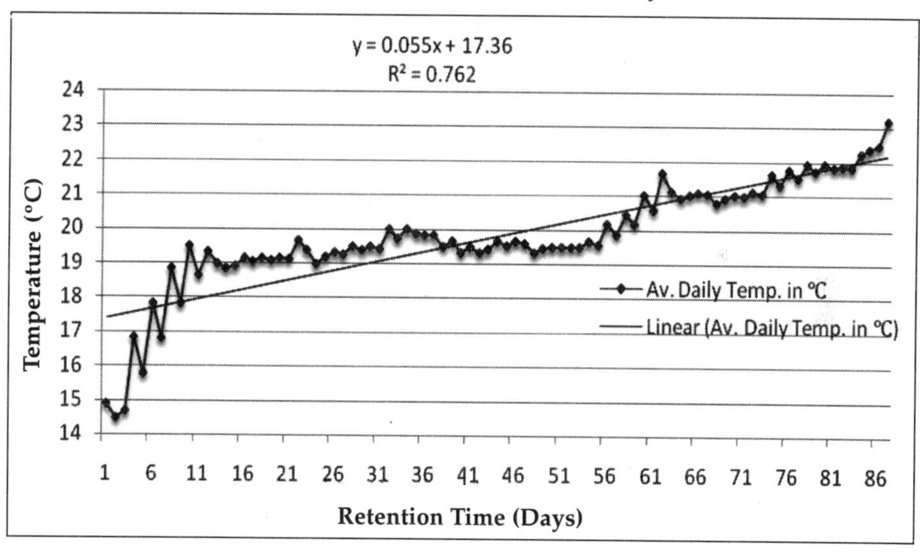

Fig. 10.2: **Average Daily Room Temperature of the Laboratory**

Also from Figure 10.2, it can be seen that the room temperature fluctuation was about 8.7°C, which can be regarded as an extreme fluctuation that may have affected the metabolic activities of microorganisms. According to Ozmen and Aslanzadeh (2009) the specified limits for fluctuation should not exceed ±2°C for the psychrophiles (below 20°C). However, NRCS (2005) recommended that the fluctuation of ambient temperature can be minimized by thick covering/jacketing of the digester by sand of about 10cm radius, which will bring the digester temperature fluctuation to less than 1°C.

Subsequently, in the present study, to minimize the temperature fluctuations, the digesters were sand-jacketed in a wooden box prepared by partitioning the chambers with a radius of about 20 cm.

The trend analysis for the temperatures indicated a significant increase from the 1st day to the 87th day of the retention time (Figure 10.2). The regression coefficient of determination (R^2) showed a significant value of 0.76, indicating the reliability of the data. Thus, the study suggested that even at low temperature (14.5 - 23.2°C), there is possibility of producing biogas by sand-jacketing the digesters to control temperature fluctuation; however, the retention time period was extended to 87 days. Earlier studies by Jigar *et al.* (2011) mentioned that the lower the temperature, the longer the retention time (62 days).

pH

The average pH variations of each digester during the reaction period (retention time), which were taken at two days time interval is given in Figure 10.3. The figure indicates that the pH value of each digester dropped in a few days of the reaction time. The drops in the pH is due to organic acid formation which is an indication for the system start up and increases as the methanogenic bacteria consumes the acids produced in the acidogenesis and acetogenesis steps for the production of biogas (Monnet, 2003).

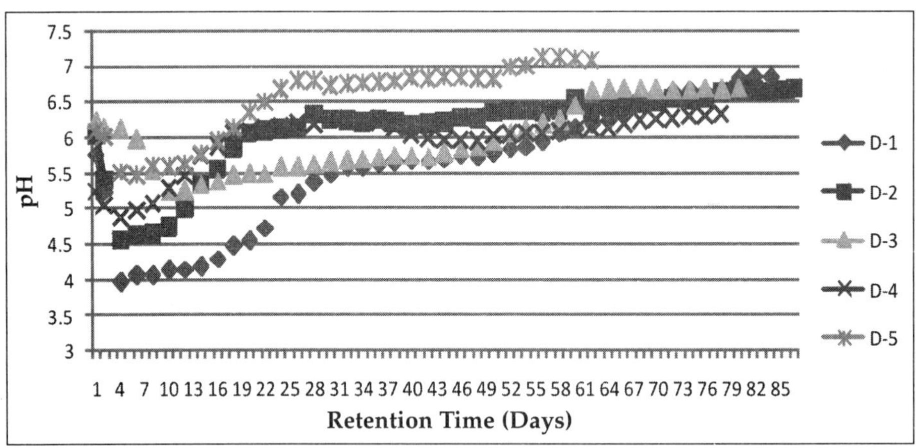

Fig. 10.3: **Average pH Values of the Digesters Throughout the Retention Time**

The decrease in pH is also the function of the concentration of volatile fatty acids (VFA) produced by the activity of hydrolytic acidogenic bacteria capable of degrading the feedstock in the first few days of incubation, bicarbonate alkalinity of the system, and the amount of carbon dioxide produced (Gomec and Speece, 2003). Nina *et al.* (2011) verified that, the presence of fat content can raise the formation of VFA, leading to a fall in pH. The present study showed that the overall pH of digesters containing TSW was lower than the digesters containing CD alone until the gas production ceased. The result shows the feasibility to produce biogas from tannery waste co-digested with CD in the pH range of 3.96 to 7.11 (Figure 10.3).

Amount of Daily Biogas Produced

The output of the average daily biogas production of each digester for about thirteen week is shown in Figure 10.4. The figure shows that the rate of averaged daily biogas production (volume) in almost all digesters increased persistently up to the fifth week, with the exceptions of D-2 and D-3, where the increments continued up-to the seventh week. The maximum and minimum reaction time periods were recorded as 87 days for D-2 (75% TSW: 25% CD) and 62 days for D-5 (100% CD). The longer reaction time period is due to the feedstock's lower bioavailability, though its theoretical biogas yield is high. On the other hand, the slow increase of the daily averaged room temperature after two weeks during the reaction time period may be the reason for the increase of the daily averaged biogas production. Michael (1979) mentioned that an increased in temperature has a positive effect on biogas yields.

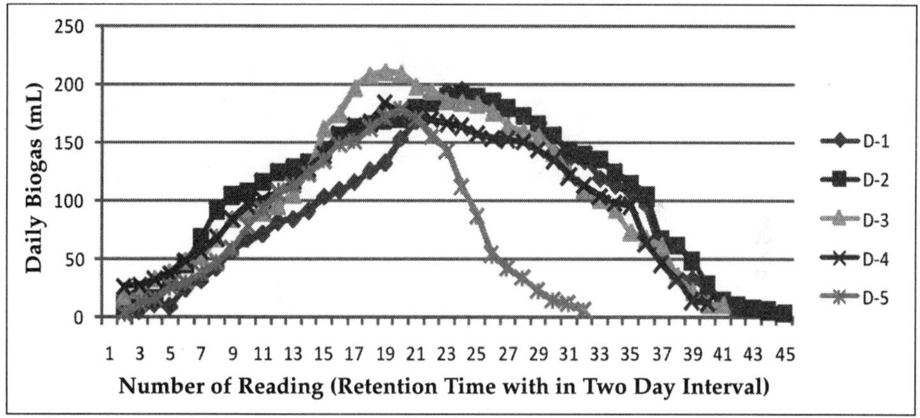

Fig. 10.4: **The Average Daily Biogas Production Potential of Each Treatment**

Maximum amount of biogas from the different digesters were produced during the 5th and 6th weeks of digestion periods; afterwards the biogas production gradually decreased (Figure 10.4). The highest values of daily biogas yield in each digester were during the 36th to 46th days of digestion period. The maximum values were 195, 192, 211, 184, and 179 mL from D-1, D-2, D-3, D-4 and D-5, respectively. Moreover, the maximum biogas was produced between the first and ninth week of the reaction period in all the digesters which was in the range of 100–295 mL, except D-5. The daily averaged biogas production in all digesters showed similar trends of gradual increments to maximum and then decreased slowly till it ceased to produce further biogas (Figure 10.4).

Total Biogas Production

Biogas production was measured for about 13 weeks of digestion period, until gas production ceased. The total biogas produced during the reaction period for all digesters is presented in Figure 10.5. The study showed that D-2 with 87 days of reaction period produced the highest total biogas (4756 ml) and D-5 with 62 days of reaction period produced the least (2539 ml) (Figure 10.4 and 10.5). Digesters D-1, D-3 and D-4 produced 3972, 4479 and 4183 ml of biogas, respectively. It is well known that the composition of biogas as well as biogas yields depend on the substrates owing to differences in material characterization in each feed (Stewart *et al.*, 1984). In the present case, the highest biogas produced by D-2 may be due to its C/N ratio of 24.18 (Table 10.1), which is in the range of C/N ratio value for digesters to produce the optimum biogas (Dahlman and Frost, 2001).

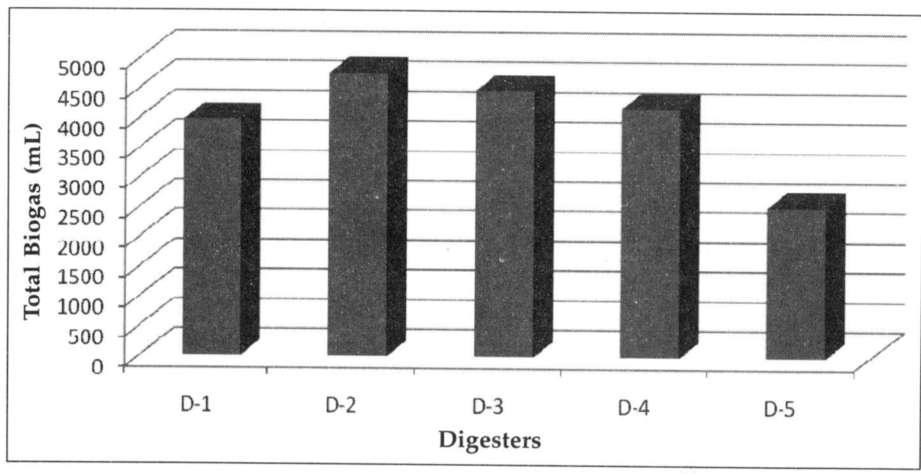

***Fig. 10.5:* Comparison of Total Biogas Production of Different Digesters**

The daily averaged biogas production rate can be obtained by dividing the total biogas by the respective retention time. Therefore, the daily biogas productions of D-1, D-2, D-3, D-4 and D-5 are 48.44, 54.67, 55.99, 53.63 and 40.95 ml/day, respectively.

Quality of Biogas Produced

Figure 10.6 below shows the weekly biogas quality produced of each digester. The quality of biogas produced by each digester in the first week of digestion period was below 50% (Figure 10.6). This indicates that, it cannot be combustible during this reaction period unless the biogas quality is enhanced by using different scrubbers to absorb the other component of the biogas like CO_2 and other trace gases like H_2S. Digesters D-1 and D-2 continued to produce biogas with quality of less than 50% until the end of 2nd and 3rd week of reaction period, respectively. Except for D-1 and D-2 the quality of the biogas remained in the range of 50 to 80% in most of the digesters from the 1st week up to the end of the digestion period (13th week). In view of that, the result of the quality of biogas of this research revealed that after the first week it is combustible except for D-1 and D-2 where the combustibility started from the 3rd and 4th weeks. In addition, depending on the system design and the type of waste feedstock, 55 to 75% of biogas is pure methane (Williams, 1998; Ostrem, 2004) which is in agreement with the results of this study (Figure 10.6).

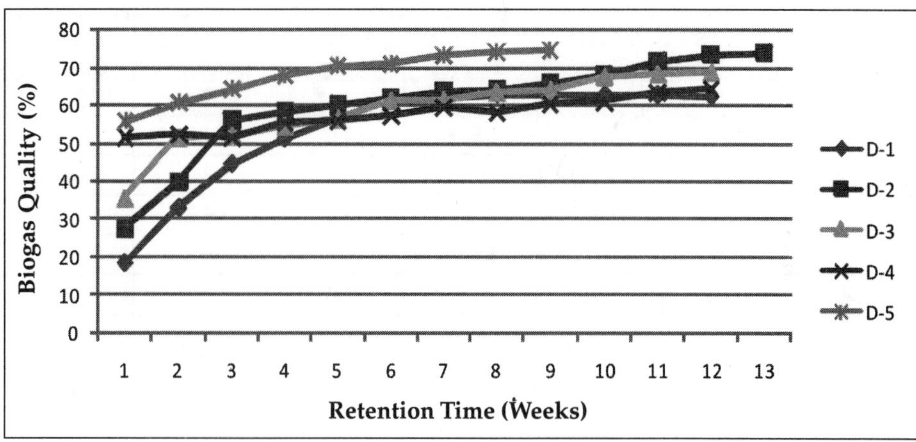

Fig. 10.6: **The Weekly Percentage of Biogas Quality Produced by Each Digester**

Moreover, the combustibility of the biogas produced was tested by connecting the gas line of each digester to a Bunsen burner head. A clear blue flame was observed during the flammability test. Curcio *et al.* (2005), suggested that the mixture of the gases (biogas) is combustible if its quality (methane content) is more than 50%.

The cumulative biogas quality produced by other digesters D-1, D-2, D-3, D-4 and D-5, were 53.23%, 60.37%, 58.78%, 57.78% and 67.31%, respectively. The highest and lowest cumulative biogas quality was produced by D-5 (100% CD) 67.31% and D-1 (100% TSW) 53.23%, respectively. Moreover, the overall biogas quality produced by all digesters was in the range of 55-75%. It is in the range of biogas quality reported by Curcio *et al.* (2005) greater than 50%, 50-70% reported by Yadav and Hesse, (1981) and 40-80% suggested by Stewart *et al.* (1984). Therefore, this result has revealed the possibility of producing high quantity and quality biogas from TSW without addition of other co-digester except a starter (inoculant).

CHARACTERISTICS OF THE DIGESTATE AFTER AD

Solids Reduction After AD

The TS and VS of each digester after the digestion period are indicated in Table 10.2. Anaerobic treatment of solid wastes converts the organic pollutants into biogas (methane and carbon dioxide). The relative higher removal efficiency of VS (%) than TS (%) in all digesters was a very good indication of high uptake rate of the organic fraction of TS and the effectiveness of the anaerobic reactor in digesting tannery waste under AD during proper operating conditions. Because about 50-75% of the original TS were converted to gaseous form, leaving 25-50% as anaerobically digested solid residues by AD (Table 2; Zhang, 2006).

Table 10.2: TS and VS Reading before and after Treatment and their Removal Efficiency

Digesters	%TS Before	%TS After	%VS Before	%VS After	Removal Efficiency of %TS	Removal Efficiency of % VS
D-1	42.96	24.8	63.83	25.6	42.3	59.89
D-2	43.26	18.5	69.24	23	57.2	66.78
D-3	53.75	18	71.95	19.2	66.5	73.31
D-4	55.12	19	61.48	14.6	65.5	76.25
D-5	12.7	3.98	58.4	7.59	68.7	87

From the percentage reduction of TS and VS, it can be put forward that AD can reduce the amount and volume of tannery waste which is disposed in dump sites. It can also reduce the cost of transport as well as the burden of the municipality's solid waste management sector.

Comparison of the volatile and total solid before and after digestion gives an indication of the utilization of the organic content in the reactor. Similarly, VS/TS ratio of TSW before and after digestion was 1.49% and 1.03%, respectively. Generally, the ratio of VS/TS before digestion was always relatively higher than the ratio after digestion, which is an indication of the utilization of the organic fraction during the anaerobic digestion; which is true for all the digesters in this study.

Capturing and combusting methane with ADs offers two benefits from a greenhouse gas emissions point of view. First, since methane has a significantly higher global warming potential than CO_2, combusting methane, rather than releasing it directly into the atmosphere, decreases direct CO_2 greenhouse gas emissions. Second, when the combustion process is used to generate heat or electricity, it displaces fuel consumption which would have occurred in the absence of the digester, creating an indirect emissions reduction. Hence, through converting waste to energy, AD has a potential of mitigating GHG emission that contributes to climate change (Monteny *et al.*, 2006).

CONCLUSION

The findings of this study show that tannery solid waste is a potential feedstock for anaerobic digestion. The ranges of mean daily room temperature and the pH during the course of the anaerobic digestion period were 14.5 to 23.21°C and 3.96 to 7.21. The results of the temperature and pH indicate the feasibility to produce biogas from tannery waste by sand-jacketing the digesters and co-digesting the solid wastes with cow-dung. The tannery solid waste (75%) blended with cow-dung (25%) produced higher amount of biogas (4756 ml) with 60.37% methane quality. The relative average percentage removal of total solid (42.27 to 76.34%) and volatile solid (47.16 to 79.23%) were found for all digesters, indicating significant reduction in the volume of tannery wastes produced in the industry. The present research will help to show the benefit of waste management vis-a-vis waste to energy, renewable energy generations (biogas) and reduction of greenhouse gas (CH_4) by tannery industries in temperate and high altitude regions of the world.

REFERENCES

Ali N., Kurchania A.K and Babel S. Bio-methanization of Jatropha Curcas Defatted Waste. Journal of Engineering and Technology Research 2010; 2(3): 038-043.

Anita Singh, Rajesh Kumar Sharma, Madhoolika Agrawal & Fiona M. Marshall. Risk Assessment of Heavy Metal Toxicity Through Contaminated Vegetables from Waste Water Irrigated Area of Varanasi. Journal of International Society for Tropical Ecology 2010; 51(2S): 375- 387.

APHA. Standard Methods for the Examination of Water and Waste Water, 20th Edition, American Public Health Association, American Water Works Association, and Water Environment Federation 1998, Washington DC, USA.

Badger C.M., Bogue M.J., Stewart DJ. Biogas Production from Crops and Organic Wastes. Journal of Science 1979; 22: 11-20.

Braun R. and Wellinger. APotential of Co-digestion; IEA Bio-energy. (2002), Task 37.

Buljan J., G.Reich, J.Ludvik. Mass Balance in Leather Processing. United Nations Industrial Development Organization (UNIDO) - US/RAS/92/120, 2000, 11-50.

Ciborowski P. Anaerobic Digestion in the Dairy Industry, Minnesota Pollution Control Agency Air Innovations Conference, August 10, 2004. www.epa.gov. Accessed 14 Nov 2011.

Curcio S., Calabro V., Aversa M., Ricca E., Sansonetti S. G., Iorio G. Optimization of Biogas Production with Bioconversion of Organic Solid Wastes (manure) and Food Industry Wastes. Journal of Biotechnology, 2010; 165-165.

Dahlman J. and Frost C. Technologies Demonstrated at Echo; Floating Drum Biogas Digester; Echo, (2001) 17391 Durance Rd, USA.

Divakaran S. Handbook of Glue and Gelating; Indian Leather, Madras, India 1984.

Durai and Rajasimman. Biological Treatment of Tannery Wastewater Review. Journal of Environmental Science and Technology 2011; 4 (1): 1-17.

Jigar Elias, Hameed Sulaiman, Araya Asfaw and Abraham Bairu. Study on Renewable Biogas Energy Production from Cladodes of Opuntia ficus indica. ISABB Journal of Food and Agriculture Science 2011; 1(3): 44-48.

Fulford D. Running a Biogas Programme: A Handbook. Intermediate Technology Publication 1988, UK.

Gomec, Y.C., Speece, R.E. 2003. The Role of pH in the Organic Material Solubilization of Domestic Sludge in Anaerobic Digestion. Journal of Water Science and Technology. 48: 143-150.

Ituen E.E., John N.M., Bassey B.E. Biogas Production from Organic Waste in Akwalbom State of Nigeria. In Ernest K. Yanful editors. Appropriate Technologies for Environmental Protection in the Developing World. Ghana: Springer Science Business Media B.V 2007; p. 93-99.

Kanagaraj KC, Velappan NK, Chandra Babu and Sadulla. Solid Wastes Generation in the Leather Industry and its Utilization for Cleaner Environment. Journal of Scientific and Industrial Research 2006; 65: 541-548.

Li Y., Park S.Y., Zhu J. Solid-state Anaerobic Digestion for Methane Production from Organic Waste. Renewable and Sustainable Energy Reviews 2011; 15: 821-826.

Mata-Alvarez J. Bio-methanization of the Organic Fraction of Municipal Solid Wastes. England: IWA Publishing 2003; ISBN: 1 900222 140.

Monnet F. An Introduction to Anaerobic Digestion of Organic Wastes, Final Report, Remade Scotland Ltd. Edinburgh, UK. 2003.

Monteny G.J, Bannink A., Chadwick D. (2006), Greenhouse Gas Abatement Strategies for Animal Husbandry. Journal of *Agriculture, Ecosystems and Environment* 2006; 112, 163-170.

Nina K., Miroslav H., Igor B. and Viera S. Utilization of Biodiesel By-products for Biogas Production. Journal of Biomedicine and Biotechnology Article ID 126798, 15 pages. 2011 August 22; [cited 2012 August] doi:10.1155/2011/126798. Available from: http://www.hindawi.com/journals/bmri/2011/126798/

NRCS Conservation Practice Standard, Anaerobic Digester in Controlled Temperature. 2005; 366: 4-5.

Ostrem, K. Greening Waste: Anaerobic Digestion for Treating the Organic Fraction of Municipal Solid Wastes; M.S. Thesis in Earth Resources Engineering Department of Earth and Environmental Engineering Fu Foundation of School of Engineering and Applied Science, Columbia University 2004.

Özmen, P. and Aslanzadeh, S. (2009) Biogas Production from Municipal Waste Mixed with Different Portions of Orange Peel, University of Borås, School of Engineering, Sweden.

Pena-Varo M.R. Advance Primary Treatment of Domestic Wastewater in Tropical Countries: Development of High Rate Anaerobic Ponds, Ph.D., Thesis, Department of Civil Engineering, university of Leeds, England 2002. Available from: http://www.leeds.ac.uk/civil/ceri/water/tphe/publicat/theses/penavaron/penavaron.html. Accessed 23 March, 2012

Pyle L. Anaerobic Digestion: Technical Options in Biogas Technology in the Third World, A Multi-disciplinary Review. Ottawa, Ont., IDRC 1978; 50-54.

Reijnders L. and Huijbregts M.A. Life Cycle Greenhouse Gas Emissions, Fossil Fuel Demand and Solar Energy Conversion Efficiency in European Bio-Ethanol Production for Automotive Purposes. Journal of Cleaner Production 2007; 15 (18): 1806-1812.

Stewart D.J.; Bogue M.J.; Badger D.M. Biogas Production from Crops and Organic Wastes; New Zealand Journal of Science 1984; 27(3): 285-294.

United Nations Industrial Development Organization (2009) Integrated Assessment of Present Status of Environmentally - Sound Management of Wastes in Africa, Sixth Session of the Committee on Food Security and Sustainable Development (CFSSD-6)/Regional Implementation Meeting (RIM) for CSD-18 Addis Ababa, Ethiopia.

Vasudevan and Ravindran. Biotechnological Process for the Treatment of Fleshing from Tannery Industries for Methane Generation; Current Science 2007; 93(11), 1492-1494.

Williams P.T. Waste Treatment and Disposal. Chichester: John Wiley and Sons 1998.

Zhang, R.H. Thermophilic Digestion of Green and Food Wastes with an Anaerobic Phased Solids Digester System; California Energy Commission Report 2006.

Zolar, S., Steffen, R. and Braun R. Feed Stocks for Anaerobic Digestion; Institute of Agro-Biotechnology Tullen, University of Agriculture, Vienna; 1998.

WASTE DISPOSAL AND MANAGEMENT *Pages:* 152-184
Edited by: **Dr. Pawan Kumar 'Bharti'; Dr. B. Tabassum;** and **Dr. Priya Bajaj**
ISBN: 978-93-5056-729-6
Edition: **2015**
Published by: **Discovery Publishing House Pvt. Ltd., New Delhi (India)**

11

Solid Waste Disposal in Delhi its Consequences on Ground Water Quality

Moharana Choudhury

INTRODUCTION

In recent years, an increasing threat to ground Water quality due to human activities has become of great importance. The adverse effects on groundwater quality are the results of man's activity at ground surface, unintentionally by agriculture, domestic and industrial effluents, unexpectedly by agriculture, domestic and industrial effluents, unexpectedly by sub-surface or surface disposal of sewage and industrial wastes.The quality of ground water is of great importance in determining the suitability of particular ground water for a certain use (public water supply, irrigation, industrial applications, power generation etc). The quality of ground water is the resultant of all the processes and reactions that have acted on the water from the moment it condensed in the atmosphere to the time it is discharged by a well. Therefore, the quality of ground water varies from place, with the depth of water table, and from season to season and is primarily governed by the extent and composition of dissolved solids present in it.

A vast majority of ground water quality problems are caused by contamination, over-exploitation, or combination of these all together. Most of ground water quality problems are difficult to detect and hard to resolve. The solution are usually very expensive, time consuming and not always effective. Ground water quality is slowly but surely declining everywhere.

North Eastern Space Application Center, Department of Space, Government of India Umiam-793 103, Meghalaya, India.

Ground water pollution is intrinsically difficult to detect, since problem may be concealed below the surface and monitoring is costly, time consuming and somewhat hit-or-miss by nature. The Wide range of contaminations sources is one of the many factors contributing to the complexity of groundwater assessment. It is important to know the geochemistry of the chemical-soil-groundwater interactions in order to assess the fate and impact of pollutant different hydrologic zones as they migrate through the soil to the water table.

The serious implications of this problem necessitate an integrated approach in explicit terms to undertake groundwater pollution monitoring an abatement programmer. A Major problem in urbanized areas is the connection and disposal of domestic wastes because of large volume of sewage is generated in a small area, the waste cannot be adequately disposed of by conventional septic tanks and cesspools. Therefore, special disposal sites are being used to collect and dispose such wastes in densely populated areas.The intensive use of natural resources and the large production of wastes in modern society often pose a threat to ground water quality and have already resulted in many incidents of ground water contamination. Pollutants are being added to the ground water system through human activities and natural processes.

Solid waste from industrial units is being dumped near the factories, which is subjected to reaction with percolating rain water and reaches the ground water level. The percolating water picks up a large amount of dissolved constituents and reaches the aquifer systems and contaminates the ground water. The Problem of ground water pollution in several parts of the country has become so acute that unless urgent steps for detailed identification and abatement are taken, extensive ground water resources may be damaged.The quality of ground water depends on a large number of individual hydrological, physical, chemical and biological factors.

Generally higher proportions of dissolved constituents are found in ground water than in surface water because of greater interaction used for drinking purpose should be free from any toxic element, living and nonliving organism and excessive amount of minerals that may be hazardous to health. Some of the heavy metals are extremely essential to humans, for example, Cobalt, Copper etc. but large quantities of them may cause physiological disorders. Apart from reported cases by different institutions, groundwater quality concerns in India was realized way-back in mid eighties with a systematic study of groundwater quality and identification of 'problematic zones' by Central pollution Control Board with reference to pollution. These (problem) areas due to their complex industrial scenario and increasing dependence on natural resources have been witness to excessive exploitation of groundwater for domestic and industrial uses.

With pollution control enforcement activities gaining momentum there were observed cases of indiscriminate waste disposal, subsurface discharge of effluent and inappropriate wastewater management by industries. This has led to severe stress on groundwater, in terms of quantitative imbalance' as well as 'quality deterioration'. Inconsideration of the potential of pollution in these problem areas, Central pollution Control Board has initiated groundwater quality monitoring in these areas. As an integral part of such studies groundwater status shall be brought out with suggested measures for pollution control.

WATER THE VERSATILE SOURCE

Water, one of the fundamental resources, is also one of the most unusual substances. Although its chemical formula is simple yet the effect of water on environment is more consequential than ever imagines. As the universal solvent', it possesses extra Ordinary ability to dissolve a broad range of substances. The salinity of the world oceans is a direct result of water's ability to dissolve rock materials as it flows overland to sea. It has the highest heat of vaporization. Because of water's high heat capacity, the presence of oceans, lakes and large rivers, prevents extreme fluctuation in local temperatures. Even within the human body (75% water by volume) water is critical in maintaining uniform body temperature.

GROUND WATER - THE BURIED TREASURE

The term groundwater is usually reserved for the subsurface water that occurs beneath the water-table in soils and geologic formation that are fully saturated. Geo-chemically, groundwater is aqueous solution of bicarbonates, chlorides and sulphates of alkaline earth and alkali metals. It supports drinking water supply; livestock needs irrigation, industrial and many commercial activities. While the degree of reliance on groundwater varies significantly, the need of groundwater as a dependable resource of fresh water has been unquestionable.In the overall go-strategic scenario groundwater has also offered a medium for many environmental solutions. It is key to understanding a wide variety of geologic processes for e.g. the generation of earthquakes, the migration and accumulation of petroleum and the genesis of certain type of ore deposits, soil type and land forms.

ORIGIN AND CLASSIFICATION OF GROUNDWATER

Groundwater, irrespective of its occurrence is an integral part of hydrologic cycle. For the origin of groundwater there are two theories. Condensation theory- supports the origin of groundwater resulting from condensation of water vapor present in the host rock at the time of their formation. According of Infiltration theory- of Groundwater results from infiltration of atmospheric water into the ground.

GROUND WATER QUALITY

The ground water quality is essential factor in determining its suitability for water supply. Groundwater has higher salt contents then surface water, as slow moving water remains in contact with the substrata for longer periods, increasing soluble minerals content until a condition of equilibrium is reached. The quantity & composition of the dissolved minerals in natural water depend upon the type of rock or oil with which it has been in contact or through which it has percolated and the duration it has been in contact with these rocks. The quality of ground water may vary from place to place, stratum to stratum and season to season. The requirement of quality of water for various purposes such as drinking, industrial use & irrigation vary widely. The water quality data also provide information about the geologic history of rocks, ground water recharge, discharge, movement and storage.

The ground water from deep tube well may not be solely representing deeper aquifers alone but it may be the mix of ground water from deeper levels.

The major source of water available, either for agriculture or human consumption is obtained from the rain that falls on the earth surface, India has a monsoon dominated rainfall pattern. The Southwest monsoon, Northeast monsoon, cyclonic depressions and local storms contribute to rain fall in the difference degrees in the various rainfall regions of India. An outstanding feature of the wind system is over the Indian Ocean and the adjoining sea and land areas in seasonal reversal of the monsoon. (Southwest from April to October Northeast during the rest of the year) About 80% of the rainfall in the most of the parts of India is contributed by Southwest monsoon. This is confined mainly to four months, namely June to September. The basic sources of water are precipitation in the form of rainfall or snowfall. Run-off from precipitations drains through streams and river or collects in surface depression forming ponds. The water from streams and rivers is stored in reservoir or is diverted direct through canal systems for irrigation. Run-off water is stored in tanks or ponds are also regulated for irrigation. A part of rainfall is stored as ground water.

GROUND WATER POLLUTION

The existence of ground water is neither unlimited nor it has foolproof protection from deterioration and degradation. The undesirable change occurring in physical, chemical and biological characteristics of natural waters, directly or indirectly as the result of human activities leads to its pollution making less useful and harmful affecting unman life, affecting the water resources and ultimately the living conditions of desirable biotic species. The sources of groundwater pollution are many and varied. Pollution by disease causing micro organisms occur when human and animal waster containing virus, bacteria and parasites come into contact with groundwater. Chemical pollutants can leach into groundwater from a variety of sources including hazardous waste dumps, sewage, land-treatment sites, injection wells, indiscriminate solid waste disposal, and percolation of pesticides and fertilizer from agricultural field and accumulation of industrial waste water on land.

IMPACTS ON GROUND WATER

The severity of groundwater pollution is of particular significance on account of the following:

- Its vulnerability to pollution
- The associated complexity in pollution source identification
- Limited feasible options for treatment of groundwater, all of which are cost prohibitive
- Complicated process in fixing geophysical boundaries:
- Difficulty in prediction of movement:
- Insufficient dilution:
- Slow movement:
- Lack of any natural cleansing capability:

Moreover, in most of cases where Groundwater is observed polluted, the area is densely populated and as commonly seen, there is no immediate fresh water substitute available at such locations. A variety of adverse impacts due to Groundwater contamination is possible it including effects on public health, the environment, agricultural productivity (e.g. due to increased salinity in irrigation water) and on the output of industries requiring high quality water.

GROUNDWATER MONITORING TECHNIQUES

Unlike surface water, wherein information on direction of movement, velocity, sources of contamination is available: monitoring of groundwater involves various investigations prior to the actual assessment of groundwater quality. The topography, soil profile, geology, aquifer characteristics, land-use pattern, source of pollution and above-all, the extent of groundwater development are some of the important pre-requisites to decide the scheme of groundwater monitoring.

MONITORING OF GROUNDWATER QUALITY

In general, monitoring of groundwater quality involves collection of representative sample and simultaneous collection of hydro-geological information about the sampling location. The sample and hence the groundwater quality data may adversely affect if one or more of the following factors are not appropriately looked into.

(a) Sample was taken from stagnant water in the open well or suddenly in case of bore well without removing the casing storage effect. The error can be largely overcome it 3 to 10 well-bore volumes are removed and in case of hand pumps- sufficient water is pumped out before taking the sample.

(b) Samples are not taken at appropriate time intervals-seasonally and at improper locations.

(c) Contamination due to entrained sediment.

(d) Hydraulic characteristics of the (soil) formation near the screen, resulting in possible dilution of the contaminant.
(e) Release of carbon-di-oxide during pumping and hence increase in PH which may cause many metallic ions to come out of solution.
(f) The samples preservation is not properly done and analyzed without considering the parameter-specific prescribed period of retention.

GROUNDWATER - INDIAN PERSPECTIVE

In India, groundwater has played the pivotal role in fulfilling the demands of domestic, industrial and agriculture sectors. At present the groundwater in India contributes more than 58% drinking water, 52% for agriculture production and unscientific management of this resource has led to development and unscientific management of this resource has led to multiple problems of decline in groundwater level, sea water ingress, in - land salinity, groundwater pollution, land subsidence etc. The measures that need to be adopted in the country to meet the increased water demand in the new millennium would include exploration of deeper aquifers, groundwater recharge, development of aquifers in flood plains, direct use of saline/brackish water, conjunctive use of surface and groundwater in canal command area, creation of groundwater sanctuaries and regulation of groundwater development.

GROUNDWATER DEVELOPMENT IN INDIA - IMPORTANT ISSUES

During the past five decades, there has been phenomenal increase in growth of groundwater abstraction structures in India. Their number has increased from 4 million in 1951 to about 18 million in 1997-99, while in the same period irrigation potential created from Groundwater has increased from 6 to 30 million hectares. Commensurate with this growth, groundwater development has been intensive in alluvial area of Indo-Ganga-Yamuna plains of Punjab, Haryana, Uttar Pradesh, Uttarkhand and in parts of hard rock terrain in southern States. Though over-exploitation of the resource in some parts of the country has created serious problems, a large portion of the available resources still remains untapped, particularly in north-eastern areas, where precipitation is remains untapped, particularly in north- eastern areas, where precipitation is high and the demand for irrigation is low and also in eastern States where fragmented nature of land holdings has been a major factor in low development of groundwater.

REVIEWS OF SIMILAR WORK

Shiddamallayya and Pratima (2008) carried out a study on physico-chemical parameters of like pH, Magnesium, chloride, nitrite, sulphate and hardness of water and fins out the great increase in all the parameters due to the various activities of urban areas.

Dhere et. al. (2008) made a study on improper disposal of solid waste in Pune city and find out the unscientific disposal of solid waste which play an important role in the degradation of physic-chemical parameter of ground water like as BOD, COD, DO, Shlphate etc. in this study it was all so found that the all parameters were directly affected due to various routine activities of the society.

Ololade et. al. (2009) have been studied on affect of household wastes on surface and underground waters and find out the majority of the water utilized for the various natural sources examined is polluted due to indiscriminate dumping of waste in to the environment.

Olaniyanet. al. (2009) have been study an surface water contamination from the Kanduna,Yola and Maiduduri landfill sites and pointed out that the solid waste sampling and categorization results as presented that food waste constitutes a major part of the wastes generated in all the cities resulting in high concentration of biogas emission from the dump sites . As presented in the table metallic waste is still very significant in the wastes generated despite the activities of the scavengers who collect them for re use by the steel mills in the country, plastic films waste especially polyethylene are another significant elements in the waste constituting environmental nuisance and clog drainage channels comparative analysis of chemical composition of the digested soil samples collected from beneath solid waste dump sites with the standard upper limits and world health organization (WHO) the parameters whose maximum values exceeded the W.H.O. international drinking water standard are BOD, COD, TDS, total hardness, potassium, iron, chromium, bicarbonate, sulphate and chloride. However the values obtained for calcium, magnesium, nitrate and carbonate are within permissible limits for drinking water.

Kumar et. al. (2010) have been studied on drinking water quality management through correlation studies among various physic – chemical parameters and pointed out that conductivity is a very important parameter to determine the water quality of any area, because it correlated with all the parameters.

Sadek et.al. (2000) made a study on the land fill sites and find out that the poorly maintained landfill sites are prone to ground water contamination through leaching action, open dumping of garbage the breeding site for disease vector such a flies, mosquitoes rats etc. methane gases also generated from the landfill waste and it is estimated that in 1997 the landfill released about 7 million tones of methane into the atmosphere which would increase to 39 million tons by 2047 to contribute to the phenomenon of global warming.

Moharana Choudhury (2014) carried out a study on solid waste dumping ground and is impact on surround area at Silchar town and found that dumping ground is unscientific which resulting contamination of water bodies and burning of wastes at dumping area directly effecting surrounding in habited area.

A SPECIAL REFERENCE OF DELHI CITY AS CASE STUDY

Delhi is the capital of India and sprawls over 1483 km^2 at latitudes 28°35N and longitude77°12′E located at an altitude of 218 m above the mean sea level. The Gangetic Plain and the Aravalli Ridge converge at Delhi and they give a mixed geological character with alluvial plains as well as quartzite bedrocks. The climatic regime of Delhi belongs to the semi arid type and characterized by extreme dry conditions associated with hot summers and cold winters. The temperature ranges between 18.7°C (mean minimum) and 40.3°C (mean maximum). It also experiences heavy rains primarily during the periods of monsoon with an average rainfall of 714.6 mm. The groundwater level in Delhi city varies between 15 to 20 meter depths. Delhi, with a population approaching to 14 million is estimated to generate about 7000 metric tonnes of garbage daily. The per capita generation of solid waste in Delhi ranging from 150 gms to 600 gms a day depending upon the economic status of the community involved and it mainly includes waste from household, industries and medical establishments.

The earliest landfill was started in Delhi in 1975 near Ring road started at Timarpur and Kailash Nagar. Till date 17 landfill sites have been filled and closed. At present there are three large functioning landfill sites in Delhi. Ghazipur, is one of the major among them none of their bases is lined, which may result in continuous groundwater contamination. These sites had not been designed systematically before being used for disposal of dumping of waste. Furthermore no environmental impact assessment had been carried out prior to selection of these sites. The Gazipur landfill started in the year 1984 and still in use. It spreads over an area of approximately 3 × 105 M^2 and situated near National Highway 24. On an average 2200 MT/day of waste is dumped and the waste fill height varies from 12 m to 20 m. It is located at the close proximity of the Hindon Canal. The waste dumped at this site includes domestic waste, e.g. kitchen waste; paper, plastic, glass, cardboard, cloths. Construction and demolition waste consisting of sand, bricks and concrete block are also dumped. Further waste from the adjacent poultry market, fish market, slaughterhouse, dairy farm and non-infectious hospital waste is also dumped. The site is non-engineered low lying open dump, looks like a huge heap of waste up to a height of 12-20 m. Trucks from different parts of the city collect and bring waste to this site and dump the waste in irregular fashion. The waste is dumped as such without segregation, except the rag pickers who rummage through the garbage and help in segregating it. They generally collect glass material, plastic and metals and sell this to the recycling units (Aggarwal *et. al.* 2005). At this landfill site two water bore wells are operational, which are used for washing of refuse removal vehicles and maintenance of heavy earth moving equipments.

Table 11.1: Details of Sampling Points Gajipur Dumping Site

Sample No.	Location	Identification	Direction	Approximate	Source	Remark
Ga 1	Gajipur Dairy Farm	General Store Kappor Medicals	N	Within 50 m –500 m	Bore Well (Motor Driven)	Used for drinking
Ga 2	Gajipur Dairy Farm	Billu Gujar's House D-36	N	Within 50 m	Bore Well (Motor Driven)	Used for drinking
Ga 3	Gajipur Dairy	Ilias's House D-50	N	Within 50 m	Bore Well (Motor Driven)	Used for drinking
Ga 4	Farm	Bheem Singh's Dairy D-48, Road 6	N	Within 50 m	Bore Well (Motor Driven)	Used for drinking
Ga 5	Gajipur Dairy	Asraf's House D-73 In front of Delhi Nagar Nigam Office	N	Within 50 m	Bore Well (Motor Driven)	Used for drinking
Ga 6	Farm	Within landfill site	N	On Site	Bore Well (Motor Driven)	Used for drinking
Ga 7	Gajipur Dairy	House of Mr. Subendra Singh B-38	W	Within 50 m –500 m	Bore Well (Motor Driven)	Used for drinking
Ga 8	Farm	Guruji Golvelkar Park	W	Within 50 m – 500 m	Bore Well (Motor Driven)	Used for drinking
Ga 9	Gajipur Dairy	ETP construction Area	E	Within 50 m	Bore Well (Motor Driven)	Used for drinking
Ga 10	Farm	ETP construction Area	E	Within 50 m	Bore Well (Motor Driven)	Used for drinking
Ga 11	Gajipur Dairy	ETP Construction Area	E	Within 50 m	Bore Well (Motor Driven)	Used for drinking

(Contd…)

Sample No.	Location	Identification	Direction	Approximate	Source	Remark
Ga -12	Inside slaughter House (Under construction)	Slaughter house	E	Within 50 m – 500 m	Bore Well (Motor Driven)	Used for drinking
Ga -13	Slaughter house Plant (Under construction)	Slaughter house for cutting animals	E	Within 50 m – 500 m	Bore Well (Motor Driven)	Used for drinking
Ga -14	Multah Colony Near canal (Harijan colony)	Pratap Sing C-641	S	Within 50 m – 500 m	Hand Pump	Used for drinking
Ga -15	Mullah colony Near canal (Harijan colony)	MulliKhatu C-380	S	Within 50 m – 500 m	Hand Pump	Used for drinking
Ga -16	Mullah colony (Mosque)	Mosque	S	Within 50 m – 500 m	Bore Well (Motor Driven)	Used for Drinking

Table 11.2: Details of Sampling Points Around Gajipur Dumping Site

Sample	Location	Identification	Direction	Approximate	Source	Remark
GB 1	N28º37.642' E 077º19.531'	Master'stable Gajipur Dairy farm	N	Within 50 m – 500 m	Bore Well (Motor Driven)	Used for drinking
GB 2	N28º37.642' E 077º19.531'	Bunda khan 'Kiran Shop' Gajipu Dairy	N	Within 50 m	Bore Well (Motor Driven)	Used for drinking
GB 3	N28º37.57' E077º19.559'	Sabir Balo's Stable Gajipur Dairy farm	N	Within 50 m	Bore Well (Motor Driven)	Used for drinking
GB 4	N28º37.532' E077º19.569'	Fajil's Stable, Gajipur Daily farm	N	Within 50 m	Bore Well (Motor Driven)	Used for drinking
GB 5	N28º44.102' E077º190.994'	On Landfil sites	N	Within 50 m	Bore Well (Motor Driven)	Used for drinking
GB 6	N28º37.415' E077º19.279' Eoevation-642m	Govelkar Gurjji Park, Gajipur Dairy Farm	N	On Site	Bore Well (Motor Driven)	Used for drinking
GB 7	N28º37.415' E077º19.401'	Gajipur Jama Masjid (GJM), Gajipur Dairy farm	W	Within 50 m – 500 m	Bore Well (Motor Driven)	Used for drinking
GB 8	N28º37.310' E077º19.364'	In front of Subi's House, Opposite to Guruji Golvelkar Park Gajipur Dairy farm	W	Within 50 m – 500 m	Bore Well (Motor Driven)	Used for drinking
GB 9	N28º37.824' E077º19.890'	Slaughter house	N	Within 50 m – 500 m	Bore Well (Motor Driven)	Used for drinking
GB 10	N28º37.379' E077º19. 825'	Mullah colony, near Canal, CR-164	N	Within 50 m	Bore Well (Motor Driven)	Used for drinking

(Contd...)

Sample	Location	Identification	Direction	Approximate	Source	Remark
GB 11	N28º37.343' E077º19.785'	Mullah Colony, near Canal, Mulli Khatun C-380	N	Within 50 m	Bore Well (Motor Driven)	Used for drinking
GB 12	N28º37.262' E077º19.723'	Mullah colony (Mosque)	N	Within 50 m	Bore Well (Motor Driven)	Used for drinking
GB 13	N28º37.450' E077º19.178'	Near STD Booth T-2, Gali No. 3, Gazipur Dairy Farm	N	Within 500m – 1000 m	Bore Well (Motor Driven)	Used for drinking
GB 14	N28º37.209' E077º19.433'	Opposite to newly constructed slaughter house, Gazipur Dairy Farm	W	Within 500 m – 1000 m	Bore Well (Motor Driven)	Used for drinking
GB 15	N28º37.230' E077º20.081'	Near Pan Shop, Sapera Basti	S	Within 500 m – 1000 m	Bore Well (Motor Driven)	Used for drinking

SAMPLING

Sampling is the process in which samples are collected from the different locations of an area. The objective of sampling is to collect a portion of water which is small enough in volume to be transported conveniently and handled in laboratory while still representative of characteristics of the water available in that water source. Water is dynamic system. Its constituents vary with time.

SAMPLE COLLECTION

Samples are collected in container depending upon the analysis it undergo (analysis of parameters of ground water) for all these analysis container is rinsed with water 2-3 times. Thereafter for heavy metals samples are taken in plastic bottles and sample preserved by adding 2-5 ml. nitric acids.. The sample is taken in a glass bottle and cap is placed over it and is covered with aluminum foil. For ground water analysis samples are taken in cans and thereafter cans are sealed.

1. **pH:**
   - Firstly warm up the digital pH meter
   - Standardize the instrument using different buffer solution of pH range (7.0.4.0.9.2.)
   - Then measure the sample pH
2. **Conductivity:**
   - Firstly warm up the digital conductivity meter
   - Then calibrate the instrument using KCl solution
   - Measure the conductivity of the sample
3. **Total Dissolve Solids (TDS):**
   - Firstly take 50 ml sample in a pre-weighed beaker.
   - Keep in oven at 105 C.
   - When beaker become completely dry increase the temperature to 180
   - C for I hr.
   - Keep beaker in dessicator for cooking
   - Then take final weight
4. **Hardness:**

   Calcium Hardness:
   - Take 25 ml sample in conical flask
   - Add 1 ml, IN NaOH
   - Add pinch of calcium indicator
   - Titrate with 0.01M EDTA
   - END-POINT: colour changes from pink to blue

Total Hardness:

- Take 50ml sample.
- Add 1ml ammonia buffer & pinch of EBT indicator.
- Titrate with 0.01M EDTA.

5. **Chloride:**
   - Take 50 ml sample in conical flask.
   - Add few drops of potassium chromate yellow color appear.
   - Titrate with sliver nitrate till light red color appears.
6. **Alkalinity:**
   - Phenolphthalein Alkalinity
   - Take 50ml sample in conical flask.
   - Add 4 drops of phenolphthalein indicator.
   - If pink color appears titrate with sulphuric acid of 0.02N.
   - Titrate till pink color disappears.
7. **Methyl Orange Alkalinity:**
   - Take 50 ml sample in conical flask.
   - Add 4 drops of methyl orange indicator yellow colour appear
   - Titrate with Sulphuric acid of 0.02N.
   - END –Point: colour changes from yellow to orange.
8. **Sodium:**
   - Firstly standardized the "FLAME PHOTOMETER" with STD.
   - Sodium solution.
   - Then measure the sample concentration.
9. **Potassium:**
   - Firstly standardized the FLAME PHOTOMETER with STD.
   - Sodium solution.
   - Then measure the sample concentration.
10. **Fluoride:**
    - Take 50ml sample in Nessler's tube.
    - Add 10ml (SPABDS+ZIRCIBIUM CHLORIDE) solution.
    - Mix well & keep for 10 minutes.
    - Set absorbance with reference solution at 570 nm
11. **Nitrate:**
    - Take 50ml sample in Nessler's tube
    - Check the absorbance in UV spectrophotometer at 220 nm & 275 nm.
12. **Sulphate:**
    - Take 50ml sample in conical flask.
    - Add 2.5ml conditioning reagent & spatula barium chloride

- Stur fir 1 minute
- Set absorbance at 420 nm.

13. Nitrite:

- Take 50ml sample in Nessler's tube
- Add 1ml sulphalinamide& 1ml NEDA solution.
- Mix well & leave for 10 min. for colour development
- Measure absorbance spectrophotometrically at 540nm

14. Ca^{++}:

- Take 50ml. of sample in conical flask if the sample has high alkalinity take 20ml. sample and dilute to 50ml. usuing distilled water.
- Add 2.0ml of 1N NaOH solution.
- Now add sufficient quantity (100-200) of mureoxide indicator
- Titrate it against EDTA solution
- Ca^{++}= Calcium hardness × 0.4

15. Mg^{++}:

Mg (mg/l) = (A-B) × 400.8/ml of sample taken × 1.645

Where (A=EDTA used in hardness determination)

(B=EDTA used in Ca^{++}determination)

Mg^{++}= Total hardness –Calcium hardness

Table 11.3: Analytical Methods and Equipment used in the Study

Sl. No.	Parameter	Method	Equipment
A.	Physico-chemical		
1.	**pH**	Electrometric	pH Meter
2.	**Conductivity**	Electrometric	Conductivity Meter
3.	**TDS**	Electrometric	Conductivity Meter
4.	**Alkalinity**	Titration by H_2SO_4	–
5.	**Hardness**	Titration by EDTA	–
6.	**Chloride**	Titration by $AgNO_3$	–
7.	**Sulphate**	Turbidimetric	Turbidity Meter
8.	**Nitrate**	Ultraviolet Screening	UV-VIS Spectrophotometer
9.	**Phosphate**	Molybdophosphoric acid	UV-VIS Spectrophotometer
10.	**Fluoride**	SPANDS	UV-VIS Spectrophotometer
11.	**Sodium**	Flame emission	Flame Photometer
12.	**Potassium**	Flame emission	Flame Photometer
13.	**Calcium**	Titration By EDTA	–
14.	**Magnesium**	Titration By EDTA	–

Table 11.4: Drinking Water Quality Standard-is: 10500-1991

Sl. No.	Characteristic	Reuqiretment	Undersirable Effects Outside	Permissible Limit
1.	Colour, Hazen units	5	Acceptance decreased	25
2.	Odor	Unobjectionable	–	–
3.	Taste	Agreeable	–	–
4.	pH	6.5-8.5	Beyond this range the Water will affect the Mucous membrane	No Realization
5.	Total Hardness (as$CaCo_3$) mg/l	300	Encrustation in water Supply structure & Adverse effects on Domestic use	600
6.	Chloride (as Cl) mg/lMax	250	Tasted, corrosion & Palatability are effected	1000
7.	Dissolved solids mg/1 Max	500	Palatability decreased & Caused GI Irritation	2000
8.	Calcium (as Ca) Max	75	Encrustation in water Supply structure & Adverse effects on Domestic use	200
9.	Magnesium (as Mg) Mg/1Max	30	Encrustation in water Supply structure & Adverse effects on Domestic use	100
10.	Sulphate (as $S0_{4)}$ mg/l	200	GI irritation	400
11.	Nitrate (as $N0_3$)mg/l	45	Methaemoflobinemia takes place	100
12.	Fluoride (as F) mg/l		High fluoride may cause Fluorosis	1.5
13.	ALK. Mg/1 Max	200	Tasted becomes unpleasant	600

Fig. A: **A Satellite Map of Gazipurdumping site at Delhi**

Fig. 11.1: **Photo Showing Gazipur Dumping Side at Delhi, Near Mother Dairy (Entry side)**

Fig. 11.2: **Photo Showing View of Dumping Site Gazipur Near Mulla Colony and Hindon Canal**

Fig. 11.3: **During Field Study at Gazipur Dumping Site (Delhi), Near Fish Market**

Fig. 11.4: **Photo Showing of Mullha Colony at Gazipur & Bore Well for Water**

Fig. 11.5: **Photo Showing Bore Well which is used for Drinking Water**

RESULTS

As per study of Gazipur Municipal Corporation of Delhi, dumping area the following parameters were found as the pH is a measure of hydrogen ion concentration in water. All the results of present study are summarized in to the table and given below.

pH indicates whether water is acidic alkaline or natural in character . As per study the pH of different areas around dumping sites was as 6.52- 7.6 which are within permissible limit. Highest value (7.76) of pH was found at the Ga14 while the minimum value was found at the Ga13.

The **conductivity** is measurement of the conductance of water electric current it assesses the extent of dissolved minerals in it. The conductivity of samples around the study site of Gazipur was found to be in rage between of 1220-2945µmhos/cm. highest value (2945) of conductivity was found at the Ga12 while the minimum value (1220) was found at the Ga5.

Total dissolve solids (TDS) refers to matter suspended or dissolved in water or waste water with high content is inferior and may be polluted. In study it was found that the (TDS) of Gazipur area in high range as1400, 1068, 1524, 1656, 840, 1106, 1540, 1330, 1900, 1960, 1914, 2061 mg/l for Ga 1,Ga2, Ga3, Ga4, Ga5, Ga6, Ga7, Ga8, Ga9, Ga10, Ga11, Ga12, Ga13, Ga14, Ga15, Ga16 respectively and above the permissible limit that of 500mg/l which may because of high concentration of dissolve solids (TDS) in water causes adverse effect in taste. Highest value (2061 mg/l) of TDS was found at the Ga12 while the minimum value (1061 mg/l) was found at the Ga2.

Alkalinity is measure of capacity of water to neutralize acids. The alkalinity range of water in different samples in around Gaziupr municipal dumping site were as minimum 164 mg/l and maximum 510 mg/l respectively. Highest value (510 mg/l) of Alkalinity was found at the Ga12 while the minimum value (164 mg/l) was found at the Ga8.

Hardness is the property which makes water forming an insoluble curd with soap and is primary due to calcium and magnesium. Calcium and magnesium contribute to hardness of water, which causes scale formation in pipes. Magnesium causes black stains on cloths during cleaning. They may affect the test of beverage made out of water hard water is of primarily concern because it requires more soap in washing and forms scales in boiler, water heater and pipes though the harness in not directly related with health concern. As per study the total hardness was found in range minimum as 360 mg/l and maximum 835 mg/l respectively. Water was found to be very hard. Highest value (835 mg/l) of Hardness was found at the Ga12 while the minimum value (360 mg/l) was found at the Ga6.

High concentration of **chloride** ions results in objectionable taste in water as per study it was found that the chloride level in water samples were in range between 60-560mg/l minimum and maximum respectively as permissible limit is 250 mg/l but some samples were above that range as Ga1, Ga2, Ga3, Ga4, Ga9, Ga10, Ga11, Ga12, Ga13 were found 370, 260, 500, 560, 490, 380, 410, 420 mg/l respectively and rest all were within permissible limit. Highest value (560 mg/l) of Chloride was found at the Ga4 while the minimum value (60 mg/l) was found at the Ga5.

Sulphate has a laxative effect on person unaccustomed to the water. It also taste and forms hard scale in boiler and pipes. Sulfates concentration of samples ranges from 43mg/l minimum to 190mg/l maximum where the permissible limit is 200mg/l and all samples were found within permissible limit. Highest value (190 mg/l) of sulphate was found at the Ga10 while the minimum value (43 mg/l) was found at the Ga2.

High concentration of **nitrite** causes methemoglobinia (blue baby) in infant's as per study the concentration of nitrite in range of 0.003 minimum to1.43 mg/l maximum where the permissible limit is 50mg/l and all samples were found within limit. Highest value (1.43 mg/l) of nitrite was found at the Ga12 while the minimum value (0.003 mg/l) was found at the Ga5.

Phosphate concentrations in samples were in range of 0.24 mg/l minimum and 1.04 mg/l in maximum. Highest value (1.04 mg/l) of phosphate was found at the Ga4 while the minimum value (0.24 mg/l) was found at the Ga6.

Higher concentration of **fluoride** causes mottling of teethe. The fluoride concentration in samples were in range between 0.12 mg/l minimum to 0.72mg/l maximum where the permissible limit is 1.5 and all samples were found within limit. Highest value (0.72 mg/l) of fluoride was found at the Ga13 while the minimum value (0.12 mg/l) was found at the Ga10.

Sodium is restricted in the diets of heart and kidney patient to avoid damages .high concentration of sodium will reduce the suitability of water for irrigation. As per the ranges of sodium concentrations were 52mg/l minimum to 360mg/l maximum. Highest value (360) of Sodium was found at the Ga4 while the minimum value (52 mg/l) was found at the Ga5.

Excessive intake of **potassium** may have laxative effect. As per the study potassium concentration in samples were found in range of 5 mg/l minimum to 73mg/l maximum. There is graphical representation of parameters is given, in which clearly represented the ranges of different parameters. Highest value (73) of potassium was found at the Ga12 while the minimum value (5) was found at the Ga6.

Table 11.5: Physico-chemical Characteristics Analysis of Ground Water Sample around Gazipur M.C.D (Municipal Corporation of Delhi) Landfill Site

Sl. No.	Parameters	Ga 1	Ga 2	Ga 3	Ga 4	Permissible Limit (BIS)	Permissible Limit (WHO)
			Physico-chemical Analysis				
1.	pH	6.66	6.67	6.84	7.06	6.5 - 8.5	
2.	Conductivity (μmhos/cm)	2000	1540	2177	2365		
3.	TDS (mg/l)	**1400**	**1068**	**1524**	**1656**	500	
4.	Alkalinity (mg/l)	404	276	264	224		
5.	Total Hardness as $CaCO_3$ (mg/l)	789	590	618	700		
6.	Calcium Hardness as $CaCO_3$ (mg/l)	367	189	261	315		
7.	Mg Hardness as $CaCO_3$ (mg/l)	422	401	357	385		
8.	Calcium as $CaCO_3$)	147	75	105	126		
9.	Magnesium as Mg(mg/l)	95	94	88	92		
10.	Chloride (mg/l)	**370**	**260**	**500**	**560**	250	250
11.	Sulphate (mg/l)	100	43	62	54	200	200
12.	Nitrate (mg/l)	1.15	0.12	1.23	1.15	45	50
13.	Phosphate (mg/l)	0.32	0.48	0.84	1.04		
14.	Fluoride (mg/l)	0.35	0.29	0.35	0.39	1.5	1.5
15.	Sodium (mg/l)	168	95	310	360		
16.	Potassium (mg/l)	17	9	8	8	–	

(Contd...)

Sl. No.	Parameters	Ga 5	Ga 6	Ga 7	Ga 8	Permissible Limit (BIS)	Permissible Limit (WHO)
			Physico-chemical Analysis				
1.	pH	7.16	7.60	7.10	6.80	6.5 - 8.5	
2.	Conductivity (µmhos/cm)	1220	1580	2200	1900		
3.	TDS (mg/l)	**840**	**1106**	**1540**	**1330**	500	
4.	Alkalinity (mg/l)	208	192	180	164		
5.	Total Hardness as $CaCO_3$ (mg/l)	370	360	440	410		
6.	Calcium Hardness as $CaCO_3$ (mg/l)	168	126	100	90		
7.	Mg Hardness as $CaCO_3$ (mg/l)	202	234	340	320		
8.	Calcium as Ca	67	50	36	34		
9.	Magnesium as Mg(mg/l)	88	90	70	67		
10.	Chloride (mg/l)	60	105	164	152	250	250
11.	Sulphate (mg/l)	59	80	56	74	200	200
12.	Nitrate (mg/l)	0.003	0.33	0.46	0.38	45	50
13.	Phosphate (mg/l)	0.42	0.24	0.29	0.26		
14.	Fluoride (mg/l)	0.33	0.59	0.28	0.14	1.5	1.5
15.	Sodium (mg/l)	52	124	98	84		
16.	Potassium (mg/l)	8	5	16	11		

Sl. No.	Parameters	Ga 9	Ga 10	Ga 11	Ga 12	Permissible Limit (BIS)	Permissible Limit (WHO)
			Physico-chemical Analysis				
1.	pH	6.66	6.52	6.43	6.70	6.5 - 8.5	
2.	Conductivity (µmhos/cm)	2014	2800	2735	2945		
3.	TDS (mg/l)	**1900**	**1960**	**1914**	**2061**	500	
4.	Alkalinity (mg/l)	224	512	412	510		
5.	Total Hardness as $CaCO_3$ (mg/l)	800	670	745	835		
6.	Calcium Hardness as $CaCO_3$ (mg/l)	272	242	265	260		
7.	Mg Hardness as $CaCO_3$ (mg/l)	548	565	357	660		
8.	Calcium as Ca	100	42	110	151		
9.	Magnesium as Mg(mg/l)	133	137	128	142		

(Contd…)

Sl. No.	Parameters	Ga 9	Ga 10	Ga 11	Ga 12	Permissible Limit (BIS)	Permissible Limit (WHO)
10.	Chloride (mg/l)	**490**	**380**	**410**	**420**	250	250
11.	Sulphate (mg/l)	120	190	175	180	200	200
12.	Nitrate (mg/l)	1.35	1.05	0.60	1.43	45	50
13.	Phosphate (mg/l)	0.38	0.56	0.86	0.73		
14.	Fluoride (mg/l)	0.31	0.12	0.45	0.38	1.5	1.5
15.	Sodium (mg/l)	245	239	260	242		
16.	Potassium (mg/l)	68	56	69	73		

Sl. No.	Parameters	Ga 13	Ga 14	Ga 15	Ga 16	Permissible Limit (BIS)	Permissible Limit (WHO)
	Physico Chemical Analysis						
1.	pH	6.42	7.76	7.26	6.98	6.5 - 8.5	
2.	Conductivity (μmhos/cm)	2835	1721	1810	1784		
3.	TDS (mg/l)	**1984**	**1205**	**1267**	**1249**	500	
4.	Alkalinity (mg/l)	432	182	179	185		
5.	Total Hardness as $CaCO_3$ (mg/l)	735	450	455	462		
6.	Calcium Hardness as $CaCO_3$ (mg/l)	258	126	220	126		
7.	Mg Hardness as $CaCO_3$ (mg/l)	557	224	319	424		
8.	Calcium as Ca	31	55	58	54		
9.	Magnesium as Mg(mg/l)	155	88	87	84		
10.	Chloride (mg/l)	450	189	195	197	250	250
11.	Sulphate (mg/l)	185	58	58	57	200	200
12.	Nitrate (mg/l)	1.30	0.23	0.68	0.51	45	50
13.	Phosphate (mgl1)	0.56	0.36	0.92	0.23		
14.	Fluoride (mg/l)	0.72	0.32	0.29	0.28	1.5	1.5
15.	Sodium (mg/l)	239	104	98	101		
16.	Potassium (mg/l)	56	20	18	17		

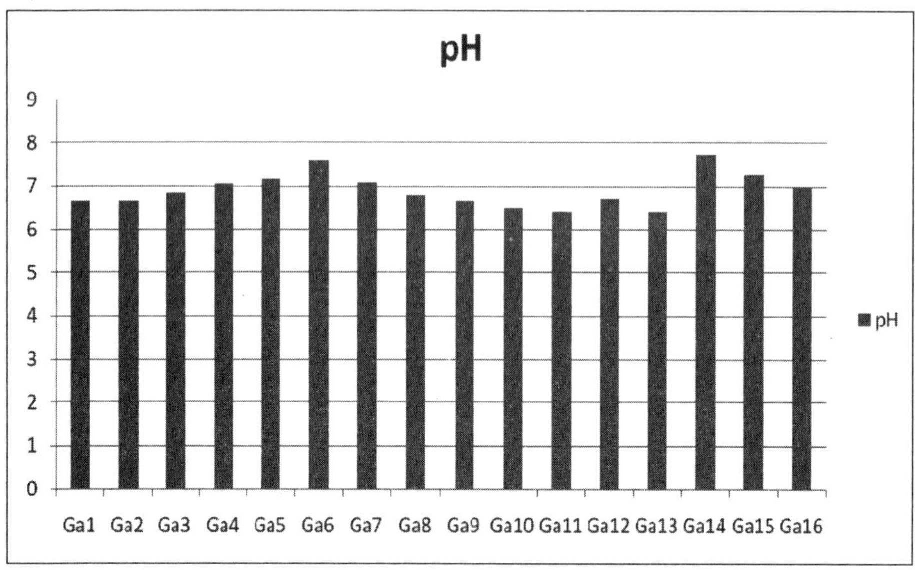

Fig. B: Graphic Representation of pH

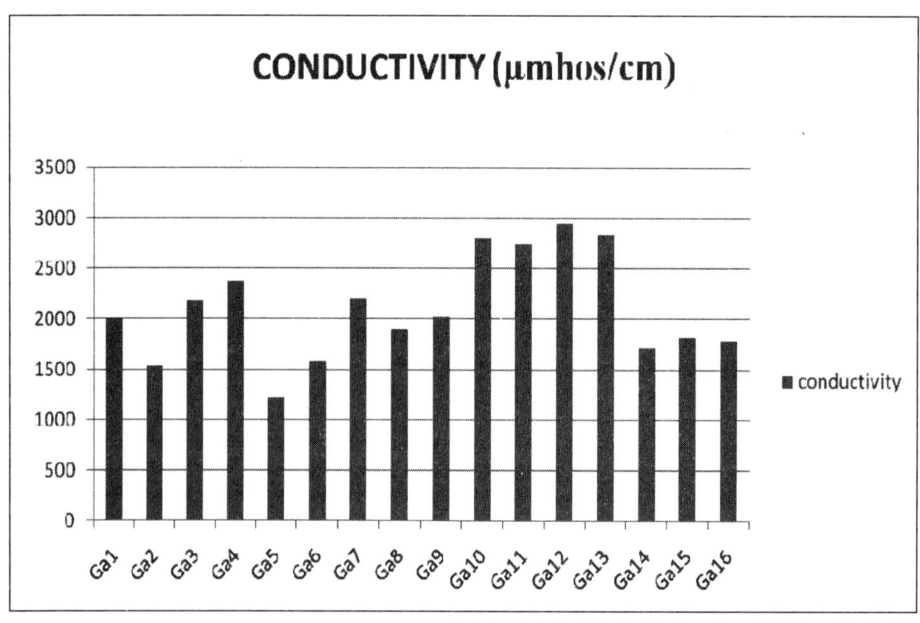

Fig. C: Graphic Representation of Conductivity (µmhos/cm)

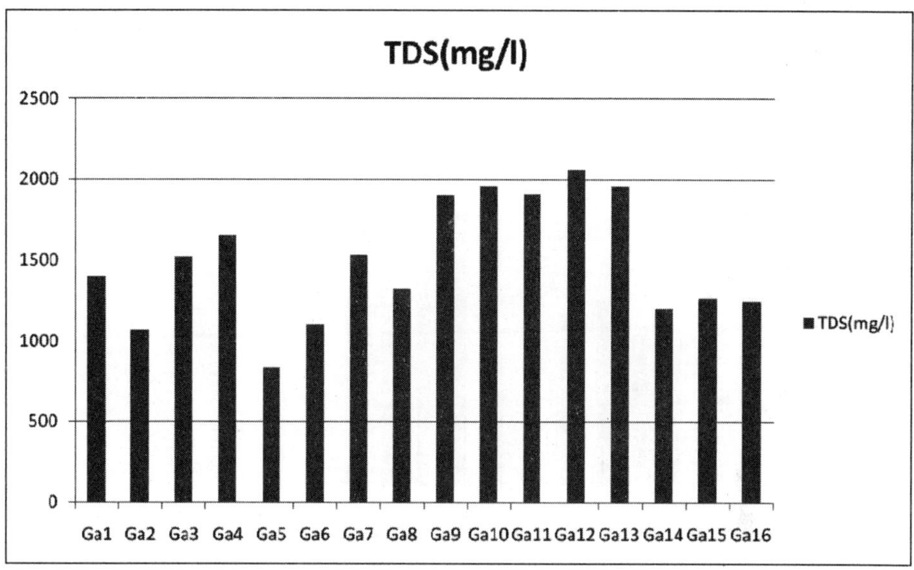

Fig. D: Graphic Representation of (TDS) in mg/l

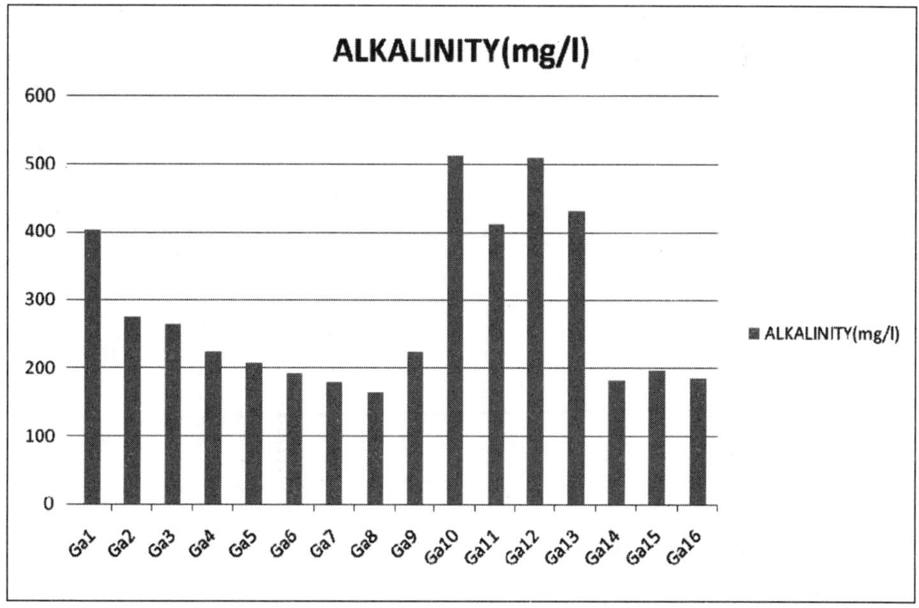

Fig. E: Graphic Representation of Alkalinity in mg/l

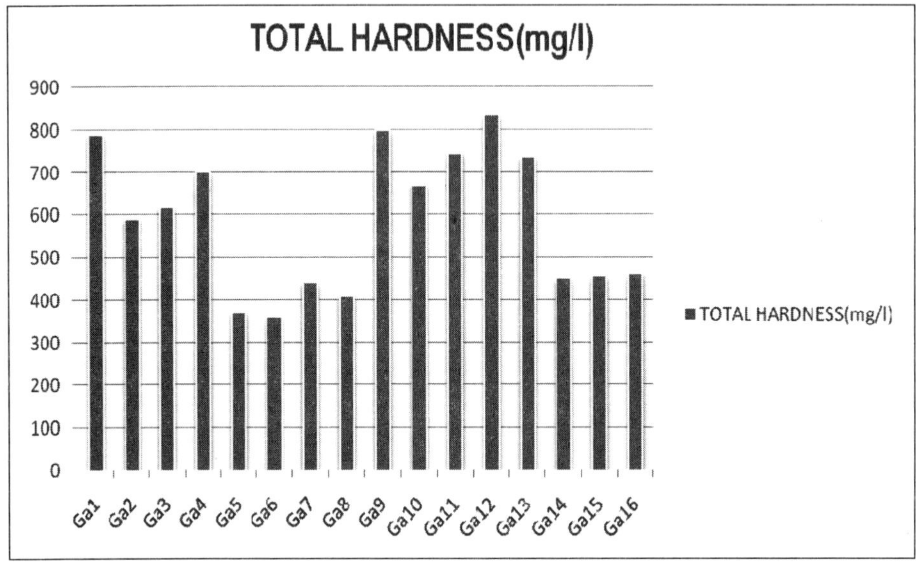

Fig. F: **Graphic Representation of Total Hardness in mg/l**

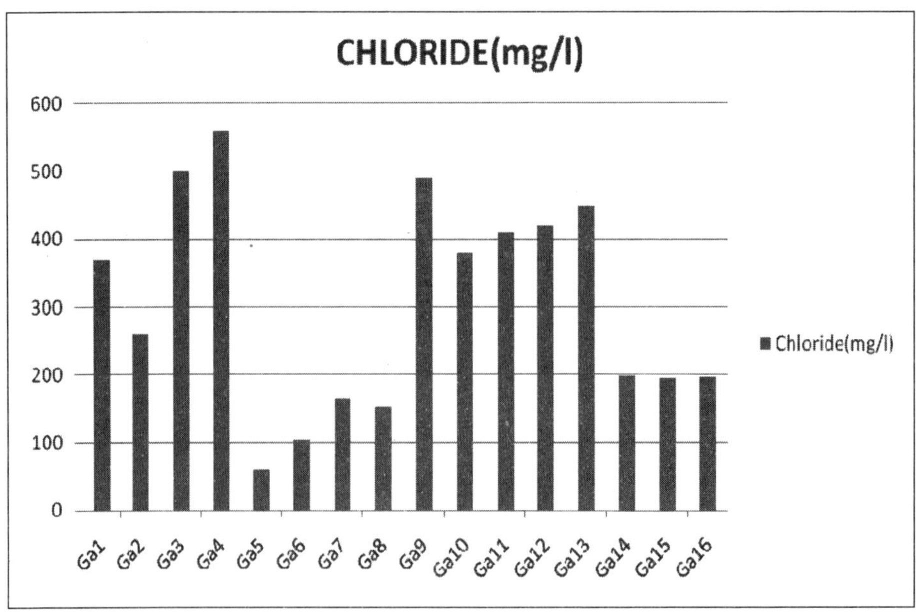

Fig. G: **Graphic Representation of Chloride in mg/l**

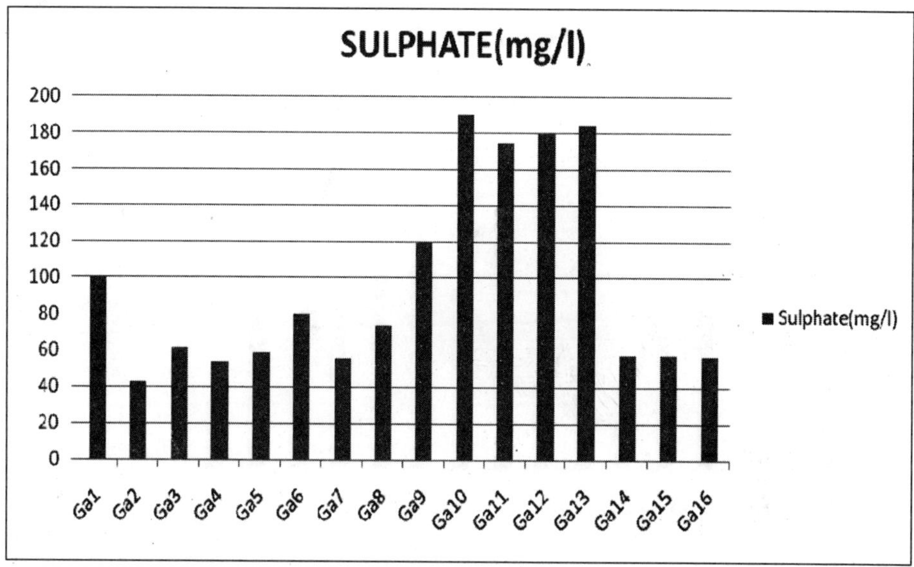

Fig. H: **Graphic Representation of Sulphate in (mg/l)**

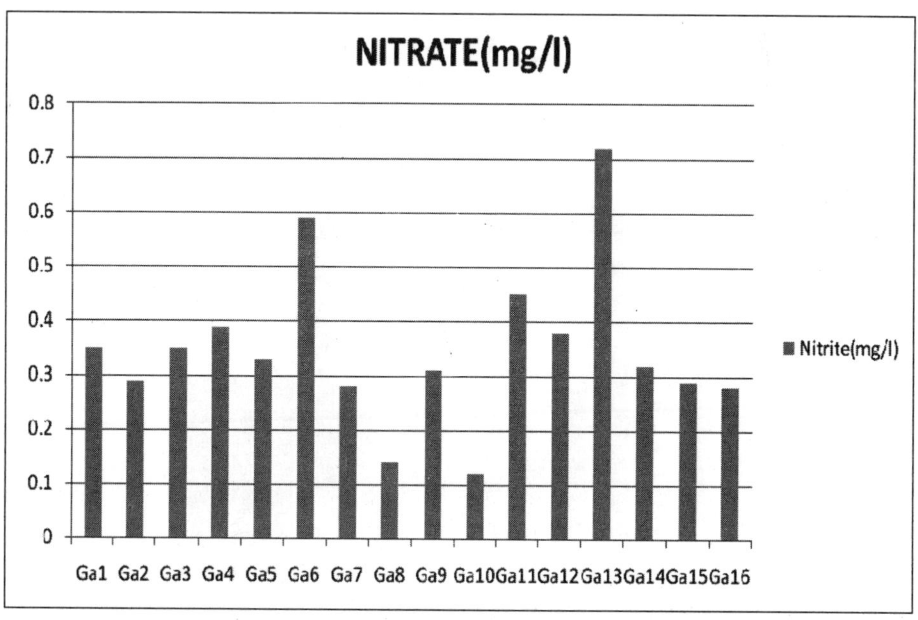

Fig. I: **Graphic Representation of Nitrite in (mg/l)**

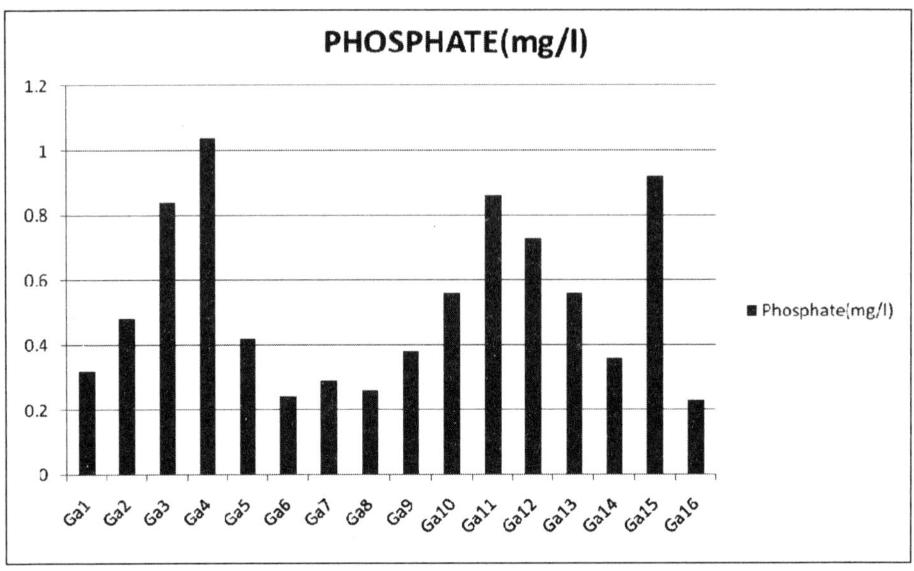

Fig. J: Graphic Representation of Phosphate in (mg/l)

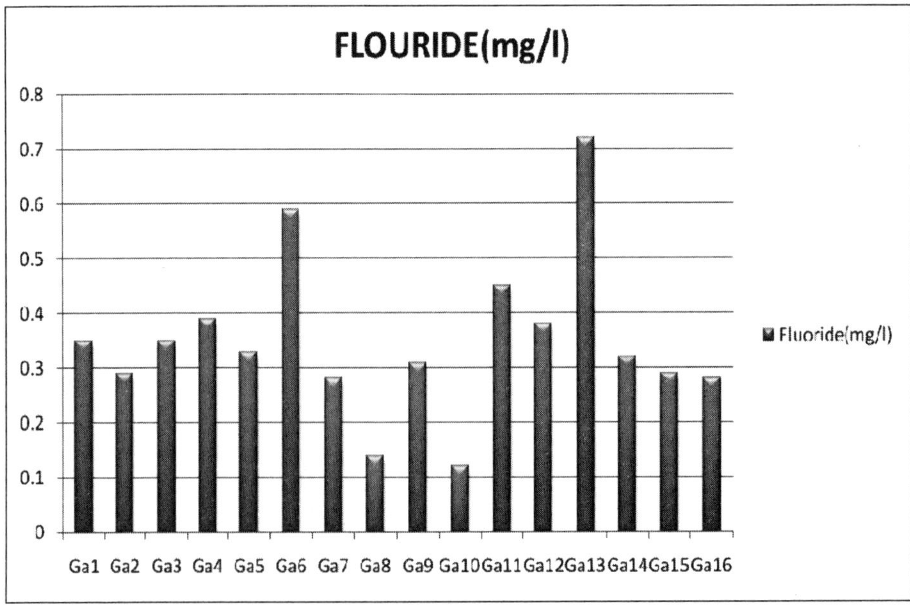

Fig. K: Graphic Representation of Fluoride in (mg/l)

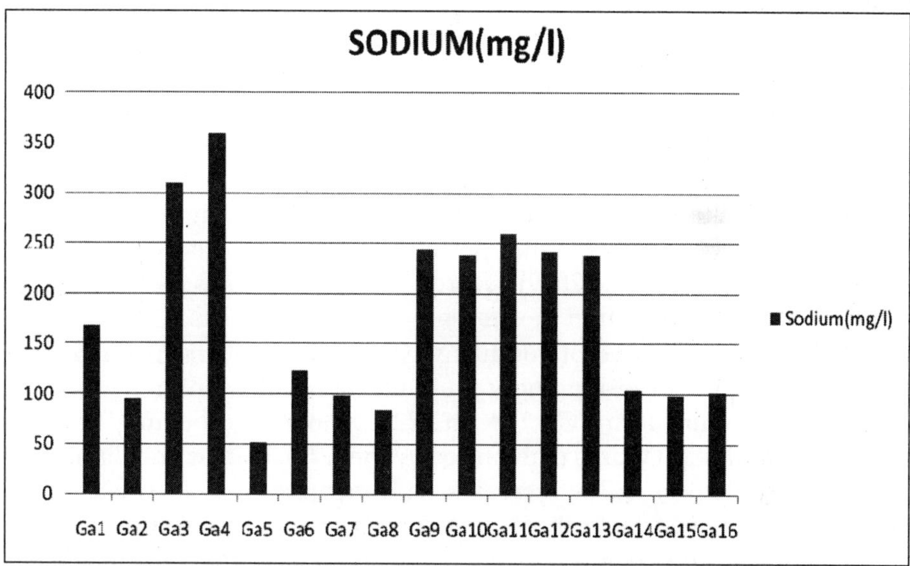

Fig. L: **Graphic Representation of Sodium in (mg/l)**

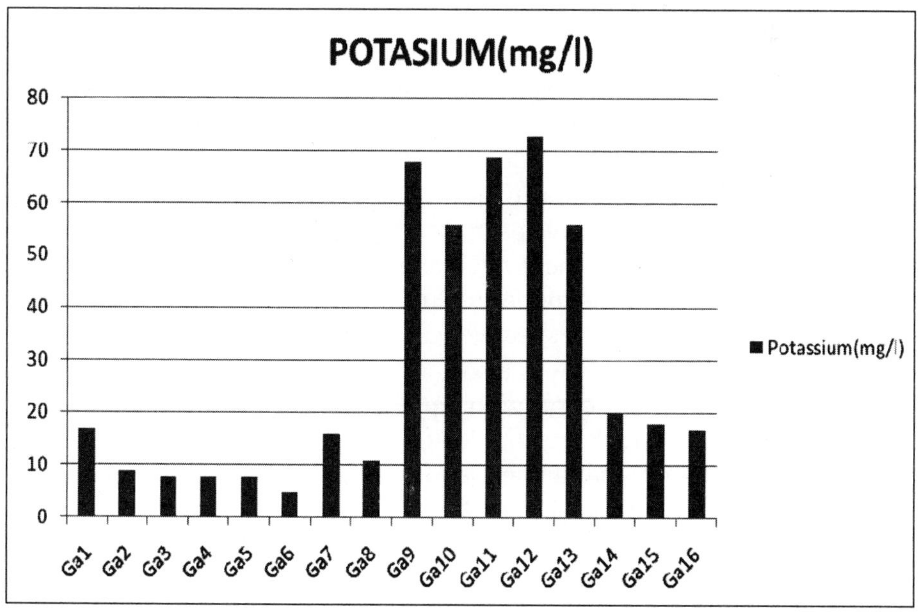

Fig. M: **Graphic Representation of Potassium in (mg/l)**

DISCUSSION

The study was conducted around Gazipur Municipal dumping site Delhi and the following parameters were studied.

The maximum value of pH was recorded from Ga 14 with 7.76 which was slightly basic and minimum value was recorded from Ga 13 with 6.52 which was slightly acidic.

The TDS value study was minimum in Ga2 with 1061 mg/l and maximum of 2061mg/l in Ga 12.This is due presence of huge amount of solid waste. Similarly, Olaniyan. I. O. (2009) recorded the TDS values as 2000mg /l in surface water contamination in dumping area.

The maximum value of conductivity was recorded from slaughtering house with a value of 2945µmhos/cm in Ga 12. While minimum value was recorded from dairy farm (Ga 5) with 1220µmhos/cm. This may be due to continuous sanitation works maintained by the farm. Kumar and Sinha (2010) reported conductivity value increases with increase in solid waste. Higher values were obtained from those areas with higher concentration of waste.

Minimum and maximum values of alkalinity were 164mg/l and 510mg/l at Ga8 and Ga12 respectively. Alkalinity also increases with increase in impurities. The values of alkalinity observed by Amar et el. (2008) in Municipal solid waste disposal, also suggest that higher the impurities the alkalinity range also increases.

Hardness was found maximum in Ga 12 with 835mg /l and minimum in Ga 6 with 360 mg/l. Kumar and Gaikwad (2004) also reported more values from more waste area. But in this present study least value was reported from an area of dumping area where the value should have been higher.

The value of chloride was found minimum in Ga 4 with 60 mg/l and maximum with 560mg/l at Ga 5. The permissible limit of chloride given by World Health Organisation is 250mg/l cultivated area may be the reason for higher record of value from farm sites.

Karthick, et al., (2007) have been studied the physicochemical parameter of water and find out the highest value of nitrite and phosphate in the related areas. In case of fluoride the highest value was 0.72mg/l at Ga 13 and lowest value in Ga10 at 0.12 mg/l respectively.

In the present study it was also found that the land fill site definitely affected the ground water quality, soil quality and create a bad environment in the related areas. Sadek et. al., (2000) made a study on landfill site and find out that the poorly maintained land fill sites are prone to ground water contamination through leaching action, open dumping of garbage, the breeding site of disease vectors such as flies, mosquito, rats, etc. Methane gas generating from the land fill waste related about 7 millions tones of methane into atmosphere which would increase to 39 million tons by year 2047 to continue the phenomenon of global warming.

REFERENCES

APHA (1995). Standard Methods for the Examination of the Water and Waste Water. American Public Health Association, New York.

Anonymous (1998). Standard Methods for the Examination of Water (20th edition) APHA; AWWA. 1200

Anonymous (2003). Pravish: Ground water CPCB, Delhi. 40 Guidelines for the Selection of Site for Land Filling (CPCB, Hazardous Waste Management Series: HAZWAMS/ 23/2002-03)

Biswas, A. (1998). Water Recourse: Tata McGrew Hill Publication Company Limited New Delhi. 1-737

CEPT (CBCB Publication) Probe 7: 23-26

Choudhury Moharana (2014).Municipal Solid Waste Generated by Silchar Town and its Impact on Surrounding Area of Dumping site at Meharpur, Silchar, International Journal of Environment and Natural Sciences 1(41-43)

Choudhury Moharana, & Nitin Kamboj (2013) Impact of Solid Waste Disposal on Ground Water Quality Near Gazipur Dumping Site, Delhi, India Journal of Applied and Natural Science 5 (2): 306-312

Dhere, M.A., Pawar, C.B. Pardeshi, P.B. & Patil, B.A. (2008): Muncipal Solid Waste Disposal in Pune City - An Analysis of Air and Ground Water Pollution. Curr. Sci. 95(6): 773-777.

De, A.K. (2010). Environmental Chemistry (Seventh Edition), New Age International (P) Ltd., Publishers, New Delhi, 364

Ground Water Hydrology (1987). Mc Grew Hill Publisher Inc, Tokyo Japan by Bower, Herman.

Khanna, D.R. and. Bhutiani, R. (2008). Laboratory Manual of Water and Wastewater Analysis. Daya Publishing House, Delhi - 110 035.

Khanna, D.R. and. Bhutiani, R. (2004). Water Analysis at a Glance, ASEA Publication, Rishikesh.

Kumar, N. and Sinha, D.K. (2010). Drinking Water Quality Management Through Correlation Studies Among Various Physic- Chemical Parameters. International Journal Envirosci Vol 1, No. 2, 253-206.

Karthick, B. and Ramchandra, T.V. 2007. Spatial Variation of Physicochemical and Hydrological Parameters with Land Use in Venkatapura Catchment, Karnataka. Asi. J. Microbiol. Biot. Env. Sci. 9 (4): 1001-1005

Kumar, S and Gaikwad, S. A. 2004. Municipal Solid Waste Management in Indian Urban Centres: An Approach for Betterment in Urban Development Debates in New Millinium (ed: Gupta) Atlantic Publishers and Distributors. New Delhi. 101-111.

Ololade, I.A., Alewunmi, O.A. and Adeleye, A. (2009). Effects of Household Wastes on Surface and Underground Waters. I.J. Phy.Sci. 4(1): 22-29

Sharma, V., Saini, P., Gangwar, R.S. and Joshi, B.D. (2010). Assessment of Municipal Solid Waste Generation and its Management in Haridwar City of Uttarakhand (India). Waste Management. 30 (4): 725-726.

Shiddamallayya, N., Pratima, M. (2008). Impact of Domestic Sewage on Fresh Water Body. J. Env. Biol. 29(3) : 303-308.

Sadek, S. & El-Fadel, M. (2000). The Normally Landfill: A Case Study in Solid Waste Management. J. Nat. Resour. Life Sci. Edu., 29: 155-161.

Todd D.K (1980). Ground Water Hydrology. Jhon Wiley & Sons, New York. 271

Trivedi, R.C., (2010): Water Quality of Ganga River: An Overview. Aquatic Ecosystem Health & Management, 13: 4, 347-351

Ward C.H. and Giger, W. (1985). Ground Water Quality. John Wiley & Sons, New York, 534

www.cpcb.nic.in

WASTE DISPOSAL AND MANAGEMENT *Pages:* **185-196**
Edited by: **Dr. Pawan Kumar 'Bharti'; Dr. B. Tabassum;** and **Dr. Priya Bajaj**
ISBN: 978-93-5056-729-6
Edition: **2015**
Published by: **Discovery Publishing House Pvt. Ltd., New Delhi (India)**

12

Rich Lands, Poor People
The Socio-environmental Challenges of Mining in India

Asif Iqbal

ABSTRACT

India is a mineral-rich country. It has a vast geological potential of over 20,000 known mineral deposits, and is in the top ranks in production of some key minerals such as coal, iron o000re, chromites and bauxite. According to the Geological Survey of India (GSI), the national exploring agency, the country is yet to tap its complete potential: it has huge reserves of important minerals awaiting exploration and exploitation. Unfortunately for India, almost all its minerals are in the same regions that hold its greenest forests and most abundant river systems. These lands are also largely inhabited by India's poorest and most marginalized people – the scheduled tribes and scheduled castes – who depend on the very same forests and watersheds for their survival. Mining in India, therefore, is not a simple 'dig and sell' proposition as it is made out to be by industry. It is, in fact, a highly complex socio-economic and environmental challenge: at stake are natural resources as well as people – forests, wildlife, water, environmental quality and livelihoods. The issue at hands requires balancing the imperatives of industrialization on one hand and the ecological and livelihood security of millions on the other. It is also about the policies, norms, procedures and institutions that must be established to ensure that mining is conducted – as far as possible – in an environmentally and socially acceptable manner. It is about writing and

Govt. Girls P.G. College, Rampur (UP) 244 901, India.

implementing new 'environmental and social contracts' to ensure that mining not only does the least damage to ecology and environment, but also contributes to the social and economic development of the areas where it is undertaken.

INTRODUCTION

In 1993, when the National Mineral Policy (NMP) was released, there was a general sense in the country that India is not a mineral rich country and this sense was reflected in the NMP, which focused on mineral conservation and the need to meet the domestic mineral requirements.

In 2006, when the high level committee constituted by the planning commission on revising National Mineral Policy released its report to the public, the sense of mineral scarcity was replaced with a sense of mineral abundance. This was reflected in the recommendations of the committee, which stressed the need to promote the mining industry for the international market rather than to meet the domestic demand.

As things stands today, there is a consensus among geologists that Australia, India, South and Central Africa, and South America belong to the same prehistoric land mass known as Gondwanaland and that these countries should have similar mineral resources in terms of quantity and grade. In fact, conventional wisdom in the mining sector is that India is endowed with large mineral resources, especially of iron ore, bauxite, stones, base metals, noble metals, and diamonds.

India's iron ore deposits are in Orissa, Chhattisgarh, Jharkhand, Karnataka and Goa. The deposits of copper, lead and zinc are mainly in Rajasthan, while the reserves of bauxite are concentrated in the states of Orissa, Chhattisgarh and Andhra Pradesh. Unlike coal and metallic minerals, non-metallic minerals show an even geographical spread across India. For instance, limestone deposits are spread from Himachal Pradesh in the north to Andhra Pradesh in the south and from Gujarat in the west to Meghalaya in the east.

With respect to concentration of mineral deposits, Jharkhand, Orissa and Chhattisgarh emerge as the three top mineral-bearing states. About 70 per cent of India's coal, 80 per cent of its hematite iron ore (high-grade ore), 60 per cent of bauxite, 40 per cent of manganese and almost all its chromites are found in these three states.

If all kinds of minerals, including sand, stone and brick earth are taken into consideration, then almost every district in the country can be said to produce one or other kind of minerals. However, out of the 604 districts in India, mining for fuel, metallic and non-metallic industrial minerals is undertaken in 274 districts (including 46 districts where coal and lignite are mined). Of these, 50 districts are extensively mined and produce large quantities of major minerals. These include seven districts in Chhattisgarh; six each in Jharkhand, Orissa, Andhra Pradesh and Madhya Pradesh; three each in Rajasthan, Gujarat and Maharashtra; two each in Goa and Karnataka; and one district each in Tamil Nadu, Uttar Pradesh, Assam, Meghalaya, West Bengal and Himachal Pradesh.

MINING, FORESTS AND TRIBALS

In general, India's major mineral-producing districts are characterized by large forest covers, big tribal populations and a high incidence of poverty and backwardness. The average forest cover of the 50 major mineral-producing districts stands at 28 per cent; the total forest cover in these districts is 11,890,400 hectare (ha) – 18 per cent of the total forest covers in the country. Six of these districts have forest cover more than 50 per cent of their geographical areas. Of the 50 districts, about 62 per cent have a forest cover that is more than the national average of 20.6 per cent. The districts where forest cover is less than 10 percent are – usually – either that where mining has been going on for a long time or those that are located in arid and semi-arid regions. Districts like Dhanbad in Jharkhand, Jajpur in Orissa and Bardhman in West Bengal fall in the first category: long years of mining have devastated their forests. In the second category are districts like Kutchh, Jamnagar and Amreli (in Gujarat) and Bhilwara (Rajasthan).

Barring Gujarat, the forest cover in the remaining top five mining states–Andhra Pradesh, Orissa, Chhattisgarh, Jharkhand, and Madhya Pradesh – is 2 Rich, Lands, Poor People: The Socio-Environmental Challenges of Mining in India above the national average. Chhattisgarh has the highest forest cover: around 43 per cent. Jharkhand has forests on 30 per cent of its land, while Orissa and Madhya Pradesh have forest cover on 27 and 26 per cent of their lands, respectively.

Mining and quarrying has destroyed large tracts of forest land in the country. One estimate by the government puts the total forestland diverted for mining between 1980 and 2005 at 95,003 hectares (ha). Other sources point to a much higher figure of 1,64,610 ha. Even this figure would be higher if it took into account the forest land diverted before 1980 when many coal mines took over vast areas of land – mostly forests. Examples are Hazaribagh and Dhanbad in Jharkhand and Bardhman in West Bengal.

Whatever the statistics say, it is clear that mining in forest land has increased significantly in the last decade. In the 17 years before 1998 (1980-97), forest clearances were granted for only 317 mines with a total diversion of 34,527 ha. Between 1998-2005, the Ministry of Environment and Forest (MoEF) cleared 881 mining projects in forest areas diverting 60,476 ha of forest area. This means that during 1998-2005, on an average, 216 mining projects were granted forest clearance annually – as against 19 clearances annually during 1980-97. Similarly, the total forest area diverted annually for mining during 1998-2005 is four-fold higher than what was diverted every year during 1980-97. This is an extremely worrying trend, since the mining industry has just begun expanding: with the new mining policy on the anvil, which is likely to give a significant boost to the industry, much more forest land is likely to be diverted for mining.

What makes things especially complicated for India is its large tribal population – numbering 84.3 million – which is approximately above eight per cent of its total population. Most of these tribes inhabit lands that are mineral-rich. Of the 50 major mining districts of the country, almost half are tribal districts.

As most tribal's also inhabit forest areas, their livelihoods and economy are closely intertwined with the fate of the forests and water sources. According to the Forest Survey of India, Dehradun, the average forest cover in tribal districts of the country is 37 percent, which is 85 per cent more than the national average.

Forest degradation due to mining and other development projects has significantly depleted the ecosystem, rendering the tribal population more socially and economically vulnerable. The impact, naturally, has been disproportionately higher on these already poverty- stricken and marginalized people. The problem is likely to get more acute as the government continues its industrialization drive, pegged at exploiting its vast natural resources – without investing much thought or action in safeguarding its people and environment.

One of the fallouts of this insensitive policy towards tribals has been the rapid rise of Naxalism in the mineral bearing areas of the country. A large part of the country's mineral-bearing areas is in the grip of Naxalism: 40 per cent of the mineral-rich districts in the top six mineral producing states are affected by the movement, which is opposing the mining industry. The militant opposition has unnerved the mining industry. A report by the risk management consultancy, Hill and Associates based in Hong Kong terms Naxalism as a "grave operational risk affecting investment climate in the core extractive sector". The report also feels that Naxalism is likely to affect foreign direct investment in the country. "The risk exposure would be greater in pockets where Naxalites have joined the tribals in opposing projectinduced human displacement ... Areas where industrialization is in the initial stages of development are more prone to stiff opposition by Naxalites," it says.

The convergence of the interests of the tribals and the naxalites are because of one simple reason: mining has failed to bring prosperity to the mining areas – infact, many would argue that it has bought poverty instead of prosperity.

MINING AND POVERTY

Across the world, the mining industry has been hard-selling dreams – of development, employment and growth. It has consistently tried to project a pro-people image by promoting the idea that mining will unleash growth in backward areas and will pull the indigenous communities into the 'mainstream', thereby improving their lives and livelihoods. But has it really done so?

At the macro level, things appear to be different. States like Jharkhand, Chhattisgarh and Orissa that have a high level of dependence on mineral resources demonstrate low per capita incomes compared to states, which do not depend completely on their mineral wealth (examples are Tamil Nadu, Maharashtra and Gujarat). The mineral dependent states also have higher levels of poverty, lower growth rates and higher levels of mortality, malnutrition and morbidity. India is not the only country where mining is linked with poverty and poor development outcomes. In most nations of the world, a high level of mineral dependence is associated with retarded economic performance. This phenomenon is so widely and commonly observed that it has been given a name – the 'resource curse'.

Resource curse is very much a reality in the mineral rich areas of India. Of the 50 major mining districts, 60 per cent figure among the 150 most backward districts of the country. Four of these mining districts – two from Orissa and one each from Jharkhand and Chhattisgarh – are among the top 25 backward districts of the country; 13 of these districts figure in the top 50 backward districts of the country. A closer look at a few districts gives a clearer picture of the phenomenon of resource curse.

Keonjhar, the most mined district of Orissa and the centre of its iron ore production, has quite a few dubious distinctions to its credit. Its infant mortality rate is 20 per cent higher than the state's average. About 60 per cent of its population lives below the poverty line and its per capita district domestic product is one of the lowest in the state. According to the 2001census, the percentage of rural households with access to safe drinking water in Orissa was 63 per cent; in Keonjhar, the percentage was a meager 39 per cent.

Dantewada is fast emerging as the most favoured destination in Chhattisgarh for steel companies due to the presence of high-grade iron ore. It ranks seventh among the 150 most backward districts in the country. Only about 22 per cent of the households in Dantewada have power connections. Provisions for safe drinking water are available for only half of the households (53%), much lower than the state average (71%). Only one-third of the population is literate – once again, lower than the state average.

Gulbarga and Bellary are two key mining districts in Karnataka. While Bellary is the hub of iron ore mining, accounting for 84 per cent of the iron ore produced in the state, Gulbarga is the largest producer of limestone in the country. Both these districts fare poorly when it comes to human development.

Gulbarga is ranked 19th and Bellary 17th out of the 20 districts of Karnataka on the human development index (HDI). Although Bellary boasts of the largest number of private aircrafts in the country, more than

45 per cent of its population lives below the poverty line. The district does not even have the basic amenities – only about 41 per cent of its households have access to power. The infant mortality rate is much higher than the state's average and life expectancy is lower. Less than 50 per cent of the population of Bellary is literate. The scenario is similar in Gulbarga, where the rate of literacy is as low as 38 per cent. Poverty is rampant with 45 per cent 4 Rich, Lands, Poor People: The Socio-Environmental Challenges of Mining in India.

Population below the poverty line (the state average is 33%). Only 63 per cent of the households in the district have access to safe drinking water, while 45 per cent have no power connection.

Both the mining districts in Maharashtra – Yavatmal and Chandrapur – not only figure among the 150 most backward districts of the country, but are also ranked 34th and 26th, respectively, out of the 35 districts of Maharashtra, on the HDI. Chandrapur, the largest producer of coal and limestone in the state, has only half of its villages linked by pucca roads, while only 43 per cent of households have access to safe drinking water. Health facilities are poor, with the infant mortality rate as high as 106 compared to the state average of 74. The per capita income of Chandrapur is more than 20 per cent lower than the state average; about 47 per cent of the families in the district are below the poverty line. Yavatmal leads in coal production, but lags behind in all other aspects. Around 44 per cent of families in the district are below the poverty line. Less than half the households have access to safe drinking water. The rate of infant mortality is 1.7 times more than the state average, while per capita income is 1.8 times lower.

Rajasthan is one of the leading non-metallic mineralproducing states of the country. Udaipur and Bhilwara are the key mining districts: the mining industry contributed 31 and 25 per cent to Udaipur and Bhilwara's GDP, respectively, between 1998-2001. But as is the case with the other states, both these districts have failed to benefit from their mineral wealth. The per capita income of Udaipur is lower than the state average. Only 32 per cent of villages in the district have access to power, while 64 per cent get safe drinking water. About one-third of the district's population is below the poverty line. Udaipur has been ranked 27th out of 29 districts in the state in terms of HDI. Bhilwara fares poorly too – with only 32 per cent of its villages with access to power and 60 per cent with access to safe drinking water. Almost half the population in the district is below the poverty line, and literacy rate is only 50 per cent.

Cuddalore, in Tamil Nadu, produces three-fourths of India's lignite. Groundwater near the lignite mines here has been depleted, leaving local agriculturists high and dry. More than half of Cuddalore's population lives below the poverty line and it is ranked 16th out of the 30 districts of Tamil Nadu in HDI.

Sonbhadra is the most mined district of Uttar Pradesh. It produces more than 20 MT of coal every year, apart from thousands of tonne of limestone and dolomite. It is also one of the most backward districts of the state. About 55 per cent of its population lives below the poverty line and its literacy rate is less than 50 per cent.

The story is similar across the country as far mineral districts and poverty is concerned. Despite the tall claims of industry as well as government, mining does not seem to usher in prosperity and development; in fact, under the current policies and practices of the government, mining districts have actually slipped deeper into poverty and destitution.

Today across the mineral belt of the country, people are protesting against mining. They don't want to give their land for mining. Apart from false promise of development, one of the major reasons for this is that mining has the worst track record as far rehabilitation and resettlement (R&R) is concerned. To start with, there are no reliable figures on how many people have been displaced by mining. There are estimates available for the period 1950 to 1991, which show that of all the developmental projects, mining has displaced the second highest number of people - around 25.5 lakh people. More importantly, not even 25 per cent of these displaced have been resettled. Of all the people displaced by mining, about 52 per cent were tribals. Mining induced displacement and resettlement has therefore created a pattern of "gross violation of human rights," and "enormous trauma in the country".

It is important to recognise the protests of people, against mining, for what they are: people in the mineral rich areas of the country are not willing to give up their land for mining. They do not believe that mining is going to improve their lot or add to the development of their regions.

MINING AND ENVIRONMENT

Mining takes a huge toll on the environment. The intensity of the environment impact depends on what is being mined, where and how. Unless it is meticulouslyplanned and carefully executed, mining can devastate lands, pollute and deplete water, denude forests, wipe out wildlife, and defile the air. Unfortunately, the environmental performance of Indian mining industry has been quite poor.

In the last decade there has been general recognition of the fact that mining has huge impact on the water resources – not so much due to consumptive use, but rather due to alteration in the hydrological profile of the area and due to pollution. Across the mining areas of the country, people are feeling the impact of water scarcity and pollution due to mining. Whether it is iron ore in Goa or Karnataka, bauxite in the hills of Chhattisgarh or Orissa, coal in Jharkhand, Orissa, West Bengal or Madhya Pradesh, or limestone and magnetite in Uttarakhand, open-cast mining has and is playing havoc with the water resources. Rivers like Damodar in Jharkhand and West

Bengal, Bhadra in Karnataka, Indravati in Chhattissgarh and Brahmani in Orissa are clear examples of water pollution due to mining. If thecurrent trend of mineral exploitation continues unabated, some of the major rivers in the country run the risk of disappearing as most of the minerals in the country are also found in watershed and catchment area of some major rivers. There have been several instances when the local community had to face hardship as mining operation changed the hydrological regime due to breaching of groundwater.

Mining operations also generates so much of fugitive dust that it often gives monochromatic appearance to the mine areas. Coal mining areas are black, bauxite and iron-ore rich region red, while limestone gives a chalky white hue. Korba, Bhilai, Satna and Dhanbad have been declared critical by the Central Pollution Control Board with respect to both suspended particulate matter (SPM) and respirable particulate matter. The iron ore mines and association transportation in Keonjhar-Sundargarh belt in Orissa and Bellary in Karnataka have defiled air in the region. Air pollution in old coalfields of Bokaro, Jharia and Raniganj has reached such levels that Central pollution Control Board (CPCB) has set 40 per cent higher ambient air quality standards for these areas as compared to new coal mines. The dust from the mines not only affects the health of the workers and local residents but also affects the agricultural productivity of the area. This has been found in Ib coalfields in Orissa, Bellary-Hospet region in Karnataka and Udai Sagar, Khamli and Chitor regions of Rajasthan through various studies.

As high grade deposits are getting exhausted, mineral industry are taking a recourse to lower grade reserves generating more wastes. For example, in beginning of the 20th century, copper ore mined by US mineral industry consisted of about 2.5 per cent of usable metal by weight, today, the proportion has dropped to 0.51 per cent.3 Similarly, Indian coal companies are digging deeper and deeper to extract lower grade coals generating as much as 15 tonnes of waste to extract one tonne of coal.4 In 2005-06 alone, the total 6 Rich, Lands, Poor People: The Socio-Environmental Challenges of Mining in India. waste generated from some major minerals alone amounted to as much as 1841 million tones. And the volume of waste is only growing.5 Unfortunately, the track record of Indian mining companies in managing its waste has been rather poor. In 2006, six workers were killed when iron ore mining waste dumps collapsed in the Tollem mines in Goa.6 Run off from overburden dumps have polluted river courses such as in Goa and in some cases even poisoned water resources as in Sukinda valley of Orissa.

However, the most serious concern for the mining industry is of mine closure. The environmental and social cost for rehabilitating the abandoned mines the world over is likely to run in trillions of dollars. A recent estimate puts rehabilitation costs just in the US, where regulation is much stringent than many other countries including India, at US$ 50-60 billion.7 India does not have a detailed inventory of abandoned mines. According to the website of Indian Bureau of Mines and reports from ministry of coal, there are 510 officially abandoned mines of major minerals and coal. However, unofficially this figure is likely to be much higher as it does not account for hundreds of mines being closed every year.

The information on mine rehabilitation in India is as sketchy as that on abandoned mines. According to the annual report of Union ministry of mines, as of September 2005, only 53 mines have been reclaimed covering an area of 660 ha. The truth is that mine rehabilitation is a completely ignored area in the country. It was only in 2003 that a mine closure plan was made mandatory for major minerals. Coal mines are still exempted from submitting a mine closure plan. Even the new regulations are a mere formality. Most of the mine closure plans today are nothing but huge pits disguised as water bodies/ water harvesting structures and massive overburden dumps disguised as plantations. The Green Rating Project of Centre for Science and Environment found during the environmental rating of large-scale cement industry that nearly all companies (with captive limestone mines) were not following proper mine closure programme.

REGULATORY ROADBLOCK

Though several legislations are in place to reduce mining's socio-economic impacts, they have not been codified clearly. The environmental law especially tailored for mining under the Mineral Conservation and Development Rules, 1998 is a two page benevolent statements, which treats every mines as a special case and leaves ample scope for interpretation by the mine owners. For example, it says "wherever possible, the waste rock, overburden should be backfilled into the mine excavation with a view to restoring the land to its original use as far as possible". The rules also say that trees cut down to make way for mining have to be replaced by double their numbers. However, there is no mention of the type of a forestation to be done. There are several such examples of ambiguity in the said legislation.

There is also an institutional confusion about who is responsible for what. Both the Indian Bureau of Mines and the state pollution control boards are responsible for monitoring the environmental aspects of monitoring. The IBM is supposed to clear the mine plans and closure plans but it the Union ministry of environment and forests, which clear s the environmental impact assessments.

SPCBs monitors the air and water pollution. IBM is responsible for waste management, reclamation and plantation, and SPCBs have nothing to do with it.

Moreover, both IBM and SPCBs do not have enough manpower to monitor even large-scale mines, let alone small and medium scale mines.

Mines require forest and environmental clearances from the Central government. On paper, this seems to be an excellent way of preserving forests and safeguarding the environment. However, today, mining is happening in every ecologically sensitive area one can think of – in and around reserve forest, wildlife sanctuaries and protected areas. The only saving grace has been the intervention of the apex court in halting mining and other developmental projects in national parks and wildlife sanctuaries. But legislatively, there is no moratorium in mining in any area of the country – be it an ecologically fragile area, wildlife sanctuaries, reserve or protected forests, biosphere reserves, national parks, critical water sources or areas inhabited by indigenous communities.

One of the biggest challenges for the lawmakers is to include safeguards in the closure legislations to ensure sustainable closure of mines. One of the key roadblocks before sustainable closure is the availability of funds at the end of life of mine. The financial assurance required by the Indian regulation is a pittance. A 10sq km mine lease area has to pay a surety of just Rs 2crores though the annual turnover of a large mine may in thousands of crores every year. The provision of forfeiting of the financial assurance is not a deterrent to the erring companies. Neither is there any system to blacklist the company for non-compliance. Another drawback of the closure regulation is the quality of mine closure plans. Most of the closure plan do not discuss alternate land use but rather focus on easier options like developing water bodies. There is also no mention of pollution control or remediation in closure plan even when there are tailings and acid mine drainage. The closure plan fare worse when it comes to socio-economic front even though a notification from IBM has made it an integral part of mine closure plan. The environmental clearance process has also several lacunae, one of the biggest being that the EIA report is prepared by a consultant hired by the company. Public hearings, an important platform for people to raise their concerns, have become a mere formality.

All these regulatory roadblocks have to be addressed to ensure better environmental management of the mines in the country.

CONCLUSION

The term sustainable mining is an oxymoron. Mining cannot be sustainable as ore bodies are finite and non-renewable. Even the best-managed mines will have environmental impacts. These are some of the inevitability that we have to reconcile with. However, another undeniable fact is that humans have used minerals from time immemorial and will continue to do so in the near future. Our dependence on minerals is so great that we cannot wish away mining. Therefore, the issue is not whether mining should be undertaken or not but rather how it should take place. It is necessary that mining should be conducted in environmentally and socially acceptable manner so that it leads to least ecological damage and also contributes to social and economic development of the areas.

Some of the new paradigm which mining companies need to keep in mind to make it more acceptable is to share the wealth generated by the mining with the local communities and to take people into confidence and seek their permission before initiating the mining operations. When people get the benefits from the project and are involved from the planning stage, they are more likely to be open to the project.

A major overhaul of the environmental regulations and regulatory mechanism is also needed. The EIA report must be made by an independent party with no vested interests. Public hearing, a component of the environmental clearance process, should be strengthened and given more space. Implementation of Environmental Management Plan should be monitored and a penalty imposed for non-compliance. It is very important to recognise critical ecosystemn, biosphere reserves and other protected areas. Like many other country, Indian too should decide 'no-go' areas for mining and other developmental projects.

There is an urgent need to codify detailed environmental management regulations for mining. Best practices such as simultaneous reclamation, collection and treatment of surface run-off, fugitive dust control, tailing waste management, etc should be adopted. There is also urgent need to enact laws to protect groundwater and water catchment from mining. The closure regulations should be made applicable for all minerals including fuel minerals and adequate financial surety and robust regulatory mechanism should be developed to ensure companies take responsibility for mine closure.

An important thing to improve the environmental performance of the mine is to restructure and revamp the regulatory institutions. A strong monitoring and enforcement system is fundamental for ensuring environmental sustainability.

One of the fundamental principles of sustainable development is 'doing more with less'. For mining and minerals sector, this translates into reduction in the requirement of minerals per unit of material output The requirement of minerals in the country can be met far more efficiently than it is being today. It can be achieved through waste prevention and recycling and reuse of existing material stocks. This will also require use of low-grade minerals and to promote this, right kind of economic incentives and disincentives should be put in place.

REFERENCES

1. National Mineral Policy, Report of the High Level Committee, Planning Commission, Government of India, December 2006.
2. Chandra Bhushan et al, 2005, Concrete Facts, The Rating of Indian Cement Industry, Centre for Science and Environment, New Delhi.
3. Gary Gardner and Payal Sampat, 1998, *Mind over Matter: Recasting the Role of Materials in Our Lives,* Worldwatch Institute, Washington, DC, p. 18.

4. Waste and Overburden Management in Mega Opencast Project – Problems & Technical Options, Director General of Mines Safety, Ministry of Labour Government of India.
5. Estimated by Centre for Science and Environment Based on Data from anon, 2001, *Overview of Mining and Mineral industry,* The Energy and Resources Institute, New Delhi and anon, 2006*, Indian Mineral Yearsbook*, Indian Bureau of Mines, Nagpur.
6. Six Killed in Goa's Mining Tragedy, India E News, December 10, 2006, http://www.indiaenews.com/ india/20061210/32003.htm
7. Abandoned Mines said Gigantic Problem, 2002, Website of Planet Ark, http://www.planetark.org/dailynewsstory. cfm/newsid/15969/story.htm
8. http://www.bdsnetwork.cbs.dk/publications/chandra.pdf

Index

❑ ❑ ❑ ❑